THE SHELL AUTO CARE GUIDE

TIPS ON EVERYTHING YOU NEED TO KNOW AS A CAR OWNER AND DRIVER

Ross R. Olney

A Fireside Book
PUBLISHED BY SIMON & SCHUSTER, INC.
NEW YORK

Material in this book is based on the "Come To Shell For Answers"
booklets.

Copyright © 1986 by Shell Oil Company

All rights reserved
including the right of reproduction
in whole or in part in any form

Simon and Schuster/Fireside Books,
Published by Simon & Schuster, Inc.
Simon & Schuster Building
Rockefeller Center
1230 Avenue of the Americas
New York, New York 10020

SIMON AND SCHUSTER, FIRESIDE and colophons are registered
trademarks of
Simon & Schuster, Inc.

Designed by Irving Perkins Associates
Manufactured in the United States of America
1   3   5   7   9   10   8   6   4   2
1   3   5   7   9   10   8   6   4   2   Pbk.
Library of Congress Cataloging in Publication Data
Olney, Ross Robert, date.
The Shell auto care guide.

"Based on the 'Come to Shell for answers' booklets"—
T.p. verso.
1. Automobiles—Maintenance and repair.   I. Shell
Oil Company.   II. Title.
TL152.0437   1986   629.28'722   86-12086
ISBN 0-671-61083-X
ISBN 0-671-62788-0 (a Fireside book : pbk.)

Contents

THE SHELL AUTO CARE GUIDE

Chapter **ONE**

The 100,000-Mile Car

Impossible? Not at all.

Unreasonable demands on your driving style? No, not if you enjoy your car and enjoy driving—and don't mind working *with* your car instead of *against* it.

You can't be neutral about driving to extend the life of a car. But with simple consideration of your car while you are driving, with routine "white gloves" maintenance, and by taking advantage of free services, you can extend the life of your car far beyond what has come to be expected today. You can forget the "50,000 mile trade-in" and at the same time be secure in the knowledge that your car will start without fail on a cold morning and get you where you're going safely and without breakdown.

Won't all this save money, too? Yes, of course.

Not only that, but you can also save a chore that most of us look forward to with apprehension—the task of shopping for a new car under pressure. Think about it. One of life's most difficult moments comes when we must hurry out and buy a car because the old one has given up the ghost. It is sitting forlornly at some service station or garage, a plastic number on its roof and an $800 repair estimate under the windshield wiper. Yet you need wheels *now*. Your bargaining position is shaky, and you know it—and so do they.

So you head off for the shopping, testing, and negotiating wars with sweaty palms and the thought that you would rather be doing something else—anything else at all. That is the moment you wish "Old Faithful" was still around, still running as it once did.

It is possible to get carried away with these life-extending matters and take all the fun out of driving. If you wish, you can baby your car from the first day, limping it down the turnpike, never going over thirty miles per hour, never hauling more than a passenger or two, always keeping it within a mile or so of home, and never, never demanding it to do the job it was built for.

Fun driving, huh? So don't worry about it. Consider the following drivers, and the fun they still have with their vehicles.

Sherwood Kahlenberg of North Hollywood, California, has a 1966 Plymouth Barracuda he drove on his honeymoon. He is still driving it more than 285,000 miles later. George Tonis of Sacramento, California, still occasionally drives his father's 1926 Model T coupe. It has gone nearly one million miles. One of the all-time endurance champions is Bob Bender of Madison, Wisconsin. He drives a 1956 Cadillac Fleetwood with more than a million miles on it. And he still uses it every day as a taxicab.

Rare cases? Not at all. Throughout the United States there are thousands of drivers who have driven their cars 100,000 miles, 200,000 miles, and even more, and who still enjoy the vehicle. You can, applying a minimum of care match these figures, and with devoted care you can double them.

Sure, to extend the life of your car you can fix every breakdown the moment it happens. That kind of treatment will certainly keep the old buggy going, but it's a risky and expensive way considering the cost of service and parts today. If money is no object, it's easy to keep a car in prime condition. Just have a mechanic ready at all times to check out every squeak and rattle—and an open checkbook. No problem at all.

There is a better way. These high-mileage drivers and thousands of others across the United States choose to keep things from going wrong in the car before it happens. That's one of the big secrets to a dependable, high-mileage car.

Norman Goldbeck, a Shell service station operator in the St. Louis area, is an expert at keeping cars going long after a mild 80,000 or 90,000 miles. Licensed as an inspector-mechanic by the state of Missouri, he says, "Anybody can keep a car going for 100,000 miles. Just keep fixing everything that goes wrong. But that's risky. It's smarter to try to keep things from going wrong in the first place. If you do that, you have a good chance of going 100,000 miles in a comfortable, reliable car, one that you're still proud of."

Here's an interesting fact you might not have considered. Drivers of exceptionally high-mileage cars take as much pride in them as most owners of brand-new cars. These high-mileage drivers love to talk about their "classic" cars, to show them off, to brag about them to anybody who will listen. Show an interest in an older car next time you see one in really good shape and you'll soon be in deep conversation with the owner.

Yet trade-in statistics show that Americans often give up on their cars after only 50,000 or 60,000 miles. These owners begin to hear noises, or they have a repair bill that frightens them, or the old bus just gradually deteriorates until it looks a little shabby—so off to the dealer they go. This is no longer economical. The average price for a new car today is about eleven thousand dollars. That is a *lot* of money to most of us. Add on interest and carrying charges and the monthly payment can be back breaking.

So why not stretch the life of your car by taking care of it, by watching your driving habits, by taking advantage of the free services available, and by paying perhaps two hundred dollars or so a year for regular maintenance?

Remember this. Without care, your car can be a nightmare to drive. It won't look good and it won't be dependable. You'll never know for sure whether it's going to start the next time you really need it.

Remember the guy stalled at the light with the long line of traffic behind him? Remember the last time you saw a car pulled off the freeway or turnpike, hood up and driver looking distressed? Or your neighbor, last time he came out in the morning and cranked and cranked and then finally knocked on your door for help? Remember the last time you had a really heavy repair bill for work done on one of your cars?

Well, consider this. One big repair bill can knock out one quarter of a car's value. That's with just *one* major breakdown. Who needs that?

FREE SERVICES?

There's one key habit to get into on the day you decide to make your car last twice as long as you might have expected. Never buy gasoline without having the service station attendant do free checks on your engine oil, radiator coolant, and transmission oil levels. It can be worth it, if you don't automatically do these checks for yourself, to pay the few extra cents per gallon at a full-serve pump. Yes, it'll cost a little more, but you'll know these important levels have been checked. If you ask, the attendant will also look at your battery and cables, tires, and other possible maintenance problem areas.

One more free service is available if you deal regularly at a favorite station—diagnosis. Most stations have a mechanic who is more skilled than the people at the pumps. They'll talk to you about your car. If you have a question, ask them. You'll be surprised at how much you can learn about care and about any specific problems with your car. A good mechanic, if the problem can't be fixed on the spot at that station or garage, can direct you to the best repair facility—and possibly even act as a middleman in the transaction.

He can watch over the repair, check it out for you, and keep an eye on the prices being charged. The garage doing the work will be aware that somebody in the business is involved, and that the job can mean more business for them if they handle it efficiently and at the right price.

MAINTENANCE

The first secret to high mileage, if you haven't guessed it already, is good maintenance. The fact is, there is no reason why a modern engine should *ever* wear out. They are built to have an indefinite lifespan. Modern automobile engines are a marvel of engineering. You don't believe it? Shell tested the performance of twenty-five cars that had 100,000 miles or more.

Clunkers, right?

Wrong!

These were everyday cars, but they had been well maintained. They had been given regular oil changes and lubrication according to the manuals. They had been driven reasonably by drivers who cared. As a group, these cars averaged 98.7 percent of their estimated original road horsepower. Oil consumption at 70 miles per hour averaged only one quart per 1600 miles. These cars were still a pleasure for their owners. A car doesn't have to be a clunker just because it has broken 100,000 miles.

Perhaps you've heard this lament before.

"I've *had* it! This is the last straw! I'm going to unload this piece of junk."

Have you ever faced this last straw? It usually occurs in the face of an expensive repair job. Or because of the overall run-down appearance of the car. Or because it refuses to start some morning when you really need it, or stalls in traffic at the worst, most embarrassing moment, or because of a pile of little problems that have stacked up.

Or a combination of the above.

The secret to long life is maintenance, and the secret to maintenance is to *do it by the book.*

THE BOOK

The book is the car owner's manual. This valuable booklet has been written by engineers from the company that built your car, people who know how to make the car perform best over the most extended period of time. In the long run, it is to their advantage if their product performs well over a longer period. They won't get you to trade for a new car quite as quickly, but if the product doesn't perform, you aren't going to trade for another of the same make anyway. So the people who write the manuals *want* your car to last as long as possible and be a pleasure to drive for as long as you own it.

Consider this advice from a car owner's manual.

- Every neglect of machinery and tires carries its penalty of annoyance and expense.

An owner's manual that remains in the glove box can lead a car to an early breakdown.

- It is not a difficult matter to operate a motor car, but the real trick is to know what to do when it refuses to go.
- On rough roads, slowing down and using good judgment will result in lighter repair bills.
- Frequent inspection is essential to safety and prompt replacements and adjustments are the truest economy.

The auto manual also says, "There is no sensation akin to that of running an automobile with full realization that you know its parts and have mastered it. It is the only way to enter the real enchantment of motorland."

Good advice today, and good advice back in 1907 when this manual was printed and included with Northern Motor Car Company's Model C.

"United States car manufacturers are doing a superb job these days of assembling a detailed picture of your car in their manuals," says V. J. Adduci, president of the Motor Vehicle Manufacturers Association. "They are blueprints of the insides and the outsides of your car and a schedule of what you have to do to make your car take you where you want to go.

"But if you don't read it, it's not worth a darn," he adds.

Take a look under the hood. There's a "watchamacallit" over there, with a "gizmo" and a "doodad" just behind it. But if you want to pour in a quart of oil, add a few ounces of power-steering fluid, or top off your windshield-washer fluid, you've got to know which cap to unscrew.

Your owner's manual will tell you, and will include tips on how much to add and how often to check the levels. Most of them have pictures and diagrams to make the jobs perfectly clear even to somebody who has no idea how the thing works.

Automakers have been tucking ownership manuals into new cars for decades, and while what's under the hood and behind the steering column may be jazzier than it was in the days of the Northern Motor Company Model C, much of that advice is still good today.

The owner's book is not a manual to get into your pocket in the aftermarket, or to promote riches for mechanics. There are plenty of those around if you want them. Nor is an owner's manual written for do-it-yourselfers who routinely tear down and rebuild their cars for the fun of it.

The car owner's manual is written for you and me, not to sell you something but to help you to help your car perform better and longer. Yet Shell asked more than one hundred drivers and found that *half* of them had not even read their owner's manual all the way through. About one in ten had never even *looked* at their owner's manual. This can be very tough on the car.

A few owners read their manual, then toss it in the glove compartment and forget it. Sure, they get an occasional oil change, but even though the manual recommends checking the transmission fluid, they ignore that and many other life-prolonging items. No wonder the car eventually fails them.

Here's an important tip. Read your owner's manual and abide by it. There are ten items that stand out in most owner's manuals.

1. Check all fluid levels regularly, in the radiator, the crankcase, the transmission, the brakes, the power steering, and the battery.
2. Change the oil and the filter on the schedule recommended.
3. Check the drive belts regularly.
4. Check the water hoses regularly.
5. Check the battery charging system frequently.
6. Flush and refill the radiator on the schedule recommended.
7. Get regular lubrications.
8. Check the brake linings on the schedule recommended.

9. Inspect the tires regularly and the pressures often.
10. Change the automatic transmission fluid on the schedule recommended.

Most drivers do not follow this list religiously, but the drivers who take care of all of these items usually double the lives of their cars. One hundred thousand miles is often the "half life" of their vehicle. There will be more specifics about this list and how to follow it later in this book.

Some owners do more than what is recommended. If there is one thing that stands out among owners of high-mileage cars, it is that they check things even more regularly than the manual suggests. Some of them insist upon changing the engine oil and filter as often as every 2,000 miles, using premium oil for longer engine life. They know that the worst enemies of a modern engine are heat and dirt. Yet, this costs extra money, possibly unnecessarily, but these owners are proud of their cars and want them to last as long as possible.

Why all the talk about engine oil changes? Engine oil does *wear out*. Or, more specifically, the additives in the oil are eventually used up. The camshaft and other hard-working parts can be damaged when the antiwear additives are all gone. Sludge and deposits can build up fast after the detergent added to the oil by the manufacturer has been used up. When the antioxidant is all gone, the oil can become too thick. Yet the average owner who changes oil when recommended, and adds oil when needed, can expect to use less than two hundred dollars worth of oil and filters in 100,000 miles of driving. That's cheap insurance.

One Shell station owner does the fleet maintenance for a huge St. Louis trucking company. These are hard-working rigs and profit goes down when the rigs go down. So a maintenance list was given to the dealer by the company. It was as long as your arm and more detailed than most owner's manuals. The list covered every possible maintenance item, every possible test and check.

Obviously, the company wouldn't be paying for something to be done if they weren't convinced by their bookkeepers that money would be saved by having a more reliable vehicle. The same is true for your car. It's hard to find a maintenance job in an owner's manual that won't pay for itself in the long run. Especially now that high costs are convincing people to hold on to their vehicles longer.

EXTRA MAINTENANCE

High-mileage car owners do more frequent maintenance, and your manual might suggest that you do the same. All maintenance is based on driving conditions. Owners' manuals usually recommend that you change motor oil and transmission fluid more often under conditions of "severe service." That doesn't necessarily mean that you constantly torture your car on the back roads of Baja or drive it every year in the Indianapolis 500.

What it does mean is that if you normally "stop and go" drive in cold weather, drive in unusually dirty, dusty, or sandy conditions, haul a heavy trailer, or do something else that puts an extra strain on your car, you need more frequent maintenance.

How much you drive can make a difference in your maintenance schedule. In most owners' manuals, service is recommended at a certain mileage or a certain time, whichever comes first. If you don't run up a lot of miles, service your car by the time intervals suggested.

Climate can make a difference in a maintenance schedule, too. In Northern cities, road deicing salt can rust the underside of any car, even if it has been "rustproofed" with undercoating. More frequent hosing off of the chassis and wheel wells, or even a later investment in more rustproofing, will pay off.

If you live in an area where the summers are real scorchers, pay special attention to the cooling system. One bad overheating can plant the seeds of a shorter engine life or a major repair job. You know the feeling. She begins to heat up and soon she's boiling. So you pull into a service station, hose down the radiator until you can get the cap off, then carefully add some fresh water. Soon you're back on the road again, home free, right? Wrong. That overheating you took care of so neatly might show up much later in a problem with hoses, thermostat, water pump, valves or rings, gaskets, or even an expensive warped cylinder head.

YOU MIGHT NEED TO REPLACE SOMETHING

Every single part of your car is probably not going to work perfectly forever. If you expect to get more than 100,000 miles from your car, you can also expect to replace certain parts that will almost certainly wear out. But not the engine, or the transmission, or most of the other most expensive parts in the drive train, fortunately. These major, costly parts will probably go the distance if you care for them.

Shell engineers created a hypothetical example using a standard 1970 Chevrolet with a 350 cu. in. engine, power steering, power disc brakes, automatic transmission, and air conditioning. They based the cost of the parts on an issue of *Motor's Parts and Time Guide*, a volume that tends to change cost figures upward as time goes on.

Assuming it takes about seven years to reach the 100,000-mile level, and assuming normal maintenance according to the owner's manual, here are the parts that they calculate will need to be replaced as time goes on.

1. Battery and cables
2. Radiator hoses
3. Alternator
4. Belts
5. Water pump
6. Distributor cap, points, condenser, and rotor
7. Heater hoses
8. Air filter
9. PCV Valve
10. Coil
11. Air pump
12. Timing gear
13. Fuel vapor cannister filter
14. Fuel pump
15. Oil filter

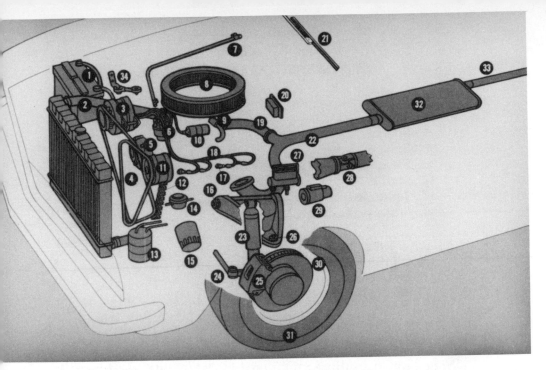

It's likely that most of these components will need to be replaced before 100,000 miles. The big-money items—engine, transmission, rear end—should make it all the way. 1. Battery and cables 2. Radiator hoses 3. Alternator 4. Belts 5. Water pump 6. Distributor cap, points, condenser, and rotor 7. Heater hoses 8. Air filter 9. PCV valve 10. Coil 11. Air pump 12. Timing gear chain 13. Fuel vapor canister filter 14. Fuel pump 15. Oil filter 16. Control arm bushings 17. Spark plugs 18. Spark plug wires 19. Exhaust pipe 20. Voltage regulator 21. Windshield wiper blades 22. Crossover pipe 23. Shocks 24. Tie rod ends 25. Pads, disc kits, linings, and wheel cylinder kits 26. Ball joints 27. Master cylinder 28. U-joints 29. Starter 30. Discs 31. Tires 32. Muffler 33. Tail pipe 34. Steering idler arm.

16. Control arm bushings
17. Spark plugs
18. Spark plug wires
19. Exhaust pipe
20. Voltage regulator
21. Windshield wiper blades
22. Crossover pipe
23. Shock absorbers
24. Tie rod ends
25. Pads, disc kits, linings, and wheel cylinder kits
26. Ball joints

27. Master cylinder
28. U-joints
29. Starter
30. Brake rotors
31. Tires
32. Muffler
33. Tail pipe
34. Steering idler arm

That's a *long* list and it looks very expensive. The trouble is, many of the parts on the list will have to be replaced more than once, according to Shell engineers. On the other hand, some of these parts won't need to be changed at all in 100,000 miles. But this is a hypothetical example, so let's average it out by supposing that you have to replace each one of them once.

Replacing everything might cost about twenty-two hundred dollars for a typical car, labor included. Do-it-yourselfers will handle many of the chores themselves, and enjoy doing it, but since this is hypothetical we'll ask a mechanic to do everything.

If it takes about seven years to reach 100,000 miles, the figures work out to $26.20 per month, or slightly more than two cents per mile. Toss in the figures for at least one, and maybe two, new cars in that seven-year period, and you can see what the averages would become.

Twenty-six twenty a month suddenly looks cheap enough, especially when you consider the extra costs in time and money of an unreliable car that might be unsafe, that stalls at stoplights, refuses to start in the morning, and is a general aggravation.

TWO BANKROLL KILLERS

Can you guess which two maintenance jobs are most often forgotten or overlooked, the results often being overheating, stalling, and even a damaged or burned-out engine—or another very expensive transmission repair job?

The most often ignored maintenance jobs are draining and flushing the radiator and changing the transmission fluid and filter. Neither of these jobs are very expensive or time-consuming (and both are recommended in most owners' manuals), but if either of them is ignored an expensive repair job might be in the future. Transmission fluid does wear out, and damage can result. Coolant additives eventually go away, and the inside of the radiator suffers even if the car still appears to run at the right temperature for some time after they are gone.

Including these two, which maintenance jobs are most important to the long life of a car? And what damage can result if they're neglected? All of the recommendations in your service manual are important, but certain ones, if ignored, can be very costly. Here's what can happen, along with maintenance tips that will probably prevent it.

The Costly Result	The Probable Prevention
Complete Engine Overhaul	Check Oil Change Oil Check Drive Belts Check Hoses Test Cooling System
Transmission Overhaul	Check Fluid Levels Add Fluid if Necessary Change Fluid Change Filter
Replace Piston Rings and Bearings	Change Air Filter Change Oil Change Filter
Valve Job	Adjust Valves
Turn Down or Replace Drums and/or Rotors	Check Linings or Pads Replace as Needed
Front End Overhaul	Lubricate Chassis
Repair Severe Rust	Flush Underneath Keep Body Clean

"We don't quibble about preventive maintenance," says Al Golub, president of Chicago Limousine Service. "A $30 transmission service may save a $400 overhaul."

REMEMBERING MAINTENANCE SCHEDULES

It's one thing to talk about maintenance, but this is a busy world we live in. It isn't easy to remember maintenance schedules. So do what fleet owners do. What truck, taxi and limousine services, and rental companies do, you and I can do. They put it all in writing. Whenever maintenance work is done, they write down the date, the mileage, the job that was done, and *when it needs to be done again.* Keep in mind that some modern warranty promises are based upon the owner keeping the vehicle maintained according to a certain schedule. No regular maintenance, no free repairs.

Auto-service insurance companies know the value of regular maintenance. They insist that their policyholders regularly maintain their cars and keep records and bills to prove it. One motorhome owner followed the schedule to the letter, changing the engine oil at exact intervals. Then the expensive

A Maintenance Record File for your car (write Shell for a free one). With it you can keep a written record of maintenance as fleet managers do.

fresh-water tank in his unit failed, and shortly afterward the refrigerator went out. Both were replaced, but not until after the insurance company had checked to be sure the engine oil had been changed at the right intervals.

THE CAR CARE DIARY

Many owners' manuals have one or more pages in which to record maintenance jobs done, including mileage and cost. If yours doesn't, a notebook or envelope in the glove compartment will do. Mark your figures in the notebook and shove the receipts in the envelope.

Here's another easy way. Shell has a Maintenance Record File to help you keep accurate records of all maintenance. It has a chart for the service job, date, and mileage, and a handy envelope to store receipts.

If your dealer doesn't have one, write to *100,000 Miles, Shell Oil Company, PO Box 61609, Houston, Texas, 77208.*

This maintenance record is easy and convenient to fill out, and it serves to remind you of when service is due again. Shell's Maintenance Record File can also be a valuable asset when it comes time to sell or trade the car.

You can own a car that will go 100,000 miles or more safely and dependably by following these tips and the tips throughout this book. Here are a few more, straight from the experts who really know cars.

"If you pump your own gas, make sure somebody gets under the hood every now and then to check drive belts and fluid levels. They might save you a lot of money," says Harold Elliott, chief mechanic for three-time NASCAR champion Cale Yarborough.

Jim Nash, superintendent of maintenance, Yellow Cab Company, Chicago, says, "Our cabs average 150,000 miles. That's *average.* One reason is the detailed, written records we keep. We know the vehicle is getting the maintenance it needs."

"The people who design the car also determine what goes into the owner's manual maintenance section," says Robert Rarey, automotive-design engineer and consultant. "So you're getting very valuable information there. They know what the car really needs."

Katie Robbins, president of the Classic Car Club of America, says, "I have one secret of long car life that I keep in the trunk: a clipboard full of written maintenance records."

Shell dealer Jim Jaskoske speaks of one of his customers, Yvan LaPointe. "Yvan is religious about regular maintenance. That's one reason why his car has gone 103,000 miles without major repairs. And he's still not thinking about trade-in."

Maintenance records can be your most important "tool" to keep your car running 100,000 miles.

Chapter TWO

To Do-It-Yourself or Not Do-It-Yourself

Experts predict that a time is coming when your car will speak to you through a dashboard speaker from an onboard computer. Of course they do that today, but in simple terms. A car might say "The headlights are on" or "The key is in the ignition" or "A door is ajar."

These are routine matters, easy for a computer chip to detect and report, but still a far cry from the past.

In the early 1920s, a farm woman was asked why her family owned an automobile when they didn't have a bathtub.

"You can't go to town in a bathtub," she replied.

Still, back at the very beginning, people were not keen on cars. Not only were they noisy, frequently scaring horses and killing chickens, but they were smelly. They broke down often and cost too much money. A fully equipped touring car cost as much or more than a new car cost in 1950.

There is probably no real "father" of automobiles, although Carl Benz is generally credited with putting the first motor vehicle powered by an internal combustion engine on the road in 1885. Other inventors, among them the Renault and Duryea brothers, Henry Ford, Elwood Haynes, Alexander Winton, and Gottlieb Daimler, had produced motor vehicles by the turn of the century.

A few more than ninety-five hundred vehicles were produced worldwide in 1900. One decade later, over a quarter million were manufactured. "The average person still couldn't afford an automobile then but the advantage was that people were getting used to them," explains James Wren, patent manager of the Motor Vehicles Manufacturers Association.

Getting people used to cars and then getting them to buy them didn't happen accidentally.

Alexander Winton, one of the early auto builders, was optimistic. "The Winton Company did not know where its buyers were to come from," he said, "but it had faith that buyers would come."

New car sales came, and they spawned used-car sales. One owner apologetically advertised in an 1889 issue of *Horseless Carriage* magazine: "A new Winton motor carriage without a mar or a scratch, been run 98 miles. Only reason for selling, owner has not time to use it. Has extra tank for gasoline for long trips. Will sell at a bargain."

The auto endurance tour was probably the best promotional gimmick for the fledgling industry. Groups of Auto Club members would travel, caravan-fashion, from city to city. The first such tour was the "Mud Lark" of 1903, a run from New York to Pittsburgh sponsored by the National Association of Automobile Manufacturers. On the second day of the tour, six-and-a-half inches of rain doused the occupants of the thirty-four cars as they traveled on mostly dirt roads. Thus the name "Mud Lark."

Charles J. Glidden was part of the 1904 St. Louis tour and had an encounter with an angry farmer along the way. "I rounded a corner into the face of a shotgun that looked as big as a cannon. The farmer back of the gun was as glum as the genuine western holdup man," Glidden later told *Motor Age* magazine.

"Give me a dollar for that dead chicken," the farmer demanded.

"What could I do?" Glidden asked, admitting he had passed the remains of many chickens along the road. "There was Mrs. Glidden, naturally worried. I knew one of our men had killed it so I dug up that dollar and was allowed to go on."

A wealthy Boston industrialist, Glidden was the automobile's greatest fan. By 1904, he had made a 50,000-mile worldwide tour in an English Napier. He crossed the Canadian Rockies in a car that could be fitted with flanged wheels to drive on railroad tracks. Glidden helped the tours get their start for two reasons. He wanted to make peace between the motorist and the resentful, watchful public. And he wanted to establish rules for automobile touring. He reasoned that tours could be scheduled each year through different areas of the nation, so the public could see firsthand the great technical advances made in the automobile.

There was harsh criticism of the early Glidden drivers. One newspaper stormed, "The lives and property of helpless people have been seriously menaced, the laws have been willfully disregarded and all this for no earthly reason other than to afford amusement to a lot of strangers."

It was amusement at that time, both to the drivers and to an increasingly interested public. "The arrival of the cars in each small town was greeted as a national holiday. Small boys in knickers cheered. Townspeople who owned cars themselves drove out to meet the tourists and escort them in," says James Wren.

Naturally, automakers of the day were anxious to cash in on the Glidden showings. The Oakland Model B touring car completed the Buffalo to Saratoga tour in 1908 with a perfect score. Ads for the Oakland shouted, "If there is any more sure test that a motor car could be subjected to than to go through the Glidden Tour, we would like to know what it is. The Oakland will give good reliable service 365 days a year." The Oakland later became the Pontiac after the company joined the General Motors Corporation.

The last Glidden Tour was in 1913. "They served the purpose to not only show the public that the automobile was here to stay, but also to promote the good roads movement throughout the country," concludes James Wren.

By the mid-teens, car prices had dropped dramatically as Henry Ford began pushing his famous Model T off the assembly line at a fast clip. And farmers continued to prefer cars to bathtubs until much later, when they could afford both.

Not only did prices drop, but cars became better and better. Yes, they talk to us today. And in the future your car will probably say, "Say, Bill, I'm running a little low on oil."

"OK," you might answer (and the computer will "hear" you by identifying your voice patterns), "I'll pull off at the next service station and add some."

It is possible you might even be able to argue with your car. You are driving down the street and go through a sprinkler watering the ivy. So your windshield wipers turn on.

"Not *now*, dummy," you might protest. "That was only a lawn sprinkler."

"OK, OK," your car might answer. "How was I to know?"

In the future, many functions of the car will be monitored by computers, and chances are they will tell you if something is wrong. Computers will keep an eye on suspension and brakes, on engine condition and tires, on exhaust and emission controls, and certainly on turbocharger and fuel-injection condition. But one thing they will probably *not* control is driving functions.

Imagine this. You are driving along with a friend. You are making a point about a business meeting you have that morning. "So I said, 'Hey, give me a *break!*'" you might say.

SCREEEEEECH! Crash!...CRASH!...*CRASH!*

The car's computer might not know the difference between "break" and "brake," to the chagrin of the drivers behind you.

But what if your car says, "My wheel bearings are hurting. Better check them, Bill."

Today or in the future, some drivers might not even know what a wheel bearing is, but they will certainly have somebody check them out. Other drivers might change the bearings themselves and save some labor charges. And enjoy themselves doing it.

Many car owners get real pleasure from working on their cars. To many, it is a hobby, and a profitable one at that. Routine maintenance, tune-ups, even valve jobs, are well within the ability of many do-it-yourselfers.

The fact is, cars talk to drivers today in more complicated matters. Perhaps not through a computer, but in their own "language" with a series of specific sounds. Instead of a computer voice saying, "My universal joints are failing," many owners recognize the car's language saying, "Clang... Buzzzzzz...Clang."

So these owners go ahead and jack up the car and change the U-joints.

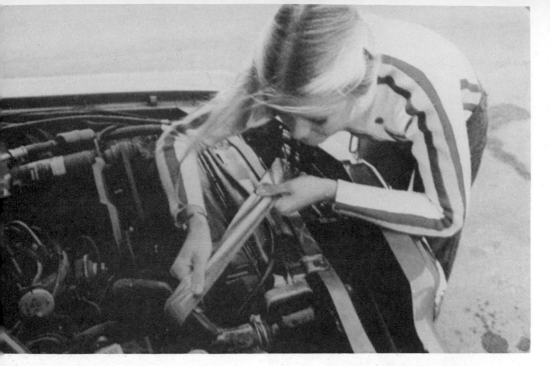

Most of us can handle the routine jobs, such as taping a leaking hose.

It is possible that some of these owners might handle a valve job, or change the piston rings, or even totally rebuild an engine.

But generally, most of us don't want to get in so deep. Most of us can handle the routine jobs, then we turn to an expert for a job that demands real skill—and expensive tools.

Carroll Hansen, a Shell dealer with a station offering both self-serve and full-serve, says, "Every year more and more drivers discover Shell self-serve as a convenient and economical way to buy gasoline. And every year, it seems more cars pull into my station—or get towed in—needing costly repairs that probably could have been avoided. Personally, I think most drivers using self-serve simply aren't taking the time to properly *maintain* their cars. They think they're saving money. But, by neglecting maintenance, they really aren't."

In his station a survey was conducted. At self-serve, certain inspections were done. Here are the results.

- 56 cars were at least one quart low on oil
- 34 were low on radiator coolant
- 27 batteries were low on water
- 29 needed power-steering fluid

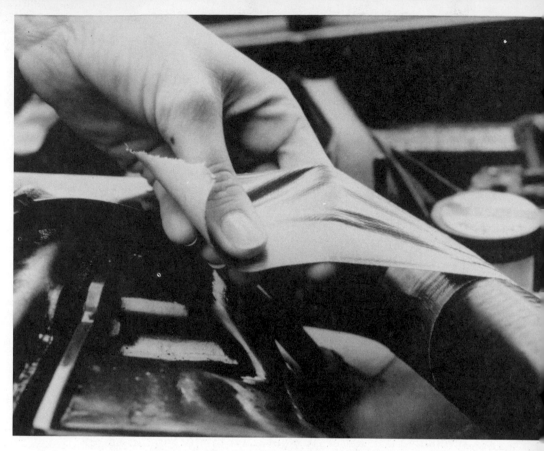

Before you tape a leak, let the engine cool. Then clean all the dust, dirt, grease, and water from the hose. Otherwise the tape won't hold and you'll still have a leak.

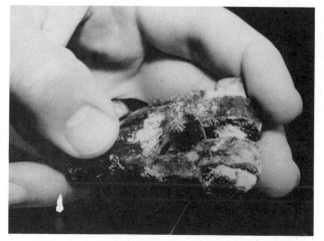

A car might not start if the battery terminals are corroded or a cable connection is loose. Clean with a knife, nail file, or an emery board.

- 28 needed brake fluid
- 33 had at least one tire well below recommended pressures.

Oddly, the simplest jobs can result in the greatest savings over the long run. Here are some routine maintenance jobs almost anybody can handle and in so doing add thousands of miles to the life of their car. The step-by-step details of these jobs will be found in chapters 5, 6, and 7 of this book. For now, and just to get familiar with what can be done by the average owner, look at the routine chores. These are jobs you can, and should, attempt.

Any one of these items could, if left unattended, result in stalling, costly repairs, or even an accident. Yet no tools are needed and the "repair" is simple.

Routine Jobs For You

Checking the engine oil
Checking the radiator coolant level
Checking the radiator hoses
Checking the battery and cables
Checking the power-steering fluid
Checking the tire pressures (though you will need a pressure gauge for this job)
Checking the brake fluid

These are simple, routine jobs that any driver can do alone at the self-serve island or in the driveway at home. They can save you *real* money. More details about each of them later in this book.

DO ANY JOB SAFELY

But before you attempt *any* car maintenance or repair job, the routine ones or the more complicated ones later in this book, keep safety in mind. Car products are generally not dangerous but if they are misused they can be deadly.

An estimated forty thousand people are burned each year in gasoline accidents. A car battery can explode in your face if you do the wrong thing with it. A car can fall off a jack and injure you. You can be cut by a whirling fan blade, or shocked by the ignition system, or scalded by hot coolant or a hot exhaust. You can, if you work in a closed area, even die from the carbon monoxide exhausted by a running engine.

"I blew up batteries, set fires with gasoline, even scalded a dummy to get a close-up look at some ways people can hurt themselves," says Dr. Jerry Berger, a Shell chemist. "Things like these fire-fighting tests always give me a better outlook on my job. Safety isn't just reports and regulations. Safety makes the difference between a healthy human being and an injured one. That difference is worth the extra effort."

SOME QUESTIONS ON UNEXPECTED DANGERS

"Is it safe to clean things with gasoline?"
Never.
Gasoline is a tricky fluid. It vaporizes easily, and the invisible vapors are heavier than air. They can spread along the floor to a water heater, an electric motor, a car's engine, or something else that ignites them.

Never use gasoline as a cleaner, a charcoal starter, or a solvent—not *anything* except fuel for a gasoline engine.

"Suppose I have a gasoline fire. What's the best extinguisher?"

It's usually best to get everybody away from the fire and call the fire department. If you must fight the fire yourself, there are four possible ways, some much better than others.

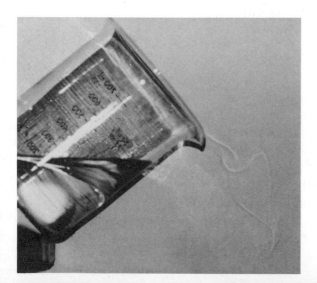

Photographed with special lighting, invisible gasoline vapors cast a shadow as they drift out of a beaker and fall toward the floor. These vapors can even "crawl" across the ground and reach an ignition source a good distance away.

1. A STRAIGHT STREAM OF WATER actually spread the fire further. Burning gasoline splashed out of the pan, floated on the water, and kept right on burning. The heat got so bad, I had to duck away. 2. A SPRAY OF WATER worked a little better. At least it didn't spread the flames. But I had to hold the hose just right, and it took a long time. If the fire had been in somebody's garage, it might have been too long. 3. A DRY CHEMICAL EXTINGUISHER snuffed out the test fire in just a few seconds. I think anyone who uses gasoline at home should have an extinguisher like this. The ones marked for "type B" fires are for gasoline and other flammable liquids. 4. A GARBAGE CAN LID killed the fire by cutting off its air supply. A shovel full of sand, a piece of plywood, a tarpaulin, anything that will cut off the air supply and won't burn easily might work. The trick is to let it sit there and smother the fire for a long time. If you remove it and let the air back in too soon, hot vapors reignite.

A straight stream of water will probably just splash the gasoline, and the fire, all over the area. Gasoline floats on water and keeps right on burning.

A spray of water is a little better. It might not spread the flames so much and it will cool down the fire. But it takes time. If the fire is in your garage or home it might take too long and the fire will spread before you get it extinguished.

A dry chemical extinguisher works well on a gasoline fire, the type marked "For Type B Fires." These are made especially for flammable liquids and should be kept readily available around the garage and kitchen.

A smothering device—a big lid, some sand, a flat board, a tarpaulin, anything that will cut off the air supply to the fire and won't ignite easily—might work. The trick is to let it sit there and really smother the fire for a long time. If you remove it and let the air back in too soon, the hot vapors might reignite.

"Then maybe I shouldn't even have gasoline in my garage?"

The best place to store gasoline in a garage is in the fuel tank in your car. You can store gasoline in other places in your garage if you wish, but only in a container made for the storage of gasoline or other flammable liquids. Yes, this is much more expensive than a plastic container (or a throwaway container used for some other purpose), but it is good insurance.

Keep only a small amount, just enough for your immediate needs. If you only use a gallon a month, what's the use of having five gallons in storage? Store your container in a place that is well ventilated and away from any ignition source, and keep it out of the reach of children even if you have to lock it up to do so. The best place is somewhere separate from your living area, such as a shed or detached garage.

A good gasoline storage safety can has a spring-loaded cap that allows pressure out but closes to resist spills. It has a flame arrestor in the neck to keep flames from following the vapor back into the can. It is short and fat and hard to overturn. It has clear labeling to help prevent mistakes.

One teenager was keeping an old car in his garage. He planned to restore it, but at his leisure. The antique had been sitting there for years. Then one day he came out to try to start the engine. It wouldn't start. Must be out of gas, he decided. The gas must have evaporated. He should have been so lucky.

GASOLINE SAFETY CAN: Spring cap lets pressure escape, resists spills. Flame arrestor in neck keep flame from following vapor trail inside. Short, fat shape makes it hard to tip over. Clear labeling helps prevent mistakes.

That's right, he took out a lighter, opened the fuel tank, and tried to aim the light down inside the tank. Gasoline *never* completely evaporates. The resulting explosion nearly blinded him, and did keep him in the hospital for several weeks.

"Is gassing up my lawn mower risky?"

Yes, but with four simple precautions you can cut the risk. First, get away from ignition sources when you fuel any engine. Don't smoke. Second, have plenty of ventilation. Do it outside, not inside. Third, and perhaps most important, don't refuel any engine that's running, or anything that is hot. Heat can set off the vapors. Take a break, have a glass of iced tea, allow things to cool down before you fill up.

Fourth, pour very carefully to prevent spills. Use a funnel. If you spill any fuel, clean it up before starting the engine, smoking, or having any other heat source nearby.

"What should I do if my child swallows some gasoline?"

First of all, separate the two. Get the gasoline away from the child to prevent any more drinking. If the child spilled some gasoline on himself, get the soaked clothing off then wash him with plenty of soap and warm water to prevent chemical burns.

Then call a poison center or a doctor right away. If there is no poison center in your phone book, get the number in advance from the operator and post it. When you need it, you *need* it, so do it when you have time.

Here's what *not* to do. When someone has drunk gasoline, do *not* make him vomit *unless* the doctor or poison center tells you to do it. Sometimes throwing up can make the matter worse. The same is true for kerosene, lighter fluid, and fuel oil. Another tip. Never start a siphon by sucking on the hose. Children aren't the only ones poisoned by gasoline.

"Can a car battery really explode?"

Yes. Battery explosions are not common, but when they happen they are dangerous. Sharp pieces of battery are sent flying like shrapnel and battery acid sprays everywhere. The chemical reaction inside a battery produces an explosive mixture of hydrogen and oxygen. This mixture escapes a little at a time under normal circumstances and no harm is done. But occasionally, when a lot of it collects around a battery and something ignites it (such as the spark from a wrong hookup of a jump starter cable), POOF!

The vent caps on some batteries have flame arrestors inside.

This battery was blown to pieces by its own explosive gases. This can happen from a spark caused by improper hooking up of jumper cables, and you could be standing next to the blast.

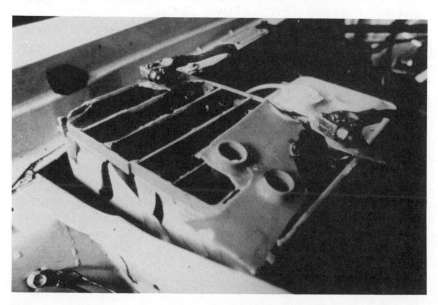

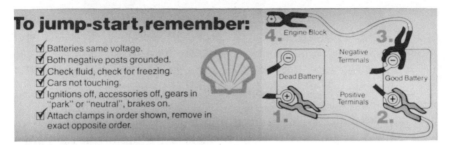

To jump-start, remember:

- ☑ Batteries same voltage.
- ☑ Both negative posts grounded.
- ☑ Check fluid, check for freezing.
- ☑ Cars not touching.
- ☑ Ignitions off, accessories off, gears in "park" or "neutral", brakes on.
- ☑ Attach clamps in order shown, remove in exact opposite order.

4. Engine Block 3.
Negative Terminals
Dead Battery   Good Battery
Positive Terminals
1.   2.

Ask a participating Shell dealer for a free sticker giving these instructions. Paste them near your battery. Then you'll always know the right way to get, or give, a jump start.

If the gases around a battery should happen to ignite, the arrestors prevent the flames from getting into the battery and blowing it apart. You might look for this next time you buy a battery.

"Then what is the safe way to jump start my car?"

The trick is to keep any sparks from getting near the battery. Here's how. Make sure the two cars are not touching. Set both parking brakes, put both transmissions into park or neutral, turn off the ignition, lights, and other accessories on both cars.

Make sure the two batteries are the same voltage.

One terminal of each battery is grounded. That is, it is connected to the engine block. Make sure the negative terminal on both batteries is the grounded one, as it is on all modern American cars and most foreign cars.

Add water to either battery if it needs it. "Maintenance free" batteries do not have filler vents, of course.

Using the red jumper cable, connect the positive terminals of the two batteries. Make sure the clamps are tight so they won't spark. Wiggle each one to get a "bite."

Connect the black cable from the negative terminal of one battery to a bare metal part bolted directly to the other car's engine block or to the block itself. This is the same as connecting it to the battery terminal, since the terminal is grounded. But this final connection is the one that sparks, so you want it as far from the battery as possible. Route the cables away from fans and belts and be careful not to touch the black clamps to the red ones.

Try to start the car with the dead battery. If it won't start the first time, start the booster car and let it run a few minutes before trying again to recharge the battery.

Once the car starts, remove the clamps in the exact reverse order. The first one you disconnect will cause a spark, so remove the one farthest from the battery first.

"What is the best way to cool my car if it is overheating?"

The *best* way is to pull off the road, shut off the engine, and wait.

Don't try to remove the radiator cap or you might get scalded. How do you know? A rule of thumb is to touch the radiator with your hand. If it is too hot to touch, it is too hot to open. Most modern cars have an overflow tank to allow you to check the level of your coolant without removing the cap. If your car doesn't have one, they are inexpensive to buy and easy to install.

If you are in a service station with plenty of water available, you can try running water over the radiator as the engine idles. This is messy, but it will cool down the engine safely and more quickly. When things are cooled down, you can open the radiator and, with the engine idling, add water.

Most modern cars cool their automatic transmission as well as their engine with the radiator. You'll see the trans fluid lines running from the transmission to the radiator and back. Running an engine that is too hot might also do real damage to your transmission. For that reason, many owners of cars doing heavy-duty work (pulling a trailer, etc.) install an extra transmission-fluid cooling radiator up front. But this might not be a job for the Saturday-morning mechanic.

OTHER JOBS FOR EXPERTS

Most of the jobs listed so far can be handled by the average do-it-yourselfer. They are interesting, even fun, and they will add years to the life of your car. There are jobs around a car, however, that only an expert mechanic should tackle. These are not "gray area" jobs that you *might* want to tackle with some practice, or because you really love working on your car. These are jobs that require special skills or special tools.

So pass these on to your local mechanic, and note in the

next chapter that this expert can and should be chosen with care.

1. Engine overhaul
2. Transmission overhaul
3. Differential work
4. Steering and front-end work
5. Valve overhauls
6. Frame work
7. Fuel-tank repairs

THE GRAY AREA

Then there is the gray area of car repair in which you might want to tackle a job if you feel qualified, or want to learn, or have done it before, or just have a feel for cars. This is an area for more serious do-it-yourselfers who have a reasonable supply of tools and a working area that will remain undisturbed for the duration of the job. Following is a list of many of these jobs along with the pros and cons of doing it yourself. Most of these are covered later in this book with detailed instructions.

Brake Work

The most important thing a car can do for you is *not* to get you from here to there. The most important thing it does is *stop.* You *need* your brakes, and working on brakes is a job that requires skill, care, and at least a reasonable amount of time, tools, and patience. In the brake shop they can swing right through a job like this, but they have extra tools and gauges, replacement parts at hand (including the little springs and clips you might break or lose), and experience.

But a brake job (other than turning down the drums or rotors, which you can hire out) is well within the realm of the serious do-it-yourself mechanic. And you can save a bundle doing it since labor is a big part of this job. You'll have to be certain you have bought the right parts, and frequently you don't learn this until you try to install the new brakes, but the job is possible.

Muffler and Exhaust-system Work

When your car begins to sound like a tractor or a semitruck, it's time to check out the exhaust system. You can do-it-your-self, but it is a dirty job that usually takes muscle as well as skill. Exhaust-system parts tend to weld themselves together. Removing the exhaust pipe from the engine can be a frustrating job, and getting the old muffler off the exhaust pipe and tail-pipe can also be a demanding chore. What's worse, you prob-ably don't have a lift, so you'll have to jack up the car, block it up (in case the jack fails), then work from flat on your back.

Labor charges aren't quite as significant as with some of the other jobs, so you won't save as much money doing it yourself, but there is a satisfaction in taking a loud, smelly engine and converting it back to a soft purr.

Another factor you will want to consider is that specialty shops do this sort of work relatively cheaply and throw in a lifetime guarantee. You can do it, and do it right, but it takes more muscle than skill.

Tune-up

This is a perfect "gray area" job. It takes some skill and some parts, but the result of careful work is a smoother running, more efficient car. Most modern cars have electronic ignitions, so you don't have to worry about installing points and con-denser. But you do have to concern yourself with spark plugs (the right type and the right electrode-opening measurements), timing (which requires a timing light), replacement of filters, service of any pollution-control devices, adjustment of drive belts, and other details.

This is an interesting and enjoyable job that, with care, most do-it-yourselfers can handle.

Changing Fan Belts

To do this right you might have to move other components on some modern cars, but this job is in the ballpark if you don't mind getting a little soiled. And it is a very important job. A broken fan belt can quickly stall a car with an overheated engine. Most owners ignore this very important part until it is too late, so if you see a worn or cracked belt, and you are an auto do-it-yourselfer, give it a try.

Changing Oil and Air Filters

Here's another job that is well within the skill of the average do-it-yourselfer. If you can do-it-yourself, you can save some money and you might do it more often, which will substantially increase the life and performance of your engine.

Lubrication

Not the cleanest job in the world, but a job that will help your car if you want to tackle it fairly often. You'll need a grease gun and a knowledge of where the grease fittings are located. Then crawl in and around and under and start shooting.

Rotating Tires

Thousands of miles can be added to the life of your tires with care like this, but there are some tricks to it. There is a rotation sequence, especially with radial tires, that must be followed. Your owner's manual will probably give you this information and from then on it's manual labor (with attention to safety, since you will be using a jack).

Flush Radiator and Engine Block and Add New Coolant

With a little attention to details and selection of proper cleaners and coolants, you can do this job in a couple of hours on Saturday morning and come out with a sparkling, efficient radiator and cooling system. It can be messy if the water splashes around, and you'll need an area for the old coolant to run off (unless you want to collect it as it drains) but the job is not tough. Your owner's manual will probably tell you where the drain plugs are, but be very careful of any hot water from the engine.

Shock Absorber Replacement

Why not? The old car is beginning to bounce like a kangaroo with every dip or bump in the road. You can do it. But remember, you are working with heavy parts here as you jack up the body, and you are going to have to crawl under to remove the old shocks and install the new ones. A service station can do this job in less than an hour. But if you want to save the money, and have two or three hours to spare, you can do it.

Body Work

This can be a challenging job that, if not done correctly, can make things worse than they were. But if you enjoy working with hammers and files, paint remover, sandpaper, fillers, and new paint, it can be done. And here you can save a bundle on repairs, since labor is the big charge for body work.

These are some of the jobs that do-it-yourselfers with a knowledge of cars can handle in their spare time. Most of them can be completed in one sitting, so the car won't be out of commission the next day. But plan to get dirty and to work with tools, heavy tools in some cases.

Chapter THREE

Where to Find
a Mechanic

If you have a good mechanic, a person you trust with your car, your pocketbook, and, in every sense, your *life*, stay with him.

It's true, you know. A mechanic who does a poor job can cost you in money and convenience, and if the job has to do with safety (brakes, suspension, etc.) the result can be an accident. Your life and the life of your family can be in his hands.

If you have a good mechanic, stick with him since you actually entrust your *life* to him.

Yet many people leave a good mechanic because of a misunderstanding over price, or a job that didn't seem done quite right, or even because of a bad breakfast that morning. A good mechanic is hard to find. Hold on to him.

Auto repair is one of the main sources of consumer complaints. The problem is, you don't need skill to call yourself a mechanic. All you have to do is print up some cards saying "EXPERT AUTO REPAIR," rent a space, gather up a few tools, and attempt to attract customers.

If you have ever fallen into the hands of one of these backyard experts, you know what can happen. You get a shaky, confused estimate, often for much lower than you expected it to be. Then you wait forever, pay a fortune or at least an amount much higher than you originally discussed, and drive away in a car that doesn't work as well as it did when you drove in.

Then you start the long battle to get the car fixed right. You take it in every morning and pick it up every night. Meanwhile, you are borrowing a car, or asking friends to haul you around. Finally, the car is "fixed," but nine times out of ten, it still doesn't work the way it should. You often end up going to another mechanic.

No wonder the auto repair business is a source of complaints.

Dr. Lee Richardson is president of the Consumer Federation of America and chairperson of the Department of Marketing, Louisiana State University. He says, "The real cost of repairs is far beyond the bill you get.... There's this great uncertainty people have because they're not sure who to deal with or what should be done. They feel it's like rolling dice.... And the consumer doesn't see any backup in the repair business. Some places may have systems in effect where the customer can bring a grievance, but they're irrelevant if the customer isn't aware of them.

"In most cities there is a place to complain. A Better Business Bureau, state, county, or city consumer protection office. They can be effective.

"Car repairs is one of the most frustrating areas consumers find themselves in. Many solutions are proposed, but they just aren't clear-cut enough."

"The shock of getting a bill that's more than you thought it would be seems to be the biggest problem," says Virginia H.

Knauer, former director of the Office of Consumer Affairs, HEW. "But we hear a lot from consumers about the nonavailability of 'loaner' cars that are advertised.

"Of all the complaints we get, only a very small percentage are about a rip-off. It's my perception that the vast majority of repair shops really try to do a decent job. If a consumer has a complaint he can't work out, he should see if there is an Auto Cap (Automotive Consumer Action Panel) in his state, put the complaint on record with the parent company if there is one, then check with his state Bureau of Consumer Protection or write to the Federal Office of Consumer Affairs."

These remarks come from the consumer's side. But the repairmen have a side, too. Richard Wagner is director of the National Automobile Dealers Association and chairman of its Public and Consumer Affairs Committee. He has also been an auto dealer for two dozen years.

He says, "If a customer has a problem following a repair job, he really doesn't know whether it's poor workmanship, product design, or an additional defect. The first thing to do is identify the problem. The customer should talk to the person in charge. Not necessarily the service manager. It should be someone away from the pressure of the service area.

"The basis of satisfactory repairs is going to someone you trust.... The customer has responsibilities. He should work out his method of payment in advance. He should arrange for alternate transportation if repairs take a long time. He should call to be sure his car is ready before coming to get it. If he notices a problem, he should go back to the facility immediately. And not let emotion aggravate the situation."

That's all true, but it puts you right in the front lines of auto repair. You are the one who has to face an unpleasant, uncooperative mechanic who feels he has done the job whether the car runs right or not. He has your car, he has handed you a bill, and the ball is in your court. You have to fight the battle on the spot, and you want it handled now, not later in arbitration or court.

One of the best pieces of advice comes from Charles Binsted, executive director, National Congress of Petroleum Retailers, board member of the National Institute of Automotive Service Excellence, and a service station operator for many years. "A

American auto owners spend *billions* each year on car repairs. You will save money if you follow the tips in this book.

consumer is better served if he selects a repair facility and builds a relationship and confidence with them.... If you don't know car repair, you should know the mechanic.

"The industry is trying to build more competent mechanics. But public education hasn't responded as well as it might have. In many schools the subject of auto mechanics hasn't been given the emphasis it should.

"The customer should have a good understanding when he leaves his car for repairs. But understanding gaps occur even with long-time customers. I advise my people to call the customer and let him know if something additional is needed. Don't give him the five o'clock surprise.... Not all people who work in service stations are mechanics. Customers shouldn't press an inexperienced man to work on their cars. It might do more harm than good."

Yet the fact remains that in many states you can't be sure—even if the guy you have hired to fix your car has a dealership, a service station, a garage, or a specialty shop. Needing a car repair is often a "right now" situation. You might not have time to shop around, or even to go to your regular mechanic.

Not that you will always get ripped off in a strange garage. Not at all. One young couple, as short of ready cash as young couples often are, were driving on vacation in another state. Their charging system failed—at two o'clock in the morning. They managed to get to the next town where they located a down-at-the-heels garage with a single bulb over the door.

"CAR REPAIRS" was all the sign said. They were frightened and concerned, but what could they do?

The mechanic came out, looked at the car, diagnosed a bad alternator, and gave them a price. He just happened to have an alternator in stock. He could have charged them almost anything, and he knew it. Yet he made the repair and presented them with a bill they considered quite fair and honest. It happens.

You can guess where they would take their repairs if they lived in that town, and for that matter where the townspeople took their cars.

It happened to another couple in a national park, when they found their engine overheating due to a bad water pump. Not only that, but they had a sick child with them and were anxious to head for home. There was only one garage for a hundred miles, so, dripping and steaming, they drove in.

The mechanic used his lunch hour as a courtesy to the couple and the repair was accomplished from stock. The price was right, and the couple were soon on their way. They could have been ripped off, but they weren't.

The majority of garages and service stations are honest. They really feel they are doing the job in the best way, at the most honest price. But not all of them.

One mechanic tried to talk a driver into a new water pump because the fan turned freely with the engine off. He said the water-pump bearing had failed. Even this inexperienced driver knew that the fan clutch was allowing the fan to turn freely. He didn't go back to that garage.

Another mechanic, new on the job and not realizing that the very same garage had just installed new shock absorbers, told a driver that he was taking his life in his hands by "driving with those worn-out shocks." The boss was embarrassed, the new mechanic was quickly jobless, and the driver was out looking for a new shop.

But there are ways to minimize your risk and calm your uneasiness.

WHAT TO LOOK FOR

You won't often get the chance on the road, but at home you have the opportunity to choose a place and a mechanic as you would a hospital and a doctor. Find a facility you trust, a place that is right for you. Here are seven things to look for.

1. Reputation. This is one of the most valuable assets of a mechanic. You can feel better about going to a shop that has been recommended by a friend or neighbor, or a shop you have heard good things about from others. If you have heard nothing at all, ask your local Better Business Bureau if there are complaints against the shop you are considering.

Most agencies won't get specific about complaints, but they will have a record of how many have been filed. Perhaps most of them have been groundless, but still, why deal with a shop where so many others have had a problem?

2. Qualifications. Are the mechanics in the shop licensed, certified, experienced? Ask around. Ask at the shop for proof of their ability to work on *your* car with *your* problem. If they resist, or chuckle at you, walk away. Unless you are stalled on a country road in a blinding snowstorm with no help for miles, they need you more than you need them.

That's something many drivers forget. Garages and service stations need the business. They value their customers. If the shop you are checking doesn't, drive on. Find one that does.

3. Equipment. Look around the shop before you make a deal. Do they appear to have the proper tools to do the job? You may not know exactly what they are, but most of us can tell the difference between a well-equipped shop and a fly-by-night operation.

This doesn't mean that the facility needs rows of electronic devices and a whole garage full of stalls and lifts. Smaller garages can do excellent jobs. But it does mean that you want more than just a simple toolbox and a roomful of promises.

4. *Cleanliness and neatness.* An auto repair garage is not a hospital operating room, but cleanliness and good order usually go with efficient mechanics. Good mechanics like to work in a clean, well-organized shop.

Generally speaking, they will keep your job and your car as clean as the place they work. This is always important, and very important when the job is a detailed one, with critical measurements involved and precise assembling necessary.

5. *Convenience.* Is the garage near enough to your home or place of work? Will you have transportation while the car is being repaired? Most garages will offer to take you to work if you get the car in early enough in the morning. But it is inconvenient, possibly even impossible, for you to give up your car for any extended period of time. Talk about it ahead of time, before you leave the car. A job will often be delayed because a part is out of stock and has to be ordered.

6. *Estimates.* You want a bill showing exactly what they figure they are going to have to do, and how much they figure it is going to cost. Many states have regulations that do not permit them to raise these figures without checking with you first.

This is, of course, one of auto-repair-land's Catch-22s. How do you know when they call with a new estimate that it is correct and necessary? On the other hand, it doesn't seem reasonable to tell them to go by the old estimate since everybody now knows that it won't help the car.

One young man was having a routine job done on his car while he waited in the customer lounge. The garage just as routinely added a few extra dollars to the bill before they called him in to pay up. It was only five or six dollars. Nobody had ever complained before. This young man did, loudly. He was there, waiting, and nobody told him. Ultimately, the garage manager apologized for the mistake and reduced the price to what had been agreed upon.

7. *Guarantees.* Will they back up their work in writing? Don't be shy about asking, and be certain they specify exactly what they are guaranteeing, and for how long. Is the labor guaranteed, or just the parts (which are usually guaranteed by the

manufacturer)? Many garages don't even mind a "come-backer" if the part has failed, since they can bill the manufacturer for labor charges the second time around.

WRITTEN ESTIMATES

This can be a problem, since there are so many "gray areas" here. One shop wrote out an estimate on a valve adjustment, then found later that one valve was burned. Obviously they stopped the adjustment, a thirty-dollar job, since it would be a waste of effort.

Must they now do a complete valve job on the engine for the estimated thirty bucks? No, of course not. But still, the owner of the car should not have to face the ill-famed "five o'clock surprise," that moment when he comes in to pick up his car with thirty dollars in his hand and faces a bill of three *hundred* dollars.

Most reputable garages will contact the owner and tell him the bad news before they go any further. The owner, in fact, can make sure of this by noting on the bill that he should be called before any additional expenses. That's all well and good, but what can you do about it then? You can either authorize the new amount, or you can come in and pick up the car— and you'll probably owe them for the work already done.

There are other secrets to a written estimate. You should check the estimate closely and be sure that every repair item discussed is listed separately, including costs of parts. If a "tune-up" is involved, be sure you know precisely what that *tune-up* includes, parts and labor.

Ask the person who wrote out the estimate to sign it so that you know who to name if a problem develops. Get a copy of the final estimate, with everything clearly listed, before you leave your car.

If you simply want a diagnosis and have no plans to get the car repaired, expect to pay for the time of the mechanic. They'll want their fee even if the repairs exceed what you wanted to spend. Their time is what they have for sale, and they have given their time to figure out what's wrong with your car. Fair is fair.

Always get a written estimate from a mechanic before authorizing repairs to begin.

CERTIFIED MECHANICS

Many service stations, garages, dealerships, and specialty shops advertise that their mechanics are "certified." This, it is assumed, means that the mechanics have been trained in auto repair, or in the specialty of the shop. Generally speaking, mechanics value the patches on their sleeves. They have, in fact, worked for them, gone to school for them, spent time learning. You can count on the fact that the mechanic has, indeed, been trained and passed tests given by auto manufacturers, oil companies, related industry organizations, or states.

This doesn't necessarily insure honesty, but it does indicate that the person knows what he or she is doing.

On the other hand, not having the certification does not automatically mean that the mechanic lacks the skill to work on your car. Many excellent mechanics are noncertified. A private garage, for example, may have superb mechanics who spend their time working on cars rather than going to school.

Certification is a sign of competence, but it shouldn't be your only consideration.

Here are some typical questions from auto owners seeking service, compiled by mechanical engineer Howard Judson. Judson was Shell Oil Company's manager of consumer relations and a member of both the Society of Consumer Affairs Professionals and the Conference of Consumer Organizations.

"What can I do to make things go smoother when I bring in my car?"

First, call for an appointment. There are around a hundred million cars on the road and only around eight hundred thousand mechanics. If possible, avoid requesting work on Mondays, Fridays, and Saturdays, usually the busiest days. Don't try to "hurry" the mechanic. If he has the proper time (even though it might be costing you a little more) he'll probably do a better job. Still, ask to see all replaced parts as proof that any work has been done. This is now an accepted practice in the auto repair business, so he won't get "mad" at you for asking, or suggest that you doubt his honesty.

In fact, it protects him as much as you, so *insist.*

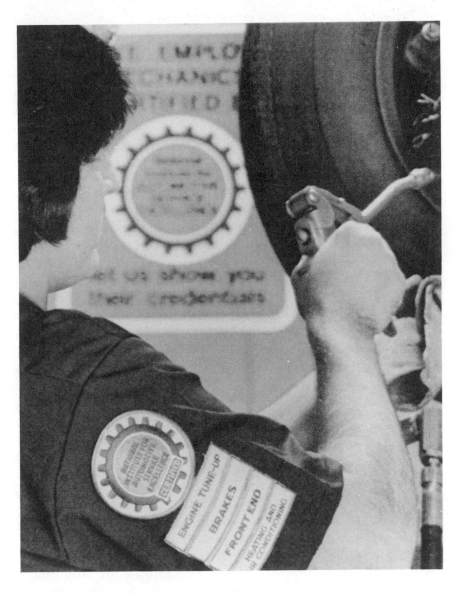

The National Institute for Automotive Service Excellence offers a certification program. The mechanic takes tests on different systems of the car. If he passes the tests and has at least two years of practical experience, he is certified and entitled to wear shoulder patches that show his expertise. And his place of business can display the NIASE sign.

One district attorney's office collected enough complaints on a local repair facility to warrant an investigation. The office had their own mechanic set up a certain problem in a car, then a volunteer drove in for an estimate. An agreement was reached and the "repairs" were done. The volunteer asked for replaced parts to be returned. But this car had marks on the parts, and this car was set up so that only one specific problem was there.

This would have been no problem at all for most repair shops, but this shop returned parts that were not even from the car being repaired. They were just old parts from the trash bin of the garage. The car was diagnosed as having much more serious problems. It was "repaired" but along with the repair a number of other things were done because they were "absolutely necessary" for safety. Of course the bill was much higher, but it was unavoidable if the driver wanted his car to run correctly.

What was worse, the needed repair was ignored in favor of the much more expensive job.

Needless to say, the garage owner was prosecuted and eventually paid a heavy fine. And the matter was publicized in the local newspaper, so you can imagine what happened to business.

This happens, and most honest mechanics cheer. They want the cheaters rooted out. They want the garages who give the whole business a bad name found out as much as you do.

"How do I tell a mechanic what's wrong?"

Most owners do not know exactly what's wrong with their car, so it is usually difficult to try to tell the mechanic. Instead, tell him the symptoms. Tell him what the car is, and isn't, doing. Tell him why you brought the car in. He's the expert, so allow him to make the diagnosis.

You should tell him exactly what has been happening, and when it happens. Does it happen all the time, or only under certain conditions? Does it get better or worse under certain circumstances? Does it happen when you are going fast, or slow, or both? Does it happen with the engine hot or cold? Did it start gradually, or all at once? Are there any unusual noises connected with what is happening and, although this is sometimes humorous, can you describe them?

With all this information, and perhaps a test drive, a good

You can get a free copy of this troubleshooting guide from Shell. It will help you to communicate with your mechanic when trouble strikes.

mechanic will have a much better chance of pinpointing the problem.

"How do I know I'm getting a fair price?"

If the price you are quoted is for a specific job, and you can still drive the car, you can always get a second opinion. We do it for our bodies, when a doctor is involved. Why not for our cars? And as you would not necessarily do with a doctor, don't jump at one price just because it is the lowest. Consider a brake job, for example. Prices can range from $30 up to about $175. Usually the higher price includes rebuilt or new wheel cylinders and machining (turning) the drums or discs.

The lower price might be limited to the purchase and installation of brake shoes only. Be sure you know what the estimate includes, since there are risks of getting only a partial job.

If the price you are quoted is truly an estimate, based on

some "labor" rate, ask them specifically what hourly rate they charge. If the job goes beyond what they anticipated, you need to know this. Remember, labor rates vary, and so can the cost of the job.

You may be one of the technically oriented customers they get, and they won't object if you ask to see the "flat-rate manual." Many regular establishments base their rates on this guide. But the only way to feel comfortable about the price is to feel comfortable about the place doing the repair work.

When a garage is using a flat-rate fee for labor charges and they make an estimate for a job, they will usually not charge beyond the amount they estimated unless the job goes into areas they did not anticipate—the valve adjustment that turned into a replacement of a burned valve, for example. Otherwise, even if the valve adjustment takes longer than they figured it would, they will usually stick with the original labor amount. Once again, fair is fair. You shouldn't have to pay extra time for a mechanic who fumbles around with the job.

On the other hand, you must keep an eye on things. Consider the man who took his car into a shop because his main ignition key switch was loose in its panel. What was needed was obvious. Somebody had to tighten the lock ring on the switch. The job was estimated to take one hour and cost thirty-five dollars in labor. No parts would be involved.

Thirty-five dollars is what the man paid when the job was finished. It was a flat-rate manual suggestion, and the garage stuck to the estimate. But wait a minute! The man had waited for the car, which he brought in at 11:30 in the morning. So he saw the whole job. First the mechanic took the car to the stall, then he grabbed a quick lunch. That took twenty minutes. Then he had to get help from another mechanic in locating a particular tool. That took another fifteen minutes. Finally, because he was relatively new on the job, he had to look up the proper procedure for tightening the switch. That took ten minutes.

At long last, in the final fifteen minutes of the hour, he tightened the switch.

True, the man brought the car in at 11:30, and by 12:30 the job was done. One hour, exactly. But you can imagine how many times he will go back to that repair facility. What happened just wasn't fair, even though the job was done within the estimate.

"What can I do if my car isn't fixed right?"

This is a tough question since so many factors, and possibly personalities, are involved. But it does happen. You OK the estimate, get the job done, pay the bill, and halfway home the noise starts again, or the shimmy, or whatever the original complaint happened to be.

If you're not satisfied with the job, register a complaint as quickly as possible with the people who did the job. Going elsewhere to get it done again, then trying to come back to the first place for a refund, only complicates the matter. Meanwhile, the first mechanic may have made an honest mistake. He may be *anxious* to correct the matter at his own expense.

Give him a chance before you carry the matter further. It is best not to shout or get angry. Calmly explain that the problem has not been corrected (as frustrating as this can be at times) and listen to what the mechanic has to say.

If worst comes to worst and you can't get any satisfaction, determine whether the repair shop has arrangements with any arbitration service such as the Better Business Bureau or the Automotive Consumer Action Panel. If they do, put your complaint in writing. Then send the original to the repair shop, with carbon copies to city, state, or federal consumer protection bureaus, or the Better Business Bureau.

A good letter can work wonders if it is addressed to the right person or agency. But remember, they are outsiders, away from the heat of the moment. A letter should be a business matter, not a tirade or a condemnation.

Here's what *not* to put in your letter. Threats. Apologies. Anger. Legal terms. Just state the facts as you know them to be, and include your name, address, and telephone number along with the name of the repair facility. The agency will also want the make and model of your car, and a total of how much the problem has cost you (including mileage, phone calls, etc.). Include a copy of the bill and any expenses you have claimed.

Keep a copy of the letter and all other pertinent data for yourself.

Usually, this type of letter will get some action. If it doesn't, you should then consider Small Claims Court. In most states, you won't even need a lawyer for this, and the fees are small. Generally speaking, you will find a sympathetic audience in the judge, who has had car repair problems himself.

LET'S GET DOWN TO BUSINESS

Where is the best place to take your car? You have a problem, you need it fixed. You need honest service, but you want good, efficient, economical service as well. You don't mind paying a price, but you want the price to be fair.

You have a choice. Depending upon what's wrong (or what you think is wrong) with your car, there are some logical decisions.

The first thing to do is to look ahead a bit. What you really want is a reliable source for years to come, not just some shop to bail you out of a current emergency. If you're stuck with a broken transmission, you probably don't have time to shop around. You need the car now. It is possible to be stampeded into an expensive decision. You'll be dollars ahead if you do a little investigation in advance of your need. For example, you're going to need a brake job sooner or later. Why not find a good, reliable source now?

Let's assume your problem is not covered by any type of warranty. Naturally, if you can get free service you should go to wherever that service is provided unless you have found them to be completely incompetent.

The Car Dealer

This establishment normally has a clean, well-run service department with modern equipment, trained mechanics, and, hopefully, a reputation to protect. But there is a hitch. The dealership will be most trained and efficient on the model of car they sell. They can work on all models, but often their equipment will be designed to take care of a certain make of car. Their parts department will have the parts for that make.

One other hitch. At a dealership they will give you an estimate, then take your car far back into the bowels of the building. You'll see it later, when the job is done, but you won't ever see it in the meantime. You won't really *know* what's happening. They'll have signs all over the place warning that "customers are not permitted in the service area."

That might not be a problem, but some drivers like to watch, or at least be around to "protect" their car.

The mechanic will readily understand the available charts and schematics since he has worked on this system in this make of car many times before. But you will probably pay a slightly higher labor rate to cover the overhead of the dealer. If the problem is complex, the dealer has a ready line to the manufacturer, but this will cost, too, in time on the job.

If you have that make of car and don't mind paying the somewhat higher rates, you should get good service. You will probably get it quicker, too, if you get your car in at the appointed time. In fact, if the problem in your car is particularly complex, the dealership may be the *only* place you can go to get proper repairs.

The Independent Garage

This is often a matter of trial and error. If you have found a garage with a mechanic you trust, where you get what you consider to be good service at the right price, then stick with them. If not, beware of the private garage unless you can find strong recommendations from people you know who have dealt there. The independent garage mechanic is not bound by factory parts, factory prices, or factory dictated work habits. He'll probably use the flat-rate book, but he can go anywhere to get what is needed for his customer's car, and he can charge whatever he feels the traffic will bear. This flexibility can be an asset or a liability, so you might consider trying some minor work at a selected garage, developing a relationship before something major comes along.

Some of these private mechanics are skilled enough to take well-considered shortcuts since they are not bound by "factory procedures." This can save you money. On the other hand, you might have to pay for hours of sniffing out an electrical short when a better equipped shop could spot it in a minute.

Many private garages have turned to specialty work, so the old-fashioned all-purpose garage is becoming difficult to find.

Many have turned to more expensive, single-purpose repairs such as rebuilding transmissions or engines, or installing mufflers or radiators.

Discount Chain Shops

Your local department store, if it is a part of a chain of stores, might have an auto service department, and this could be a good deal for you. They often have specials—muffler work, tune-ups, tire work, radiator work, and the like. If you happen to need that service at that time, this could be a good bet for you. The mechanics are relatively well trained in lighter types of work, though often you will find scheduling difficult. They may be less concerned that you need your car tonight than you are.

There is one big plus with these stores. If you have a credit card with that chain, you can usually charge all the work and pay it off by the month. The only other place you can generally do this is at your local service station.

It is possible to mess up the type of jobs these stores tackle, but it isn't easy. A muffler is either installed or it isn't. A radiator cools or it doesn't. Shock absorbers either absorb shocks or they don't.

If the place comes recommended, or offers an ironclad guarantee, or best yet, both, and you need that type of service, you could do worse.

Specialty Shops

This is an age of specialization. Everybody wants to be an expert on something or other, and mechanics are no exception. So the revered old general-purpose mechanic is fading from the scene. He's not going out of business, he's just getting into something he enjoys doing. Then he only takes on that type of work. A mechanic might work for years on all parts of a car, then open a radiator shop or a muffler shop.

Why? Because he has found over the years that he enjoys that job most, and that there is plenty of that type of profitable work available.

He might even open a franchise shop and deal in only one type of part in the repair work he enjoys. If you want an expert for a job, you will generally get an expert job at a specialty shop—but you will pay more for it. These shops often charge 20 to 30 percent more for the same job, though you will probably get your car back quicker, and generally with a solid guarantee. If money is no object, and you want somebody to be very critical of every single component in your brake system, replacing any part he chooses and hang the expense, choose the specialty brake shop. They are in business to sell complete brake jobs, and you might be shocked at just how "complete" a brake job can be. But, and this is important, you will come out with a very fine brake job.

You *could* come out with just as fine a brake job, for less money, at your local service station. Is your service station mechanic an expert at brake jobs? You'll have to decide.

Transmission shops specialize in selling complete rebuilds. You are pretty sure to "need" one if you take your sick transmission to one of these shops instead of taking it to your local service station mechanic for an initial diagnosis. But at the specialty shop you will end up with a fully guaranteed transmission, often good anywhere in the United States if the shop is part of a chain.

But beware of the specialty shop that advertises heavily, offering "free" inspections of your transmission, brakes, or whatever. These shops have been known to tear down your unit for nothing, then you will be pressured and badgered to buy new equipment. There have been cases where they handed a reluctant customer his parts back in a basket. The "free inspection" didn't include putting the unit back together again.

Generally speaking, it is not very often that a component needs to be torn down completely in order to diagnose what is wrong. Be sure any fee you agree to covers putting the thing back together again, repaired or not.

Specialty shops will probably do a good job but it will be a complete job costing more money, as a general rule. They will offer you a good guarantee on the work.

The Chain Service Station

A phenomenon of the eighties is the automotive service station now provided by many major chain and discount department stores. They sell gas and oil and they sell some light repair work though, they usually specialize in tires and other "add-on" items, and not in real auto repair work.

Following the lead of Sears & Roebuck and Montgomery Ward, many of these centers have reasonable facilities. But they vary widely in service. Their "mechanics" are usually paid less than at other facilities, indicating that this is often used as a training ground before they move on to better paying jobs. Prices are usually competitive or even lower, but choose one carefully and watch over what they're doing to your car.

The Service Station

Many modern service stations have come full circle back to the old-fashioned station that did all types of service and mechanical work. You could pull in for a quick few gallons of gasoline, or a complete overhaul. Although some modern service stations might pass on the overhaul, most of them are staffed and equipped to do far more than pump gas and change oil.

Service station mechanics (real ones, not those who just call themselves mechanics) charge about two thirds the hourly rate of car dealers' mechanics in the same area of town. Minor work, done not by the mechanic but by the one who watches over the pumps, is even less. This could include spark plug changes, tire repairs, and other uncomplicated repair work.

So lighter repair work, tune-ups, brake work, shock and muffler installations, wheel alignments, etc., as well as oil and grease, might best and most economically be done at your local full-serve gasoline station. They have the equipment, as a general rule, and they have the skill.

Find a good one, with a staff you can trust, and use them for this type of service. The cost will be less, and the service as good as anywhere else—sometimes even better because the local service station might be even more experienced in general light repair work.

But most service station mechanics tend to be younger, with less experience in heavy repairs—internal problems like engine rebuilds or transmission repairs. Rear-end jobs might confuse them, and in the long run cost you more money, too. They will refer to books and service manuals often, and this time spent in studying and learning will be on your bill.

The fact is, most of your automotive dollar, after the original purchase price of the car, is spent at service stations. Much of this can be put on a credit card, an important consideration for an expensive job. This isn't a pure blessing, though. Use of a credit card costs the station money, especially if it is MasterCharge, American Express, Visa, or the like. The dealer is going to make up this extra on your bill. He has to do it, since profit margins are low. By the same token, paying cash at your local service station will often get you a discount. It may or may not at your service station, but it never hurts to ask.

USE YOUR SERVICE STATION AS A DIAGNOSTICIAN

Here's one of the best tricks of all. It works for you and it works for your "subcontractor." Once you have found a full-serve station you trust, a facility that does light work to your satisfaction and within your price range, use them as a diagnostician on any heavier work you need done. Ask them to look at your car first, figure out what's wrong, then farm out the work.

Remember, they know your car from the work they have done before. They are skilled in tracing down problems with your car. They may even have been keeping track of that strange noise or that increasing drip of oil. They will probably be glad to recommend a garage that can handle the problem.

Even better, they will often serve as your "general practitioner," a true business friend who will refer you to a specialist when the need arises and who will then follow through on the job, protecting your interests. They will accept your car, deliver it to the specialist, keep an eye on the estimates and the job, and hand your car back to you repaired.

The specialist wants to keep the relationship with the service station, so they do a good job, and the service station wants to hold on to you as a customer, so they keep a close watch on the job.

Yes, you'll pay a little extra for this since the service station has to tack their time onto your bill when it is presented. But it can be well worth it, for one reason if for no other: If the job should go sour, or if the repair should fail, you go back to your local service station and not to the special garage that did the work. Your service station must argue with them. And your service station is much better equipped for this type of negotiation.

Chapter **FOUR**

Roadside Emergencies

It can happen to anybody. If it hasn't happened to you, it probably will sometime during your driving life. You have cared for your car, followed all the recommendations in the owner's manual, checked the fluids regularly, and never succumbed to the temptation to race, overload, or otherwise abuse your car. You watch your gauges and you follow their lead.

In fact, your car could be said to be in showroom condition, considering the few thousand miles on the odometer. You wouldn't be afraid to drive it from New York to Los Angeles.

Then you set out on a trip. It never happens when you are near home and help, or near a repair facility. Nine times out of ten it will happen out on the road, far from home and a garage known to be friendly.

Your car *tricks* you. You are sailing along when you notice a slight rise in the engine temperature. You worry a little, considering your location and the fact that now, of all times, you don't need any problems, but it doesn't appear serious. Still, you watch things carefully. The needle creeps up higher and higher. Yet, it never quite reaches the pin. So you drive on, watching for an open service station. Then it happens.

With a serious sounding "Clunk! Grind! Groan!" your car limps to a stop. The engine gives one final gasp and dies. It could happen on the darkest, coldest night of the year, on the loneliest country road, at midnight, with not a house in sight.

Maybe it will start in a minute. You try ... and try ... and try. No, it isn't going to start. In fact, it sounds as though it is really *sick* inside.

Occasionally, even a well-maintained car will trick you and break down.

You have a *roadside emergency.*

It could be serious, but don't panic. Don't rush away from the car to seek help or immediately begin to attempt to flag down passing motorists (unless it happens to be a police officer). You might be able to help yourself. You'll learn exactly what caused the problem above at the end of this chapter.

THE FIRST THING TO DO

At the first sign that your car is going to give up the ghost and stop completely, get it off the road. More people have been hurt or killed in and around stalled cars than you would believe. It goes against the grain to pull off on a lonely road, but that is your only choice. Once you are completely off the road and away from the danger of getting hit by another car, do the following:

- Raise the hood
- Turn on the emergency flashers
- Tie a handkerchief or a piece of white cloth to the radio antenna or the door handle.

These have become universal signals that a motorist has had a breakdown. Most police officers will recognize the signs, and so will many passing motorists.

If you *must* stop in the roadway, use the warning flares or reflectors you have in your emergency kit (see the next section, p. 70). Place the first flare ten feet behind the car. Then walk back about three hundred feet and set another flare. Be very careful of traffic and of any strangers lingering about as you accomplish these chores. Finally, put a third flare about one hundred feet *in front* of your car. If you are using flares instead

This is the correct way to inform other motorists that you need help.

of reflectors, check to be sure you aren't setting any of them in or around any spilled gasoline.

One driver's problem was a broken fuel line. The car stopped, of course, caused by a lack of gasoline to the fuel pump. Where was the gasoline going? Out on the road. Where did he place his first flare? Ten feet back, and right on top of the fresh trail of gasoline. The flames quickly moved to the car, and the resulting fire attracted plenty of attention. But it took a wrecker to get the burned-out hulk to a junkyard.

To go for help or not to go for help? If you know where you are and know of help nearby, and there are no lingering strangers around, you can use your judgment about going for help. If you see the lights of a house in the distance and feel you can cover the ground safely, there is probably a telephone there. Perhaps you can get your car started again. But if it is a lost cause, you might want to try for the house. Remember though, you don't really know who's in there or what their reaction might be. It is a strange world we live in and caution is always a good policy.

Better yet and especially if you are in strange territory with no idea where help might be found, stay in the car with the doors locked. The raised hood, the flashers blinking, and the cloth on the door will tell people you need help. If another motorist does stop, roll down the window just enough to ask him to telephone for assistance. If the other driver is sincere, he will. If he is not sincere, you still have the doors locked— and the horn to attract attention in case of real trouble.

Most of these creeps don't like a lot of noise.

EMERGENCY KIT

Every driver should carry the following items in the car. You may never need them. If you don't, wonderful. But if you do, they can be lifesavers. The whole kit will cost less than forty dollars. A single towing charge will cost more.

- A working flashlight
- Simple tools (wrenches, adjustable pliers, screwdrivers, duct tape)

To go for help, or not go for help, that is the question.

Emergency items every car should have: jumper cables, flashlight, siphon pump, distress flag, flares, duct tape, wire, paper clip, tire inflator, plastic water bag, screwdrivers, adjustable pliers. See also page 88 for an even more complete list.

- Warning flares or reflectors
- A jack
- A lug wrench
- A set of jumper cables
- Some spare electrical wire
- A paper clip or two
- A pressurized can of tire inflator
- A set of fuses for your car
- A siphon pump
- A folded plastic water bag
- A fire extinguisher

FLAT TIRE?

If you can get far enough off the road to change the tire, then do so. But remember, it isn't going to help if you get so close to an obstruction at one side that you can't work. It also won't help if the other side of the car is so close to the highway that you might get killed while working.

On many superhighways or freeways, it is impossible to get far enough off the road to work on a tire. In that case, drive on. Yes, you'll ruin the tire, but a ruined tire and wheel is

I'VE NEVER HAD TO CHANGE A FLAT TIRE. HOW DO I DO IT?
First, check your owner's manual. It should show you exactly what
to do to change a tire on *your* car. But generally, there are nine
basic steps to follow: 1. Park on level and solid ground. If you have
an automatic transmission, put the car in "park." If not, put it in
gear. And always put your emergency brake on. You should also
block the wheel on the opposite corner of the car to keep it from
rolling. A piece of wood or large stone will do. 2. Take the wheel
cover off. Usually you can use a screwdriver or the tapered end of
the lug wrench to pop it off. 3. Take the lug wrench and loosen each
lug nut one turn. 4. Take the spare tire out first, it's easier and safer
that way. Then place the jack on solid ground and jack up the car.
(Follow owner's manual instructions.) When you finish, the tire
should be at least two or three inches off the ground. 5. Remove
the lug nuts. (Put them in the wheel cover so you won't lose them.)
Then pull off the flat tire. 6. Put the spare tire on and tighten each
lug nut snugly, being careful not to jar the car off the jack. Jack the
car down until the tire is just touching the ground. Then finish
tightening the nuts. 7. Tighten the lug nuts as tight as you can. Don't
tighten them in circle sequence. That could cause the wheel to come
loose as you drive. Tighten one, then the one opposite it, and so on.
Finish lowering the car. 8. Don't put the wheel cover back on. Put
it in your trunk. Every time you see the wheel without it, you'll be
reminded to get that flat fixed. 9. Put your jack, tools, and flat tire
back in the trunk. You're ready to travel again. But get that flat
fixed right away. Driving without a spare tire is asking for trouble.

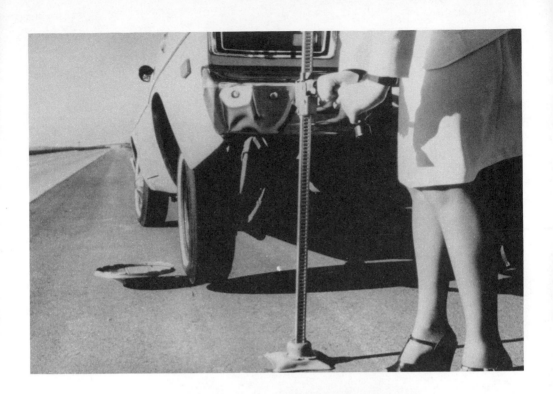

much better than an injured driver. Turn on your flashers, stay in the slow lane, drive slowly, and keep going until you get to help.

Did you ever change a flat? It isn't that difficult if you take your time and don't panic. Your owner's manual can be a big help here, so get it out and look it over. You'll see the proper jacking points and correct procedures for removing the wheel.

No owner's manual? Here are ten basic steps to make the job as easy as possible.

1. Park on ground that is as level and solid as possible. If you have an automatic transmission, set it in "park." If you have a manual transmission, put it in low gear. These actions will help keep the car from rolling off the jack.

While you're at it, set the emergency brake and block the wheel on the opposite corner of the car with a rock or a piece of wood. All you have to see is a car that has rolled off the jack with a missing wheel to know how important these initial steps are. If you get through the roll-off uninjured, you'll have a great time trying to get the jack back under the frame now that it's almost resting on the ground.

2. Take the wheel cover off. You can use a screwdriver or the tapered end of the lug wrench as a lever to pop it free.

3. Using the lug wrench in your kit, loosen each lug nut one turn. Normally, you will turn to the left to loosen, no matter which side of the car you are on.

OK, let's be reasonable. The nut might seem to be welded on. It isn't, so if you have to hit the wrench, or stand on it, do so. Just be very careful that it doesn't fly free and hit you or the car.

4. You've done all this *before* you set the jack. Now remove the spare tire from the trunk. It is easier and you have less chance of shaking the car off the jack if you wrestle the spare out before you raise the car. Only then, with the spare tire alongside and ready, will you set the jack on solid ground and jack up the corner where the flat tire is located. Your owner's manual can be a help with specific jacking techniques. The flattened tire should be two or three inches off the ground. Remember, it is flat. You'll need that extra clearance to mount the inflated (and it is, isn't it?) tire.

5. Finish unscrewing the lug nuts and store them in the wheel cover so they won't be misplaced during the operation. If worst comes to worst and you do lose one, all is not lost. You can drive on, slowly, with one missing lug nut. The next service station will have a replacement.

Pull off the flat tire and set it aside.

6. Put the spare tire on and tighten each lug nut as snugly as possible with your fingers. Be careful during this operation that you don't slam or jerk the car. It can still fall off the jack. During the entire operation while the car is on the jack and the wheel off the car, keep your hands and other body parts out from under the car. Cars have slipped off jacks and pinned the hand or foot of unfortunate drivers, or worse.

7. Jack the car down until the tire is just touching the ground, then finish tightening the nuts. The slight weight of the car on the tire will keep the wheel from turning during this operation, something it will otherwise do even if the emergency brake is on during the tightening operation.

8. Lug nuts should not be tightened in a circular pattern. Follow your owner's manual or, if you can't find the manual, like this: tighten one, then the opposite one, then the next opposite, and so on until they are all tight. This will square the wheel on the drum and prevent it from coming loose as you drive.

9. Lower the car and then store the flat tire in the trunk, but don't put the wheel cover back on. Store it in the trunk, too. Every time you see the wheel without the cover, you'll be reminded that the tire in the trunk is flat. It should be repaired as soon as possible.

10. Put the jack, your tools, and anything else you have removed (luggage, etc.) back in the trunk. Drive on, but remember to get the flat repaired.

Driving with a flat spare in the trunk is begging for trouble. If you've ever had two flats in a row, that is when it will happen.

You do have a can of pressurized flat-tire inflator compound in the emergency kit in your trunk, so if you find your spare tire is flat, you can try it out. Many drivers swear by the stuff. The pressurized air inflates the tire and the sealing compound seals the leak—at least until you can get some help with the flat. Naturally you wouldn't want to drive very far with this stuff inside your tire, but it should work for awhile.

If you use it, replace it with a new can in your kit.

Here are a few common questions about what to do if your car begins to fail.

"If my engine starts to sputter, is a breakdown on the way?"

You are probably beginning to run out of gas, but you still have a moment or two. Get off the road, near help if possible. Some states have emergency call boxes to help motorists along the road, but try to have an idea of where you are before you call. Call boxes are also numbered, and that information will be a big help to the operator.

"What should I do if the engine starts to overheat?"

There are a number of reasons why a modern engine overheats, not one of which can be ignored. You could have a dirty radiator on the outside and the air is not flowing through fast enough to cool the engine. You could have a dirty radiator inside, and the coolant is not flowing fast enough to cool down before it is returned to the engine block. Or you could be loosing coolant and the reduced amount isn't enough to cool the engine. It is even possible that you don't have enough *oil* in the engine, and the heat-producing friction cannot be overcome by a perfectly operating cooling system.

In any case, if the engine begins to overheat, driving faster will not help, as some backyard mechanics insist. Driving in a lower gear for a short time *might* help, under certain conditions. Try it briefly if you wish. This will speed up the engine (and water pump), force more coolant through the radiator, and also drive the radiator fan faster to suck in more cool air. This probably won't work, so the best thing to do is pull off in a safe place and allow the engine to cool down.

The driver at the beginning of this chapter nearly ruined his engine, though the heat gauge never did reach the top. He should have pulled off sooner, for he would have found a rapid leak in one of his heater hoses. As the coolant drained out, the heat sensor in the engine block was sensing hot *air* instead of hot water. So it never did go all the way. Meanwhile, this driver was cruising along with a blistering-hot engine. The engine finally just gave up and stopped. The car needed a new head gasket (expensive) and the driver was lucky at that. The great heat could have warped the engine head, or even caused some pistons to score the cylinder walls.

So if the gauge goes up, or the heat light comes on, pull off and see if you can spot the trouble. If you can, and you can fix it (temporarily tape a hose, tighten a connection, etc.), and if you can then find some water to replace what has been lost, you can drive on. All you have to do then is replace the hose and add more antifreeze to bring the percentage back to normal, but you can do this at a more convenient time.

It might not be the best thing in the world for your radiator, but even water from a *ditch* will do the job temporarily. Any water is better than no water at all.

"What do I do if my alternator light comes on, or my ammeter shows a discharge?"

Don't stop. If you do, you might not be able to get started again. If possible, keep driving until you locate a garage or service station. Watch the other gauges as you go, since an alternator "failure" might be a drive belt failure instead, and your fan, water pump, etc., might not be operating properly.

A car will run on the electricity from its battery for many miles, especially in the daytime with no lights. Naturally you'll want to turn off every accessory you don't need (radio, air conditioner, etc.) to save as much electricity as possible. When the battery is used up, the car is going to stop because you no longer have power to the spark plugs. Once the alternator is fixed, or whatever was wrong with the charging system, the battery will probably recharge and you can go on your way.

"What do I do if my oil pressure light comes on, or my oil pressure gauge shows a drop in pressure?"

Stop. Turn off the engine. An engine can be ruined quickly if it is operated without oil pressure. When you are safely parked, check the oil in the engine (see chapter 6). Do not drive your car until you have brought the engine oil back up to normal. If the dipstick shows that you have oil in the engine, the problem could be anything from a gauge failure to an oil pump failure. Don't drive until you know.

If the oil light is flickering when you are stopped at a light, your engine may be low on oil or your engine could be idling too slowly. Drive slowly to the nearest service station and check the oil. If it is low, add oil. If it is OK, ask the attendant to give a nudge to the idle adjustment screw. Then keep an eye on the light or gauge to be sure that the problem has been solved.

"What causes most breakdowns on the roads today?"

This might surprise you. Most breakdowns are caused by problems that could have been easily and inexpensively handled, and that were merely neglected by the driver. They are:

1. Running out of gas. Watch your gauge. Fill up when you are down to a quarter of a tank. Don't take a chance "running on fumes." Some modern cars have a light that comes on when you are down dangerously low, but the best way will always be to know how much gas you have. What if the light doesn't work?

2. Flat tire. Keep an eye on your tires, their inflation and condition. New tires rarely get flats. Old tires frequently do.

3. Overheating. Overheating is most frequently caused by deteriorated hoses, broken fan belts, or dirty radiators. All three are easy to keep track of, and to correct before they lead to trouble.

Here's a safety tip for any breakdown at night. If you must walk to get help, stay well off the road and tie a white armband around your arm. This will make you more visible on a dark road.

"How can I prevent a breakdown?"

Nobody is breakdown-proof, but there are some things you can do with your car to help prevent them. Here's a checklist:

- *Instrument Panel Warning Lights*
  Most cars have instrument panel warning lights (oil pressure, ammeter, brakes, etc.) that come on when the key is turned on, then go off when the engine starts. Be sure yours come on, indicating they are working correctly.
- *Tires*
  Correct air pressure isn't enough. You should also check for tread depth (you'll have far fewer flats with good

Oil level should be *between* the "add" and "full" marks, not below the add mark or over the full mark.

treads) and tire wear. If you're down to the last sixteenth-inch of tread you'll be able to see the "wear indicators"—flat bands of no tread—on the tires. If they show across two or more grooves, shop for new tires. Be sure you have a good, properly inflated spare in your trunk, plus the tools to change the tire.

- *Windshield Wipers and Washers*
  Check them periodically, even in dry, clear weather, only to see that they are working when you need them. If you've ever been caught in the rain with no windshield wipers, you know that the best thing to do is pull off the road and wait for the shower to end.
- *Motor Oil*
  This is the lifeblood of your car's engine. Check the dipstick to be sure the oil level is between the "add" and the "full" marks. Do it when the car is parked on level ground if possible. Not checking the oil level would be like a doctor not taking your pulse. This is the single most critical measurement in your car.
  Your service station or a neighbor can show you where the dipstick is located, generally down along one side or the other of the engine. It'll be easy to locate, and easy to use.
- *Outside Lights*
  All lights should be working, including the emergency flashers and the brake lights. You'll need a friend to check the brake lights, unless you do it with the back of the car near a wall so that you can see the light reflected as you apply the brakes. Give your lights a wipe when you stop for gas. It's amazing how much light can be lost with dirty lenses. If you're driving at night, you'll see the difference.
- *Brakes*
  Push the pedal down. If it goes more than halfway to the floor, it's going too far. Push down again and count to ten. If the pedal keeps going down, you could have a leaking master cylinder or wheel cylinder. You can check

for leaks, but the best thing to do is head for the brake repair shop. (Note: With power brakes, you must have the engine running for these tests.)

• *Power-Steering Fluid*

There is a cannister with a dipstick for checking the fluid level in the power-steering system. Many drivers never check this, and indeed never even know the dipstick is there. It's easy to do while the engine is off, as it should be since you'll be working near the fanbelt (which is as dangerous as the fan). The power-steering pump is lubricated by the fluid in its own system, so you can save a bundle of money—and even a breakdown—by keeping it at the proper level.

• *Belts*

Press down on each drive belt with your thumb (with the engine off, of course). The belt shouldn't give more than a half inch. If any one of them does, it needs to be tightened, a simple job for a service station. If any belt appears worn or cracked, or if chunks are missing, you should have it replaced before you drive again. A broken belt can stall a car just as quickly as a thrown connecting rod or a broken piston.

Your car may not look exactly like this, but the parts should look basically the same. Use this diagram to help you identity: 1. Radiator 2. Radiator cap 3. Battery 4. Battery cables 5. Alternator 6. Upper radiator hose 7. Distributor 8. Fan belt 9. Oil dipstick 10. Spark plugs 11. Spark plug wires 12. Gas line 13. Carburetor 14. Choke valves 15. Air cleaner 16. Transmission dipstick 17. Brake fluid reservoir.

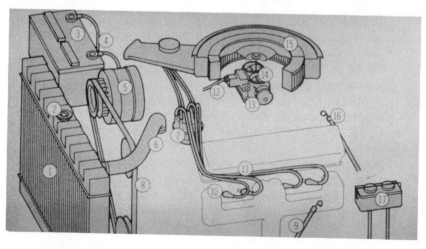

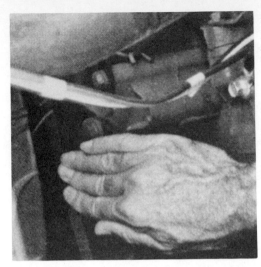

A belt shouldn't give more than about a half-inch when you press it with your thumb, with the engine off, of course.

If the battery is filled to the proper level, the fluid should just touch the filler neck and "pucker" a little. Less than that and you can see the fluid is flat and doesn't reach the filler neck.

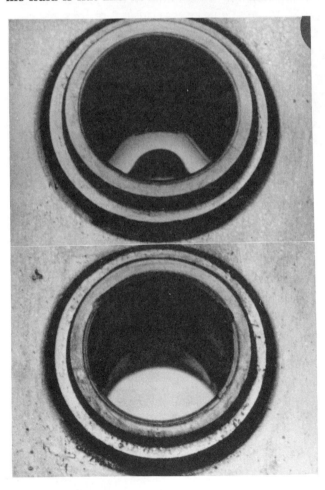

- *Battery*

  If you have the type of battery that takes water, check the level in each cell. If it's low, add distilled water to bring the level back to the bottom of the filler hole. Next, check the battery cable connections for tightness and cleanliness. A little baking soda made into a paste with water, then dabbed around the post, will quickly clean away any corrosion on the terminals.

- *Radiator*

  When the engine is cool, remove the radiator cap and look at the coolant. Dip your finger in. It should come out clean and not besmudged with rust or corrosion. If it is dirty, clean it yourself with radiator cleaner from the auto parts store, or have it "boiled out" at your service station. Then add new antifreeze and water in a 50-50 mixture. This is an inexpensive way to assure long radiator and hose life, and a cool running engine.

- *Hoses*

  Hoses carry coolant to and from the engine block and to and from the heater core. You'll see big ones for the engine and smaller ones for the heater. There is a big hose from the top of the radiator to the engine, and another from the engine back to the bottom of the radiator. Look them over. Squeeze the big ones. They should be dry, clean, free of cracks, and solid (not "spongy"). If you detect any leaks, or if the hoses feel old and worn-out, they should be replaced.

  Chances are the upper one will go first, since it is under more hot pressure than the lower one (which also may have a coil spring inside it to keep it from collapsing when the pressure lowers).

- *Horn*

  Blow it. If it doesn't work, get it fixed. You might even want to check out the wiring to the horn to see if you can figure out the problem. Sometimes one of the bayonet clips to the horn simply comes loose, so the repair is easy. Just slip it back on.

- *Emergency Flashers*

  Try them periodically to be sure they are still working. You'll rarely need them, but when you do, you'll *really* need them. Chances are, if they are not working the problem is in the little flasher unit under the dash. It is easy to replace if that is the problem.

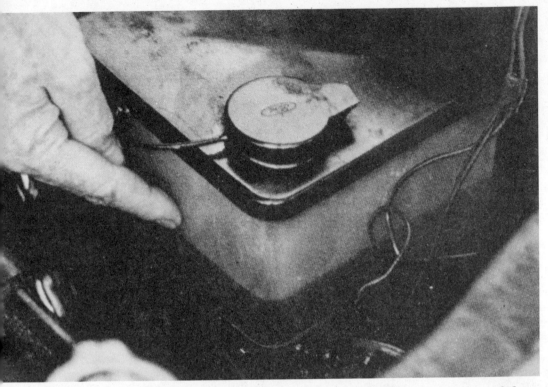

If your car has an overflow tank, check the coolant level there...but be *careful*. This is hot stuff.

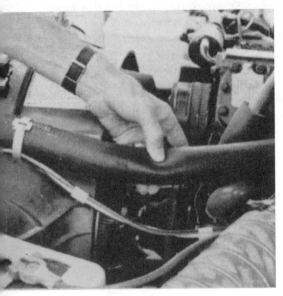

Squeeze the big hoses. They should feel firm, not "spongy," and be dry, clean, and free of cracks.

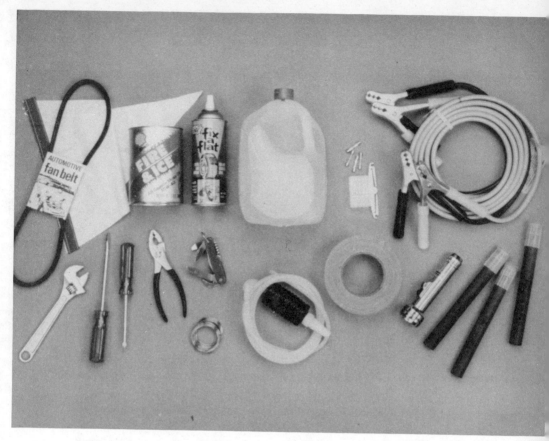

Don't leave home without these emergency repair items in your car: Jumper cables, flashlight, adjustable wrench, insulated pliers, two insulated screwdrivers (one Phillips head, one standard), distress flag, distress flares, duct tape, siphon pump, plastic jug full of water, tire sealant-inflator, light fuses (check size in owner's manual), fuse puller, pocketknife, all-purpose wire (to lash down a sprung trunk door or whatever), at least one quart of oil, a spare fan belt (even if you can't put it on yourself, you'll be ready with the right size when the tow truck arrives).

- *Spare Tire and Changing Equipment*
  Check again to be sure you have a good, properly inflated spare and the equipment to mount it. One of life's great frustrations is to have a flat and have no air in the spare.
- *Emergency Kit in Trunk*
  While you're there, be sure you have the other tools and

flares or reflectors for any emergency situation. They'll probably lay there for years without use, but when you need them you'll congratulate yourself for being so far-sighted.

YOU CAN DO IT

Dick Hall, who has long owned and operated service stations and worked as a consultant to other dealers, decided to see if the average driver can keep a car running even under emergency breakdown conditions.

"I've been working in and around service stations for almost forty years," says Hall. "In that time I've seen lots of people stranded on the road because of some little problem they might easily have fixed themselves."

So Hall asked six California college cheerleaders, three from USC and three from UCLA, to help him with a troubleshooting demonstration. None of the six had had any previous mechanical training, but all six were regular drivers. They were given a "quickie" two-hour course in how a car works at Shell's Service Training Center in Anaheim, California. Covered were most of the same things covered in this book.

Then, for the next two days, the six were put to the test. They drove from Anaheim to San Diego in "rigged" cars, cars fixed to manfunction along the way.

In every case, the students figured out what the problem was and what to do about it. Not once were they stalled since, as Hall explains, "Some car repairs are often no more difficult than wrapping a gift or reading a thermometer. You just have to know where to look, what to look for, and most important, what to do when you find it."

LET'S DIAGNOSE A FEW COMMON
EMERGENCY PROBLEMS

"I turn the key and nothing happens."

First of all, turn on your headlights to see if the battery is OK. And also check to be sure your automatic transmission is in park or neutral. Both OK? Then it could be the neutral safety switch in the transmission, if your car is an automatic. Sometimes jiggling the gear shift lever in park or neutral while turning the key to start will help.

If your lights go dim while you are trying to start, you may have a loose battery connection or corroded battery terminals. For either, loosen the bolts, carefully pry the terminal clamps apart, and lift off the cables (grounded side first). Then clean the contacting surfaces until they are bright metal again, both the clamps and the battery posts. Reattach them securely (grounded cable last) until they won't turn on the post. If your lights still go dim, you probably have a low battery.

If the lights don't go on at all, your battery is probably dead and you'll need a jump start so you can get to a garage where the battery can be checked and charged.

"My engine turns over, but the car just won't start."

You could have one of three problems: air, spark, or gasoline. A strong gasoline smell probably means that you have "flooded" the engine. Raise the hood and if gas is on the engine, get help. If not, try cranking the engine for ten seconds or so with the gas pedal *all the way to the floor.* Don't pump the pedal or you will flood the engine even more.

If the engine still won't start, try tapping the carburetor lightly near the gas line. Then repeat the entire procedure.

To see if you are getting spark to the plugs, remove one spark plug wire. To do this, grasp the wire by the "boot," the rubber cap at the end, and twist it as you pull it off. Pull open a paper clip and push it so that the bend at one end is firmly into the boot, touching the metal inside. Hold the boot with a cloth rag, position the other end of the paper clip about an eighth of an inch from any nut or bolt on the engine, and ask somebody else to crank the engine.

Watch for a spark to jump from the paper clip to the bolt. If you don't see one, call for help.

It is possible that you have some loose or broken spark plug wires that are preventing a spark from getting to the plugs, or an unattached wire between the coil and the distributor. Look them over, especially the one between the coil and the distributor, and reattach any that are loose.

There is a chance the engine is not getting enough gasoline, so be sure you have fuel in the tank. You can try removing the air cleaner atop the carburetor to see if the main butterfly valve in the throat of the carb is stuck open. If so, push it shut and try to start the engine. If that's not it, open the choke completely and look down inside the throat while somebody pumps the gas pedal. You should see the gas squirting down inside the throat, the big tube in the top of the carburetor. If you don't, call for help.

If an engine suddenly quits or begins to sputter on a hot day, it is possible you have a "vapor lock." This is a condition where bubbles have formed in the fuel line because of the heat and are blocking the flow of fuel. You can simply wait for the engine to cool, the bubbles will dissipate, and you can start again. Also try cooling down the fuel lines where they pass near the engine, often near the exhaust manifold. Some drivers who are plagued with this problem wrap the fuel lines with an insulating layer to help prevent vapor lock.

"My brake warning light just came on. Now what?"

Don't panic. First, be sure the parking brake is completely off. If it is, then remember that modern cars have two separate hydraulic systems for the brakes—one for the front, one for the rear. If one system should fail, the other system is still there to stop the car. If you have such a system and the red warning light comes on, it could mean that one system has failed and needs work. But you should still have enough brakes to stop the car without problems as you very carefully drive to the brake shop.

Test your brakes to see if they work, then head slowly for a mechanic to get the system checked. It might be something as simple as low brake fluid in the master cylinder, which has allowed the equalizing switch in the system to drift to one side and turn on the light. You can correct this by adding brake fluid to the brake fluid reservoir over the master cylinder under the hood. Just lift off the lid and fill the reservoir. If the trouble is more serious, you want to know about it and correct it.

On the off chance that your brakes go completely out, shift into a lower gear to help slow down the car, then pull to the side and gradually apply the emergency brake. Don't drive farther. Have the car towed to a shop where it can be checked out.

"My temperature gauge is reading too high, or the heat light is on."

If your engine overheats, pull off the road, turn on your flashers, and turn off the key. Then do these three things, in this order.

1. Look for a water leak under the hood, usually around the radiator or the radiator or heater hoses. If you find a small leak in a hose, use the duct tape from your emergency kit to tape it up, after waiting for the engine to cool down. Then loosen the radiator cap one notch to relieve the pressure in the system, and drive to the nearest service station.

2. When the radiator is cool enough to put your palm on it, check the level of the coolant. If it's low and you have water handy, fill it up.

3. Check the fan belt that drives the cooling fan. If it's broken, but the radiator is still full and the cap is back on tight, you can drive the car slowly until the warning light comes on again or the heat gauge climbs into the hot range. Then stop and let things cool down again. By driving this way, you can probably get to a service station for a new fan belt.

If your engine overheats in traffic, or on a long hill, turn off your air conditioner and turn on the heater. This may make it uncomfortably hot inside the car, but it is causing coolant to be circulated, and cooled somewhat, by going through the heater. The extra heat you feel could have been going into the engine and keeping it that much hotter.

Put the transmission in neutral and rev the engine up a bit to speed the flow of water through the engine and heater core. The temperature should go down. But if the warning gauges still read "hot," pull off the road and stop. Heat is the major enemy of an engine, and too much of it can do very expensive

A geyser of steam and engine coolant can scald you if you aren't careful, and the engine doesn't have to be this hot to be dangerous. With the cap off, the pressure is reduced and coolant can instantly boil.

damage. Don't try to start until the engine has cooled down, and then watch the gauges carefully as you drive to a service station for aid.

"My engine stopped after I splashed through water."

This will take a little bit of work, but it isn't a serious problem. The engine ignition system has been soaked, and the spark is going to ground instead of to the spark plugs. You'll have to wait for it to dry, or you'll have to dry it yourself. Do this just the way it sounds. Get some dry rags or paper towels and start drying parts. Dry the ignition wires top to bottom. If the distributor cap is accessible in your car, dry it off. Inside and out, if possible. The engine should start. If it doesn't, wait a few minutes and try again. Sometimes the heat of the engine will help in the drying process, but it takes a little time.

HIGHWAY RIP-OFFS? SURE

Most complaints received by consumer agencies do not involve pure cheating, but it does happen. Especially at strange, roadside repair facilities where the mechanic knows he will never see you again. They even have terms for such practices.

- *"Honking"*
  While he is checking your air pressure, the attendant punctures your tire with a sharp tool. The solution? Check your own air pressure in unfamiliar garages or remote roadside service stations.
- *"Slashing"*
  While checking under the hood, the attendant cuts your fan belt so that it hangs by a thread. Then he points it out to you, and what can you do but pay to have him replace it? The solution? Get out of the car and watch as the attendant checks under your hood.
- *"Short Sticking"*
  This is a neat one that sells extra barrels of unneeded oil, and little does the attendant care that too much oil in your engine is harmful. While he is checking your oil, he shoves the dipstick in but not quite all the way. Then, when he shows you that the oil level is below the "add" mark, you tell him to put in a quart. The solution? Watch as he checks the oil. If it comes up low, ask him to check it again, and watch very carefully that he inserts the dipstick all the way into the crankcase.
- *"Shock Treatment"*
  A little oil squirted on a shock absorber will make it appear that the shock is leaking. Then the attendant will try to convince you that you can't drive another mile without risking a serious accident since the seal in the shock is broken. The solution? Most shock leaks will be older and dust coated, not appearing as fresh oil. Wait till you get to a friendly garage to have the shocks re-

placed, if they need replacement. Besides, driving with a bad shock is seldom dangerous.

- *"Battery Boil"*
An attendant at a highway facility might drop a seltzer tablet into your battery. This will neutralize some of the acid and cause it to boil over in a fizzing foam. It looks terrible, but if you haven't noticed any problems with your charging systems, drive on. Batteries don't normally "fizz" without other warnings.
- *"Hot Oil Filter"*
An attendant might tell you that your oil filter is overheated and that you must replace it immediately. Don't believe him. If the engine has been running normally, drive on. In any case, oil filters do warm up to the operating temperature of the engine. There is no such thing as an "overheated oil filter."

STRANDED

There comes a time when ingenuity is your only answer to a stall. You are stuck, and that's that. Even then, though, you might still have a chance. Let's take a look at two drivers with two different problems. See if you can figure out how they resolved their apparently insoluble problems.

Driver 1. It is a cold, rainy night. She pulls into the driveway, happy to be home at last and safe and secure. She shuts down the engine, sets the parking brake, grabs a newspaper to hold over her head, and rushes for the front door in the icy drizzle.

Then she crawls into a hot bath and forgets the terrible weather outside.

The next morning she awakens and looks out the window. The world had become a wonderland of icy crystals. It is cold, pristine, white and beautiful, and although she dreads the drive to work, she isn't worried. She has taken good care of her car. The battery is up, the engine freshly tuned, and she has no doubt that it will start quickly. It does when she goes, bundled against the cold, to start the car. No problem.

But when she shifts into gear and starts to back out of her driveway, the engine struggles and dies. Again she starts it, engages the transmission, and tries to back out. Again the engine dies. It is as though the brakes are on, and indeed they are. When she pulled in the night before and set the parking brake, the shoes were wet. They have frozen solidly against the drums. The car is going nowhere.

Driver 2. It is a warm spring morning and although he is running a bit late, he still has to stop at a co-worker's house for some papers. The co-worker is heading for the airport that same morning, and the papers are needed at work. He pulls up the gentle incline of the co-worker's driveway, stops, puts the transmission in "park," sets the hand brake, and goes to the door.

Papers in hand, he returns to the car and starts the engine. Yes, he is a bit late, but he still has time. He starts to put the car in "reverse" but the shifter won't work. It is stuck solidly in place. He tries again, but it is no use. Even with a little force, the handle won't move.

The friend comes out to help, but he can't move the handle either. The situation is becoming critical, for the co-worker must get his own car out of the garage for the trip to the airport, and Driver 2 is blocking the garage door. The problem? The car was put into "park" before the hand brake was set, and a slight roll backward on the incline has locked the parking gear cog in the gears of the transmission. No amount of force can seem to release it.

These two drivers are stalled.

But not hopelessly.

Driver 1 is smart when it comes to cars. She suspects her brakes are locked and she figures they are frozen. So she goes into the house, takes the hose from the vacuum cleaner, and holds it to the end of the exhaust pipe. She puts blocks on the rear wheels. She directs the other end at the backside of the rear wheel. Before long she hears a sharp "click" as the ice thaws and the return springs pull the shoes from the drum. Then she aims the heat from the idling engine at the other wheel. "Click!" Both brakes are free and she drives off to work.

By very lightly riding the brakes the first few blocks, she dries any remaining moisture inside so the problem won't happen again at work.

A neighbor has noticed the plight of Driver 2 and his friend. He suggests the easy solution, though there are others. He drives his car up behind the car of Driver 2 and gently touches the bumper. Then, as he pushes very slightly, taking the car's weight off the cog in the transmission, the shifter can be moved and the car backed out of the drive.

Without the help of the neighbor, the two men could have taken a post or two-by-four board and levered the car forward from the rear to take the weight off. Or they could even have used a block and tackle from the front bumper to the garage or any other nearby solid object to momentarily pull the car and allow the shifter to move.

You can get stranded in other odd ways.

•Against a Wall

Your car slides sideways up to, but doesn't *quite* touch, a solid wall or fence. The engine is still running, and so far no damage has been done, but you are stuck. No matter how slightly you turn the front wheels to drive away, the back fender is going to scrape. If you turn the wheels the other way and try to back away from the wall, the front fender is going to scrape.

You can't move the wall or fence, and you don't want to scratch your car. What do you do?

If you're lucky, the solution is simple. If there is a solid object close to the car and on the other side of the car from the wall, you can attach the rope you have in your trunk to that object, then, with no slack, to the off-wall rear bumper. Keep it tight.

As you turn the wheels and ease the car away from the wall, the back end will also swing away. In only a few feet you will have enough clearance to unhook the rope and drive away.

This will work from the front of the car if you try to back away from the wall. You can also take a two-by-four block and wedge it between the wall and the wheel. As you move slowly and carefully forward, steering away from the wall gradually, the block will wedge the car outward away from the wall. You might have to reset the block two or three times, but gradually you will move the whole car far enough away from the wall to drive away cleanly.

•Locked Bumpers

Many cars still have bumpers that will lock to each other under certain circumstances. This effectively stalls both cars until you can figure how to release them. There is the old-fashioned way of crawling up on a bumper and bouncing till they unhook, but this can be risky.

Why not look to see if there is a crown of a driveway or hill or an incline nearby. Drive both cars to the crown and as the back end of one rises, the bumpers will free themselves. If you can move both cars and there is no hill nearby, try driving the rear wheels of the front car up onto bricks or blocks, or even up over a curb. This will lift the back end of the front car and free the bumpers.

Then there is the easy way. Where you have two cars you probably have two jacks. Merely put a jack under each end of the upper bumper, and with two people jacking at the same time, one on each side, raise the upper car until the bumpers are unlocked.

•Blown Fuse

A blown fuse at night can stall a car because of the danger of driving without running lights. Rarely will the headlights burn out, but under some driving conditions (narrow road, winding road, rain, fog, etc.) driving without tail and running lights can be very dangerous. Headlights, incidentally, are usually on a separate, very heavy circuit or circuits, and they will almost never all go out at once.

Wrap the fuse in aluminum foil? No, this is not a good idea. There was a reason why the fuse blew, and if you do that you may dead-short the circuit and possibly do serious damage. Better to go to your fuse box and pull a fuse from another circuit. You can live without the air conditioner, for example, to have working lights at night. If you are "fuse-snatching" be sure the fuses are nearly the same electrical and mechanical size. Then, next service station, replace the fuse—and if you are at home, ask them to determine why it blew in the first place.

•Fender Dented into Wheel

One of the most unpleasant ways to get stuck (and many stock-car racing drivers face this) is to have a body panel banged into a wheel. Nothing will move. But there is a solution beyond brute force, and it doesn't have to be what racing mechanics do. They swarm over the car with sharp cutters and merely snip away the offending metal. The car roars back into the race.

You can be more gentle since you probably have a little more time. Get out your jack and mount it between the frame and the bent fender. Then just jack the fender out of the way of the wheel. You're going to need body work anyhow (see chapter 11) so an extra ding or two won't matter.

•Frozen Out

One of the most embarrassing ways to get stuck is to get locked out of a car with a frozen door lock. The engine is fine, the street is clean and dry and though it is cold, you are ready and so is your car. But you can't get in because moisture has collected and the lock is a block of ice.

Don't use a lighter to try to heat the lock. This can ruin the paint. Instead, heat the key with your lighter or a match, then insert it in the lock. Gently try to turn it. Do this over and over until the heat from the key is transferred into the lock, melting the ice. After a few times, the key will turn and the door will open.

There is an even quicker way if you don't feel the heat will hurt the paint. Stick the key in the lock, then heat that part sticking out. The heat will carry into the lock and melt the ice quickly. Think you look stupid out there heating a key? Not as stupid as you'll look breaking your own window to get into your perfectly good car.

By the way, before you do any of this, try the door on the

other side. Many people assume they have been frozen out of a car because the driver's door lock is frozen. But the other side might be dry.

Chapter **FIVE**

Driving Tips

The start of the annual Memorial Day 500-mile race at the Indianapolis Motor Speedway is one of the most exciting moments in all of sports. The tradition is iron-bound. Thirty-three of the fastest race cars in the world are poised and ready on the starting line. Celebrities cruise around the track in open convertibles. The National Anthem is played. As the clock ticks down toward the start, a singer of note sings "Back Home Again in Indiana." "Taps" is played by a bugler or by a full band. Final interviews are conducted before a crowd of more than three hundred thousand racing fans and millions more on radio and television.

Then comes the dramatic call.

"Gentlemen, start your *engines!*"

The racers roar to life and move slowly away behind a fleet of pace cars. Mechanics and pit crewmen hurry back behind the wall as the sleek racing cars in three long rows, eleven cars in each row, pick up speed. Every one of the thirty-three drivers is highly skilled and ready. Most have driven thousands of miles on this same track and other similar tracks. Each knows his car as perfectly as possible. If a driver is a rookie at the speedway (and he can be a world driving champion and still be a rookie at Indy), he or she has gone through an extensive series of driving tests and practice sessions during the previous thirty days of May.

Every driver knows that if victory is achieved, riches will follow. But failure can be worse than mere mechanical problems and an early exit from the race. Failure can mean injury or death.

After a couple of parade laps to get engines warmed, all but one of the cars pull off. Behind it, the field sets out on the final pace lap. Around the fourth turn they come, increasing speed. The last pace car pulls down into the pit lane, the green flag waves frantically, and every driver punches his accelerator to the floor. Turbochargers scream, engines thunder, and like a single massive machine, the field roars down the long, narrow, concrete-walled straightaway, battling for position. To every fan watching, it seems a miracle that they all reach the first turn without crashing.

No place for defensive driving, right?

Wrong!

Racing drivers are among the most highly skilled defensive drivers in the world, and Indy drivers are among the best in racing. One mistake by any them can result in several cars spinning and crashing. One mistake can result in injury and death at the Indianapolis Speedway. These drivers must drive defensively. Their lives can depend upon it.

And so can *yours*.

Watch a race driver in action. Don't just watch his car, but watch him. You'll see him constantly looking about, his helmeted head jerking back and forth as he checks his mirrors, his position on the track in relation to the other cars and the walls, and watches the traffic ahead. If there is a problem, you will see him react instantly, attempting to steer clear (often by steering right *at* the accident). At the same time you'll notice him acknowledging the drivers coming up from behind.

Watch Mario Andretti, a superb driver who has won at the Speedway, at many other tracks in other types of racing, and who became the world driving champion in Formula One racing, said by knowledgeable fans to be the most dangerous of all. Andretti rarely makes a mistake on the race track. But others do make mistakes around him. Yet Andretti seldom crashes. He has the ability to anticipate problems, and to avoid them. It almost seems to be luck, but those who know racing know that luck is a very small part of Andretti's victories. As aggressive as he is in a racing car, Mario Andretti is still a marvelous defensive driver. He drives his own racer and he mentally drives all the others as well. He knows what he is doing, and he constantly tries to know what the other drivers are doing, or what they might do in any situation. Andretti has crashed, of course, but it is almost always caused by a mechanical failure in his racer or, rarely, a completely unavoidable situation. Those who know racing say that Andretti has never suffered "brain fade" and caused a crash for himself or anybody else.

Andretti, other skilled race drivers, and most regular passenger-car drivers who understand defensive driving attempt to build a moving oval of space around themselves. This oval is one of the keys to successful driving.

THE MOVING OVAL OF SPACE

If you are closely surrounded by other cars, pinned in by nearby traffic, you have no space in which to move your own car. If something happens to you or to anybody else, you have no way to avoid it. Wise drivers continually try to position themselves so they have space all around. This space allows them to move right or left, faster or slower, to avoid trouble.

Wise drivers never hover between heavy trucks or buses, or allow themselves to be locked in between cars in front and to the rear. Wise drivers look for space on the road, and the minute the space is occupied, they find new space.

Doesn't this make driving hard work instead of pleasure? Yes, in a sense, it does make driving more challenging. But driving isn't supposed to be done in a doze. Driving is something you should do as alertly as possible, with your senses attuned to the potential danger all around. You are in a vehicle that can become a deadly projectile if something should go wrong. You are in command of this projectile. You are in charge.

The further away from other such projectiles you remain, the safer you will be. That's why smart drivers try to keep themselves in that relatively safe moving oval of space.

But there is far more to this matter of defensive driving. The National Safety Council says to drive defensively is "to minimize risks by anticipating the actions and errors of others."

If a car is coming directly at you, it is usually best to steer to the right.

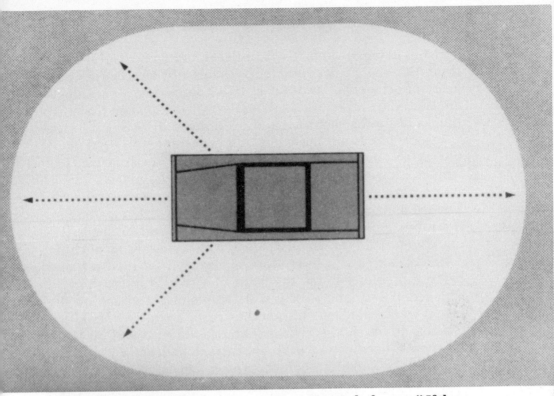

Never allow anybody to invade your "moving oval of space." If they do, move to a new space.

How often have you heard these statements?

"He won't dim his lights, so I don't plan to dim mine!"

"I'm sure the road is clear...let's pass."

"Don't worry about the speed, this car can stop on a dime."

"Don't be silly, nobody signals anymore."

"I'll just speed up a bit and we can make that light easily."

"No thanks. Seatbelts muss my dress."

Or the classic, "He'll stop since I obviously have the right-of-way."

Can you imagine the possible aftermath of each?

Specifically, defensive driving means watching the other drivers on all sides; it means being ready to give in any situation. Defensive driving is being prepared to back off, even if you are right. It means backing off even if you have the right-of-way. It means forgetting about your own "rights" and adjusting your driving style to that of other drivers around you.

Here's a statistic from the National Safety Council. You might think that mechanical problems, poor tires, etc., cause a majority of accidents, but the fact is 85 percent of all accidents are caused by driver errors. These errors cause more than fifty thousand deaths each year and millions of disabling injuries.

Yes, accidents are caused by odd occurrences. A light plane towing an advertising banner flew too low in California. The banner hit a high power line and caused the plane to crash into a freeway. The plane smashed head-on into a semitruck. The truck driver wasn't doing anything but driving along on his route, safely within his own moving oval of space. He couldn't possibly have anticipated an airplane falling into him.

In another case, a heavy roll of steel fell off the back of a truck and bounced onto the hood of a small car, crushing it. The occupants, who were just driving along well behind the truck, were killed. In still another case, a couple was killed when a driver suddenly swung across the road and hit them head-on. There wasn't even an instant to react. In an even more bizarre situation, which proves that anything can happen, an airplane part fell, hit a car, and caused an accident.

All this and more happens on the road today. In cases such as these, it can truly be said that a poor driver had little to do with the accident.

No driver heads for the street or highway expecting to be involved in, or to cause, an accident. Nobody would go out on the road if that were the case. Each one of us feels reasonably certain that we will get where we are going without problems— and certainly without crashing. Most of us hope we will never even *see* an accident. We almost never give thought to being involved in one. Even those of us who consider the possibility of an accident try to think positively.

It will happen to the other guy, right?

Where few of us are so smug that we imagine ourselves perfect drivers, most of us are confident in our own driving skills. We feel that if only the other guy will obey the laws, we will all get safely where we are going.

Yet drivers like us are involved in accidents every day.

Defensive driving has little to do with physical driving skills, with the ability to steer and brake and speed up and slow down and parallel park. Defensive driving is a mental attitude, a developed conditioning. It is a feeling as you are driving, an anticipation of any problems that might develop around you. It is watching other cars, imagining what you might do if they move a certain way, however erratic. It is an awareness of weather and road conditions, or visibility and density of traffic. Defensive driving is a knowledge of the mechanical condition of your own car.

The defensive driver, and for that matter the Indy car racer, never drives "automatically." Indy drivers have said one of their biggest problems, later in the long race when traffic has thinned out, is keeping their concentration. They know that concentration, not driving automatically, is the key to winning—and even to survival.

The defensive driver remains aware and alert (but not nervous). He is not one of the "average" motorists whom safety experts estimate make at least one mistake for every two miles of driving. Unfortunately, if the expert at defensive driving does not make that average of one mistake every two miles, then somebody out there is making more than a mistake every two miles, just to maintain the average.

Defensive drivers are confident of their ability to avoid trouble, but never overconfident. They constantly consider the situations, drivers, and cars all around and instantly recognize potential hazards. Because they have anticipated a hazard, they will have an extra second or two to act even if the action they take is no more than a routine maneuver.

Backing off slightly, just feathering the brake pedal, is a defensive maneuver if you see somebody ahead drifting about. Probably nobody even noticed your move. Defensive driving is safely changing lanes if a big truck draws alongside. Defensive driving is speeding up a bit and moving over if somebody comes in too close behind and begins to "tailgate." Defensive driving is slowing a bit if somebody wants to take the lane in front of you.

HOW TO DRIVE ON A COUNTRY ROAD

The situation you find yourself facing on a country road is hopelessly out-of-date and dangerous beyond compare. Yet most of us encounter it frequently. Here it is.

As safe as a road might look, you must be prepared for any hazard.

You're traveling fifty miles an hour on a two-lane road. Suddenly, often within the length of a football field, you see another car approaching. He, too, is traveling at fifty. So you are rushing toward each other at a closing speed of one hundred miles per hour. In seconds you must pass each other within three or four feet. You could in many cases reach out and touch his hand if he reached out to you—all at one hundred miles per hour. You think an Indy driver is crazy?

This type of driving is a throwback to the past when the Tin Lizzie was the queen of the road. But you are no longer traveling at Tin Lizzie speeds.

Meanwhile you might be facing bad lighting, questionable paving, animals wandering into the roadway, and farm vehicles just around the bend. You might be on an off-camber curve, where the banking is opposite of what it should be, with no shoulders to pull off on, heavy trees alongside the road, and potholes. You probably have no escape route at all. Two-lane country roads usually follow the paths of old wagon trails and strike right into the heart of small villages. There you will almost certainly find an ill-timed stoplight (and frequently an ill-tempered local policeman).

Don't you believe that modern, high-speed superhighways, turnpikes, and freeways are the most dangerous to drive. They are truly the *safest* on which to drive.

Can you spot the nine two-lane road hazards in this photo? 1. Car passing you in no-passing zone may cut in front of you. 2. Narrow shoulders—escape route limited. 3. Car making right turn at intersection—oncoming traffic could swerve to miss it if it comes out. 4. Poorly loaded truck—something may fall off. 5. Car approaching intersection at right may not yield. 6. School bus—you *must* stop when lights are flashing. 7. Oncoming truck has wide load—keep to right. 8. Traffic behind slow-moving truck may try to pass. 9. Right curve ahead—excess speed could force you into an oncoming lane.

On a country road you might pull up behind a slow-moving motorhome or travel-trailer. Passing them becomes a challenge. If there is a shoulder, it might be soft or gravelly. Every mile or so there will be a crossroad, often with entering traffic. This traffic is probably local, with drivers who know the road well and take automatic chances. Most of these crossroads won't have a traffic light, and many have no signs or signals at all.

Who has the right-of-way? The *other* guy, at least until you are certain of what he is going to do. That's defensive driving.

There is one long country road in the Midwest that goes for miles in a straight line with no crossroads. Then it rises up over a low railroad bridge in a gentle curve, straightens out on the other side, and goes on for more miles. The curve in the road, safe at normal highway speeds, became so dangerous, especially for visiting drivers who often flew through the rail and off the bridge, that officials put in a signal. Although it seemed a foolish place for a red light, local traffic officials placed one right at the top of the bridge. But this signal was different.

For one thing, it could be seen for miles. For another, it never stopped any traffic. It was set to turn green as the car approached the end of the bridge from either direction. So as any driver approached, at any rate of speed, the bright red light was obvious far ahead. The driver would slow down anticipating the stop that never came. Only when he reached the foot of the bridge did the light turn green. By then the car had slowed down enough to negotiate the gentle rising curve without problems.

The installation of the light cut accidents drastically, though nobody ever actually stopped for it.

Here are some tips for country road driving.

- Slow down. The slower speed limits on country roads might seem ridiculous to you, a visiting driver, but they are right. They have been set by local people who know the road and the conditions. Obey them.
- Pay extra attention to road and traffic condition signs. These also have been placed by people who know the road best and must not be ignored. If a sign says "SLOW—DANGEROUS CURVE" you should slow down, even if

the curve looks safe. Local officials know something you don't know, perhaps that the roadway is tilted the wrong way, or that a country road enters just beyond where you can see, or even that there is constant debris or dirt on the road.

- Pass with great care. You'll never be in a more dangerous situation than passing another vehicle on a country road. The frustration of being stalled behind a slow-moving vehicle is grating, but it's better than being dead in a head-on collision.

- Drive curves as though you were on ice. The road might be off-camber, a very tricky situation in a fast-moving car. Or the road might be oily. Maybe the road is rough and chuckholed. In that case, your suspension will bounce and your control will be minimal.

- Watch out for animals on the road. But if you must hit something, hit the animal and not a tree or another car. Remember, country roads are often not fenced like high-speed roads and animals roam freely, especially after dark. There is little more frightening than speeding up to a poor confused cow standing in the center of the road. The cow doesn't know it, but you know he could wind up in your back seat.

- Beware of heavy equipment, farm machinery, and equipment or cargo that might have dropped from these vehicles. A bale of hay can do real damage to the front end of a car. Accidents have happened because of roadway debris on all roads, but this is especially true on country roads.

- Defer to the local road hog. He knows the road, wants the road, and will *take* the road. He lives there and is accustomed to having his way. Give it to him.

- Don't expect rural roads to be as well marked as modern superhighways. State budgets may not cover the cost of extensively marking local roads, since state officials know that local roads are most often traveled by local drivers. It is best to know where you are going before you start out.

- Don't expect as many service or repair facilities on a country road, and remember that mechanics might not be as skilled (or even as honest). Be sure your car is in shape before you venture off the high-speed roads into farm country.

- Railroad crossings are common on country roads. Even if you miss the train, the crossing can damage your suspension if you hit it too fast. It is always best to slow down for a railroad crossing if you are on a strange road.
- Intersections can be killers, so be especially aware. Use your horn more frequently. You don't have to be impolite about it, but the horn can warn others of your presence, and it's better for them to think you are a bore than to have an accident.

HOW TO DRIVE ON CITY STREETS

You'll face a different set of conditions here. Instead of cows and rural landowners, you will be dealing with double-parked trucks and careless teenagers. You'll face doors opening directly in front of you, wobbling bicyclists, and smoke-belching buses pulling out without looking.

The dangers are different, but just as important.

One of the real hazards of driving on city streets is the fact that other drivers are often preoccupied and in a hurry. They don't think as carefully about what they are doing and are often so impatient that they will take a chance. Generally they have driven this route a hundred times before and so they do it "in their sleep." That's when they suddenly appear in front of you, or blow their horn in anger because you won't move the way they want you to move.

Take stoplights for example. Stoplights are intended to expedite the flow of traffic. In most cities, their location and timing are established only after detailed traffic pattern analysis. They are there to help both the motorist and the pedestrian.

Yet many city drivers seem to take traffic lights as a personal affront to their driving skill, a direct insult. They fume the entire time the light is red and crane their necks to get the first glimpse of yellow around the corner of the light. Then they gun the engine, leap forward, and perhaps barely miss a pedestrian.

Meanwhile, another impatient motorist is hurrying down

This city street has nine driving hazards. Can you spot them?
1. Frisbee in air means kids could run after it. 2. Skateboarder in
driveway could be in street quickly. 3. Driver at wheel of car in
driveway may be backing out. 4. Bicyclist on sidewalk could come
out into street. 5. Dog in front of oncoming traffic—pickup could
swerve into your lane. 6. Parallel-parked cars on both sides of street
force traffic into middle. 7. Car with hood up—owner may walk
into street. 8. Car at stop sign may not yield. 9. Ice cream truck—
children may be around it or running toward it.

the cross street. He, too, sees the yellow, but he hates the
thought of waiting the thirty-odd seconds through the upcom-
ing red light. So rather than slow to a halt and wait, he accelerates so that he can make the green light. What he really
plans is to enter the intersection sometime before the yellow
turns red.

After all, there may be a policeman around, and he doesn't
want to get cited for running a red light.

That is the scenario of the typical fender-bender on a city
street. There is a screech of brakes, a squeal of tires, and the
sickening sound of $500 fenders tearing. An hour later the

There are eleven driving hazards in this downtown driving photo. Can you spot all of them? 1. Street repair—traffic will be forced around it. 2. Driver in parked car—could open door or reenter traffic. 3. Pedestrians jaywalking 4. Taxi may stop quickly—door may open on street side. 5. Bus at stop will soon enter traffic. 6. Parking garage exit—cars may come out. 7. Car making left turn—traffic in left lane will stop or change lanes. 8. Pedestrians crossing against "Don't Walk" sign—be careful making right turn. 9. Construction fence—trucks or workers may enter street. 10. Delivery truck—driver may walk around truck. 11. Right lane is right turn only—some traffic may move into left lane.

shouting is over, licenses and insurance have been exchanged and recorded, and the police have completed their investigation, if they even bothered. The impatient drivers are on their way again, not thirty seconds late but an hour late.

With foolish-looking crunched fenders.

The most foolish part of the whole thing is that traffic lights are designed to move traffic smoothly. Each one of these drivers would probably have been caught at the next light anyhow, since they both tried to jump this one.

Smooth driving is most important for car and passenger security on city streets. There is a simple race-driver test to see how smoothly you really do drive your car. It's very easy, yet it indicates the true skill of the driver—and humbles the driver who thinks he is better than he really is.

You can try this without telling anybody, when you are alone in the car so nobody ever knows. You might be surprised.

Stand an empty glass on the floor, then drive around town. Imagine the glass is full of some foul-smelling liquid that will forever stain your rug with a nasty mark and a terrible odor. Try to keep the glass standing. It might be a little tougher than it sounds, yet a really smooth, skilled driver (and we should all be this way) can do it with ease. With the glass sitting there, you will have to start off smoothly, avoid sudden hard turns, take corners easily and without strain, and stop gently without harsh braking. If you don't tip over the glass, you have passed the test.

Can you imagine how much longer your car would last if you drove this way all the time? Can you image how much more comfortable you and your passengers would be?

City drivers are faced with crowded streets, the possibility of children darting out from the curb, bicyclists who demand the right-of-way (give it to them), crossing guards, double-parked cars and trucks, poorly marked crosswalks, street repairs, cars changing lanes, pedestrians who think your car will magically stop just because they are in a crosswalk, tailgaters, a jumble of signs and signals, and other unnerving hazards.

Here are some tips for city driving.

- Assume there is no such thing as a right-of-way rule. Give it to whoever wants it. Sure, we all know the driver on the right is supposed to have the right-of-way, but if the guy on the left insists, give way.
- If you are going to stop more quickly than normal and have the time, tap your brakes once to let the guy behind know. The flash of your brake lights will give him at least some warning.
- Use your signals to indicate a turn or a lane change. Most traffic officers will say that you can't use your signals too much in city driving. Better to oversignal, even if it makes you look like a beginner.

- Beware of hidden intersections, such as parking garage entrances, driveways, truck loading docks or other un-marked vehicle entrances. About the time you arrive in a doze is when a big, heavy truck is going to pull out.
- Don't trust a green light. There may be oncoming traffic that doesn't see the red, or plans to ignore it. The best drivers always look both ways, even if the light gives you the right-of-way. It's much better to slow down or even stop at a green light than to fight it out in court later. What if you get hit from behind? That could happen, but even that is better than a "T-bone" at an intersection.
- Remember the left-right-left rule at all intersections. Look left, look right, then look left again before proceeding. It's amazing how many good drivers look right, left, right, and then pull out in front of a car in the nearest lane. Perhaps that other innocent driver pulled out of a nearby driveway, or away from the curb. Always look left *last*.
- Check your rearview mirror every five seconds. Most good drivers get into the habit of "sweeping" their vision front, one side, rear, then the other side and quickly back to the front. They do this constantly, just like a professional race car driver. They want to know what's happening *all around*.
- Drive about a block and half ahead of your car (at thirty miles per hour). This is the old trick of anticipating what's happening, or what might happen, up front. You can avoid many accidents, and even putting on your brakes too firmly, by driving a little ahead of your car. Anticipation is one of the best ways of keeping the glass standing tall.
- Stay in the center lane on four-lane city streets. This gives you a chance to see cars or people coming out into the street. The center lane, if you are not blocking traffic, is where you will find the biggest safety oval.
- Beware of UFOs (frisbees, balls, kites, etc.), and expect a child to follow. Children can be taught by parents to look both ways before crossing, then dart into the street after a ball without a thought for oncoming traffic. The ball is the most important thing. Most good drivers are almost *afraid* to drive down a street where children are playing.
- Beware of any parked car with a person behind the wheel. He could pull out, or he could open his door. Sure, it will be his fault, and he will probably have to pay for the damage to your car as well as his own, but such an ac-cident can sure ruin a day.

- Anticipate a door opening on every car that has pulled over to park. They'll be parking because they want to get out. With this sure and certain knowledge, you might avoid an accident.
- At a left-turn intersection, don't turn your wheels before you start to make your turn. If you are struck from the rear, you will be driven straight ahead, and not over into oncoming traffic and a head-on collision. Once again, it might not be your fault, but you might not be out of the hospital in time to fight the case in court, either.
- Only foolish drivers swing over to the left into another lane to make a right turn. You don't need that much road in a car, and you could be inviting disaster. Most vehicles that routinely make wide right turns are marked with prominent signs to inform following drivers of the fact. Look for them.
- Right turns can be hazardous to your car and to the motorcyclist or bicyclist cruising along in the "bike lane." Always look to the immediate right rear before making a turn, and when you do make it be sure to be all the way over so there is no room for a two-wheeler in between you and the curb.
- Beware of other drivers cutting in front of you, but if they do, back off. If somebody else cuts into the safety oval you have allowed yourself, back off again. It's irritating, but you'll live.
- Follow the "Three Cs" of driving—Cooperation, Communication, and Concentration.

HIGH-SPEED ROADWAY DRIVING

You are probably safest on roads that many consider to be the least safe. These are interstates, freeways, turnpikes, superhighways, and other high-speed, multilane roads. Although you are going faster, you truly are safer.

These roads are designed for higher speeds by traffic engineers of today, not yesterday. As a general rule, they have smoother surfaces and are fenced, they are engineered and banked for curves, they have collision barriers, they do not usually allow pedestrians or bicycles, and some even restrict or prohibit trucks. There are no traffic lights or intersections

There are ten driving hazards in this freeway and turnpike photo. Can you locate them? 1. Car in your mirror will soon be in your blind spot. 2. You're too close to car ahead—keep a minimum two-second following distance. 3. Motorcyclist is often overlooked—keep an eye out for him. 4. Car changing lanes—could cut in front of you. 5. Left lane closed ahead—traffic will be squeezed to the right. 6. Car parked on shoulder may reenter traffic. 7. Exit ahead—right-lane traffic may slow down; left-lane traffic may cut across to exit. 8. Truck has brake lights on—slow down until you're sure there's no danger. 9. Recreational vehicle has limited visibility, larger blind spot. 10. Car on entrance ramp may not yield.

to consider, and they are usually well-lit at off-ramps. Where there are signs, they are generally large and easy-to-read and contain off-ramp and destination information.

Theoretically, there is no stop-and-go driving on modern high-speed roads (though some early morning and late afternoon commuters might reasonably argue this point). If an accident and the inevitable "rubbernecks" slow traffic to a near stop and you are an hour late for work, you know about stop-and-go traffic, even on a six-lane highway.

Still, high-speed roadways do have inherent hazards, most often because drivers ignore the laws and regulations. Drivers exceed the posted speed limits, they tailgate at high speeds, they cut in and out of lanes to gain a car or two, and they stay

What's the right way to enter a crowded freeway? As you enter the ramp, be sure to check in front, to the sides and behind you as the red car is doing. Time your approach to blend into the traffic in the merging area. Don't make any sudden stops in the acceleration lane. Being smooth and alert are the keys to entering a freeway properly. What's the right way to exit a freeway? Use all of the deceleration area as the blue car is doing. A quick exit at freeway speed, as the yellow car is doing, means you'll be traveling too fast when you reach the ramp. The red car should be traveling at ramp speed, which is considerably lower than freeway speed.

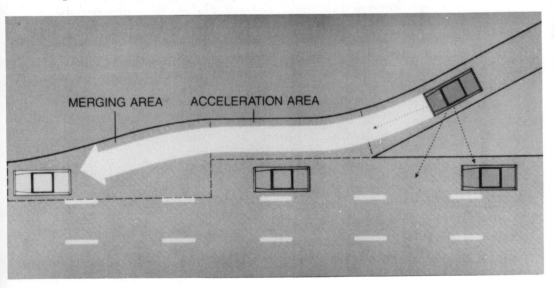

in the fast lane until the last minute and then cut across several lanes all at once to make their off-ramp. Plus they ignore weather and traffic conditions.

Because of this, driving on high-speed roadways does place certain demands on your driving skill and knowledge. There are techniques for this type of driving just as there are techniques for country road driving and city street driving. Nor should you be afraid of driving on high-speed roadways merely because it is faster driving than the others, or sometimes more crowded than the others. Superhighways, though sometimes boring to the point of danger, will get you there quicker and safer if you keep the following tips in mind:

- Know where you are going, where you are going to get on, and where you are going to get off. This allows you to plan your driving moves. Most such roadways are well marked, with signs telling you that your off-ramp is coming up two or three exits ahead. This gives you time to make moves gradually and safely.
- Don't make sudden lane changes. More high-speed roadway accidents are caused by erratic drivers jumping from lane to lane than any other single thing except driving under the influence of some substance.
- Plan your entrance by getting up as much speed as possible before you hit the slow lane. Then blend in smoothly. Don't believe the old wives' tale about the car on the on-ramp having the right-of-way. The car on the road has the right-of-way in every case. Do it like an Indy driver does it. Get up speed and then blend into the traffic flow.
- No hole? Don't slam on your brakes on the access road. Instead, use the emergency lane to the right of the right lane until you can blend in. Most drivers will allow you in. They don't want a collision any more than you do. In any case, entering a freeway or turnpike can be risky business, so do it gently and with care.
- Select your lane and, as much as possible, stay in it. But don't poke along in the fast lane, or speed in a slower lane. OK, here's a common question. Who's at fault, the driver going the speed limit and blocking traffic behind, or the driver who tailgates and honks trying to get the one in front to move over so he can go on faster than the speed limit? Answer? The one behind. If you are going at the speed limit, according to highway patrol officers,

you do not *need* to move over to allow a faster driver behind to speed on. But courtesy, also according to police officers, suggests you move over. They'll take care of the speeder, and meanwhile you won't be causing a dangerous situation. Besides, you and I are not trained or responsible for seeing to it that other drivers obey the laws. We have ourselves to look after.

In some states it is illegal to drive in the left lane unless you are passing.

- Change lanes with extreme caution by looking in the mirror, making sure there is plenty of room, signaling, then glancing over your right or left shoulder before the actual change. As pointed out before, changing lanes on high-speed roads is one of the most common causes of serious accidents.
- Never tailgate, even in bright, clear weather, and especially to harass the driver in front into moving over. If lane changing is most dangerous, tailgating is also high on the list. You've heard of the terrible multicar accidents on high-speed roads. If nobody had been near anybody else, they might not have happened.
- Remember that the driver in front, in the next lane, may not be able to see you because you are in his "blind spot." He may cut over in front of you. Avoid this spot at all times—like the plague. This spot, of course, is not within

Here, I accelerated to 35 mph before braking. Dry road: skid distance, 54 feet. Same road with thin film of oil, then moistened: skid distance, 96 feet. Same road after heavy water washing: skid distance, 69 feet.

your own safety oval anyhow, because the other guy is there.

- Be especially careful after a light rain on a high-speed roadway. Light moisture tends to mix with the oil film and make the surface "icy." Heavy rain, though, will finally wash the oil away. Take a tip from motorcyclists here. You'll see the experienced ones avoiding the center of each lane, since that is where the oil has dripped from countless cars.
- Beware of "highway hypnosis" on long drives on high-speed roads. You can be lulled into a false sense of security and lose your concentration. Stop frequently and walk around the car. If you feel drowsy open a window, change the radio from soft music to hard rock. Roll your head around. Clench and unclench your fists. Best of all, stop and get a cup of coffee, or doze for a few minutes at a rest stop.
- Resist the urge to "rubberneck" accidents. Those folks have as much trouble as they need, and that includes another nearby accident because a driver slowed down to see what was going on. Unless you can truly help, move along as quickly as traffic conditions will permit.
- If you have a problem and must pull over, pull completely off the road, get out on the right side of your car, raise your hood, and wait for help. Generally, don't attempt repairs alongside a high-speed road. A passing truck can even blow your car off its jack.

DRIVING EMERGENCIES ON ALL ROADS

There are seven driving emergencies, any one or more of which anybody might face at some time or another during their driving career. The trick is to know what to do about them when they hit.

1. "*My* brakes *suddenly won't work!*"

Remember these four words: Pump. Park. Shift. Swipe.

Pump the brake pedal. This will sometimes put enough pressure back into the brake system to stop the car. *Park* refers to the parking or emergency brake. This is usually a manual system and can be used, if you don't just jam it on, to stop the car. Jamming on a parking brake can cause a spinout, though, so apply this brake carefully, and not on a curve if you can avoid it. *Shift* into a lower gear, or a lower range on your automatic. The drag of the engine will slow you down. Do all three of these as quickly as you can.

Sideswipe as a last resort. Swipe something, anything (a guardrail, a curb, even a parked car) to rub off your speed. The indirect blow is better than hitting a brick wall or an oncoming car. And damaged car parts are much better than damaged people parts.

In any case, if the first three work, they'll take up to four times more distance than normal to stop the car. This means you must react quickly.

2. "*A tire has just* blown out!"

When a front tire blows, the car will pull hard to the side of the blowout. It can jerk all the way across a highway. The steering wheel will vibrate hard. Hang on tight. Don't panic. Stay *off* the brakes. If you jam them on, a natural reaction to the emergency, you might lose control completely. Get off the gas and concentrate on staying in your lane as you gradually slow down and pull off the road.

If a rear tire blows, also a very dangerous situation, the back of the car will vibrate and weave back and forth. Handle this situation the same way.

Working with stunt drivers and special cars at test tracks, Nancy Curry, a Shell dealer representative, tested these tips with a car that had tires purposely blown out with explosives.

"My car jerked across the yellow line of our 'highway,'" she reported, "but the tips work."

3. "*That car is coming* right at me!"

Right is usually the right way to go. Try to escape to the right if possible. Remember that almost anything is better than a head-on collision. If you dodge to the left, the other driver might correct back into that lane at the last second. Swerve to the right, even if you have to hit something on the roadside or another car going the same way you are. You might tear up your car, but chances are you'll survive.

While you dodge, blow the horn and if you can't avoid a collision, brake hard. Every mile per hour you slow down will reduce the impact.

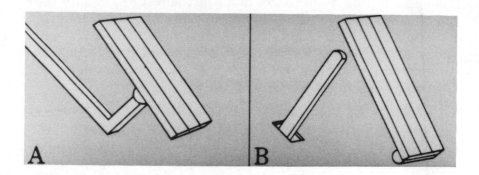

Two kinds of accelerator linkage. Check your car in advance to see if you can lift the pedal to unstick the accelerator.

4. "*My* accelerator *is stuck!*"

First of all, try to unstick it. You might be able to pull it back up with the toe of your shoe. Or maybe a passenger in the car can reach down and pull it up. Don't take your own eyes off the road to reach down yourself.

If you can't get the accelerator unstuck, you can shift into neutral or press down on the clutch. The engine will race by itself while you pull off and stop.

Don't forget this. If you turn off the key on some cars, the power systems will stop and you will have to fight the steering. Turning off the key could even lock your steering wheel. Modern power-equipped cars (steering and brakes) will still steer and brake without the power, but the effort it takes to do these things will seem to be ten times as much as if the car didn't have the power in the first place.

5. "*I'm starting to skid sideways!*"

Don't panic and slam on the brakes. That will only aggravate the situation. Instead, take your foot off the gas and turn the front wheels into the skid. This will bring the back end of the car around and into line with the front end again.

Be careful, though, that the back end doesn't snap around too far and begin to skid in the other direction. If it does, whip the steering wheel back the other way, into the new skid, and gradually regain control.

This is not an easy reaction. The first thought will be to hit the brakes and steer the wrong way. That's why performance

Turn in the direction of the skid to recover control, and stay off the brake.

driving schools have "skid pads" to train drivers the correct way. With practice, the technique comes.

6. *"My car has fallen into deep water!"*

More than three thousand people each year face this emergency. Get out a window as quickly as possible. Some cars will float for a moment or two, giving you a bit of extra time. Use that time to escape. Remember, power windows might short out, so get them down as quickly as possible.

If you can't get out a window, a door is the next best bet. Water pressure might hold the door shut for a time, but don't panic. As the water fills the passenger compartment, the pressure will be equalized and the doors will open. Remember, the door is the *second* best way. Try to get out the window first.

Meanwhile, as the pressure is equalizing there will probably be an air pocket near the roof. Use it while you wait, though this requires a great deal of cool and calm action. If you have children in the car, shove them out first. They'll float for a moment, and in any case, at least they have a chance outside the car.

7. *"My hood flew up!"*

Stop the car as quickly as possible, of course. But on a crowded road, jamming on the brakes might only make the matter worse. Try to stop smoothly, meanwhile peeking through the opening between the hood and the dashboard. Or lean out the window to steer. Next time you are in your car, check to see which vantage point is best so that you will know in case the emergency happens, as it does to thousands of drivers every year.

Here's a preparedness checklist. Look it over and ask yourself the following questions about you and your car.

Ask yourself about yourself:

1. Am I very tried? Or sick?
2. Have I been drinking, or taking drugs, or consuming any substance that might make me groggy or impair my driving?
3. Where am I going? Should I prepare for dangerous roads?

If your car goes into deep water, get out the window, FAST.

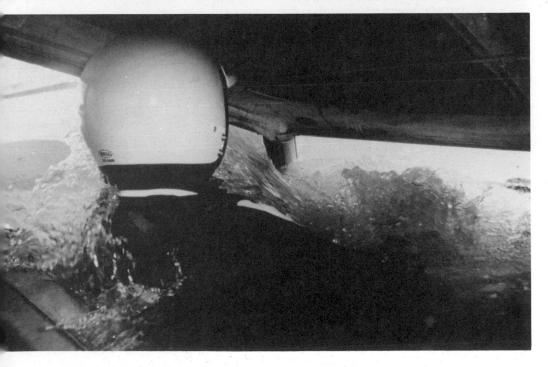

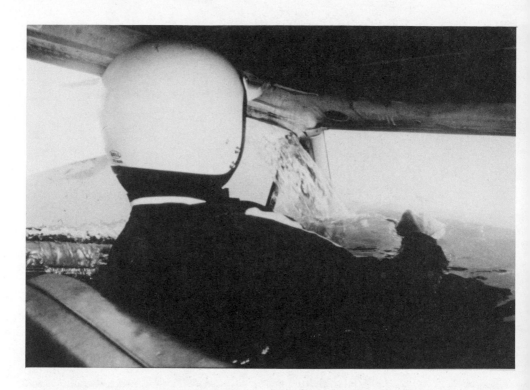

4. How's the weather? How will it be on the way back?
5. How are the other drivers? Am I likely to encounter sleepy ones, or drunk ones?

Ask yourself about your car:

1. How are the brakes? Does the pedal go more than half-way down? Does it continue to sink under pressure?
2. Is the parking brake working?
3. Are the wear indicators on the tires showing?
4. Are all the lights working?
5. Are the windshield wipers, washers, and washer fluid all in good order?
6. Does the horn honk?
7. Are the tire pressures correct?
8. Are the shock absorbers in good shape?
9. Are any fluids leaking?
10. Are the driver belts frayed, cracked, or loose?
11. Is there enough power steering fluid?

DRIVING IN FOUL WEATHER

Driving in snow, rain, or fog puts extra demands on a driver. It can be dangerous no matter how good you are, and if you are not careful you might find out the hard way that Mother Nature isn't easy to handle.

But there are ways to minimize the risks.

Bruce Galbraith drove a tank truck for seventeen years in all kinds of weather. He knows firsthand the problems bad weather can cause, but he handled it well. Galbraith logged more than three quarters of a million miles without a single accident.

Here are some things he learned over his driving career.

1. *Fog, day or night.* Use the low beams on your headlights since they shine downward and do not reflect as much of the fog back into your face. With your brights on, the lights shine directly into the fog and the glare cuts your vision. If you have fog lights, use them. They cut into the fog and light the way better without glaring back at you. If you drive in fog regularly, consider installing fog lights on your car. Mount them low,

beneath the headlights but no lower than about twelve inches off the ground.

When driving in fog, drive slowly but keep moving. Massive accidents have been caused on high-speed roads because a driver stopped. Even in the day, turn on your lights and your windshield wipers, and use the defroster to cut down on the condensation on the inside of your windshield.

Here's another fog driving tip. If you must stop, get off the road, then *turn on your emergency flashers and not your lights.* Many drivers follow the taillights of the driver in front in a heavy fog. Somebody might drive off the road and into the back of your car before they realize you have parked. Be especially careful with cars creeping along through the fog at a snail's pace. It is surprising how quickly you can bear down on another car moving much slower than you are moving.

2. *Rain.* It doesn't have to rain very hard to make the roads slippery. In fact, a light rain can make a highway more slippery than a heavy rain, which tends to wash off the oil film that causes the condition. The first few minutes of any rain are the most dangerous, since water mixed with the dirt and oil that collected when the road was dry can make a soapy, slick film that takes a while to wash away.

Decrease your speed and increase the interval between you and the cars around you.

Even with new tires, you can "hydroplane." This is a condition that causes the tires to ride up on a film of water just like water skis. Control of the car can suddenly be lost, without warning, when hydroplaning begins. The back end can whip around before you realize it and you can go spinning down the road.

If you feel yourself starting to hydroplane on a wet road, often beginning with a "lightness" in the steering wheel and a drifting of the front wheels, take your foot off the gas but don't touch the brakes or turn the wheel. As you slow, the tires will begin to cut through the water, get a grip on the road, and give you control again.

You can avoid hydroplaning by driving much more slowly on a wet road. Don't overload the rear end of your car in an effort to get more traction, since this will make the front tires hydroplane more easily. And remember, worn tires are *much* more likely to hydroplane than tires with full tread.

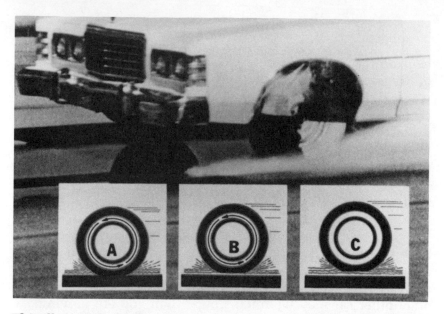

This illustrates what happens during hydroplaning: A) At low speeds, the tire cuts through the water and remains in complete contact with the road surface. B) At speeds around 30 mph, a water wedge may penetrate the tire-road contact and partial hydroplaning occurs. C) At speeds around 55 mph, the water wedge can increase and the tire can lose contact with the road surface, causing total hydroplaning. At this point you have virtually no control over the car. NOTE: In the photo, the car is traveling at 60 mph and the front wheels (riding on a layer of water) are not turning at all. This is total hydroplaning.

Try to avoid making sudden moves with the steering wheel. This can promote hydroplaning. In fact, if you are safely able to follow directly in the tracks of a vehicle in front of you, you'll help yourself. These tracks will be drier, having been "squeegeed" by the first car's tires. So keep an eye on the road, don't tailgate, but use this advantage if you can.

If you must go through deep water, do it slowly and carefully. If you go too fast, you might splash water up on your ignition system and short out the ignition system. Then your car will just die, right there in the middle of the puddle, and it'll be tough to dry things out to get going again.

After you have gone through deep water, pump your brakes a few times to be sure they are dry and won't fade if you need them. If they fade, shift into low gear and ride the brakes gently to dry them out.

It is true all the time, but especially in wet weather: Wipe your headlights clean periodically. The low, dirty spray thrown up by other cars can cut your light nearly in half.

3. Snow. Did you know that in California and certain other "warm" states, they *tell* you when to put chains on your car? This is humorous to Eastern drivers, who feel they know better than anybody else when to chain up (and they probably do, too), but that's the law.

In these states, you can get a traffic ticket for not installing chains when you are instructed to do so. "Chain monkeys," young men and women who make a good living from the job, station themselves at a wide spot in the road near the chain sign and charge from five bucks and up to do the dirty work of installing chains. This service is, of course, only for drivers who do not want to get out of their warm car and get under.

Wherever you are, driving in snow can be a challenge. Here are some tips that will help.

This lady is snowbound but she knows what to do. A. She's keeping the exhaust pipe clear. B. She's wearing a plastic garbage bag as protection from the wind. C. She's turned the dome light on to keep an eye on her passenger. D. She's cracked the window for ventilation. E. She's put out a flare so she'll be more easily seen.

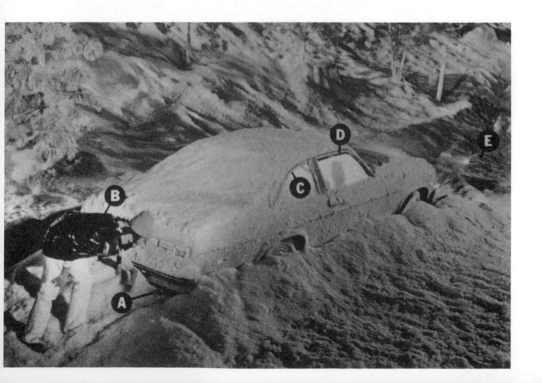

- Keep a basic emergency kit in your trunk in snow country, and know how to use it. The kit should contain the usual tools, and these extra items: a steel shovel, matches, candles or several containers of canned heat, a metal coffee can, two plastic trash bags or a large sheet of plastic, and some sand in a bag.

  The shovel and sand will help you get out of snow if you get stuck. The candle or canned heat will work to melt snow in the coffee can for drinking water (but don't *eat* snow since it will just chill your system further). The candle and coffee can will also double as a foot warmer. The trash bags or plastic will be great insulators against a cold wind if you must step outside your car.

  If money is no object, include some extra warm clothing in your kit, some nonperishable foods, a compass, and a CB radio.

  Why all the precautions? Every year, people die in stalled cars in snowstorms. If you get caught in a situation like this, don't panic, and don't leave your car. It is your best shelter.
- Meanwhile, run your engine and heater for only ten minutes or so every hour. You'll keep from freezing and since you might be stuck for an extended time, you'll have fuel. But while you are running your engine, keep a window slightly cracked for fresh air—and be sure your tailpipe isn't jammed with snow. If it is, deadly exhaust fumes could back up inside the car.
- Keep an eye on any other passengers in the car to be sure they are in good shape. It is best if they don't sleep under these conditions. Frostbite can sneak up without a person realizing it, and then it might be too late.
- Tie a colored scarf or cloth to the fully extended antenna and light one of the flares from your kit occasionally. Even an airplane might be looking for you, and passing traffic will certainly be alerted.
- If you live in snow country, keep your fuel tank at least half full all the time, even if it requires more frequent gas stops. If you do get stuck, you'll need the gas to help run the heater at intervals to keep from freezing.
- Remember that a wet road is most slippery at just about thirty-two degrees. The water will not be frozen completely, but will make the road that much more slick. In these conditions, drive very slowly, or find a motel and wait out Mother Nature.

- Bridges and overpasses freeze quicker than solid roadbeds because the air is cooling them from both above and below.
- On glare ice, snow tires won't even compete with chains or tire studs for car control. At twenty miles per hour, it can take a car with snow tires up to 151 feet to stop. The same car with chains can stop in *half* that distance.

Here are a few more easy tips for snow and cold country driving.

- Keep your windows clean and free of snow and ice on all sides.
- It's a lot harder to get moving in snow or ice, so try to avoid parallel parking and other full-turn maneuvers.
- It won't help to cut down on tire pressure to try to get more traction. You won't get any more bite on the road, and you will wear out your tires sooner.
- Spinning your wheels only makes matters worse.
- When stopping, let off the accelerator slower and earlier than normal, then pump your brakes gently instead of jamming them on.

Chapter SIX

More Driving Tips

The driver you and I see on the street every day can learn a lot from professional racing drivers. The pros drive for a living. They make their house payments that way. What's more, their life can depend even more than yours or mine on their driving skills. They often have to do the right thing, make the right driving decision, or *die*.

Of course, that can be true with us, too, though we hope not.

Four-time Indy winner A. J. Foyt once tried to bodily lift his crashed racer from the track. Foolish? Not at all. One of the cardinal rules of race driving is to "clear the track." This is also true in highway driving. If you possibly can, get out of the way of other traffic if you are having any type of emergency, or if you have a minor accident where your car will still move. No sense turning a fender-bender into a fatality.

Yes, you are supposed to remain at the scene and not move the vehicles under normal circumstances, but the police will tell you that if your car is causing a traffic hazard, it should be moved out of the way.

It's also true that ol' A.J. had an extra motive for his frantic actions at the scene of the crash. His team car, another car owned by him in the race, was in second place and the 500-mile race was nearing an end. If his wreckage wasn't cleared quickly, the race would end under a yellow flag, and his team-mate wouldn't have a chance to win. Racing cars aren't allowed to pass anybody when the yellow flag is out.

So Foyt all but *muscled* his car out of the way, with the help of some nearby track workers. The race roared on and his teammate, Jim McElreath, won. Foyt's hard work paid off.

Race drivers often learn the hard way, and we can learn from them. Take "rubbing off speed" for example. Race drivers learn that if they *must* hit something, they should hit something that will gradually reduce their speed instead of something that will stop them instantly. A slower stop, even if it doesn't seem to be that much slower, will do considerably less damage.

Would you rather hit a brick wall or a row of small trees? Would you rather hit a bridge abutment or a line of parked cars? None of these choices are very attractive, it's true, but trees and cars have some give to them while brick walls and bridge abutments do not. Race drivers know about this technique. They call it "energy absorption." They learn to attempt to hit things that will absorb their speed more slowly, and we can do the same when possible. If all appears to be lost, and you know you are going to hit something, hit something as soft and giving as you can.

Often you do have choices, even in a quick-moving emergency. If the choice is between a car coming from the other way, for example, and a car going the same direction as you are going, choose the one going the same way. The damage to you and to your car (as well as the other car) will be less. If you must swerve, and have the choice between swerving into some bushes, or some trees, pick the bushes. They are softer, and will absorb more of your energy as you come to a stop.

Watch a modern race car during some of the terrible accidents shown in newspapers and on television. You will see body panels flying one way, wheels another, and the engine another. In the old days, the car just plowed into a wall in one piece, with few parts breaking off. Imagine the force it takes to throw a tire and wheel, or an engine, high into the air. That force being expended on the flying part is some of the force developed by the car and its speed. There is only so much, a certain given amount of force in that car at that moment, and some of it is being used to throw parts around.

Modern race cars, by breaking into many pieces, absorb some of the energy that might have gone into injuring the driver. The same science will work for you and me.

Race drivers always try to visualize escape routes. You and I should do the same. This is a continuing process as you are driving down the road. Constantly sweep the area with your eyes, imagining where you would go if something should happen. Many race tracks are *built* with such escape routes, short roads at the end of a long straightaway, an open area outside a high-speed corner, a break in the wall at a common "spin off" point. Normal highways generally are not. But there are escape routes everywhere as you drive along if you just look for them.

Make it a game. It's fun and interesting, and it could save your life. Imagine at every moment what you would do if a drunk driver suddenly swerved across into your lane. Watch out for driveways, barnyards, shallow ditches (an excellent energy absorber in an emergency), wide spots in the road. As you drive along, constantly select potential escape routes. Soon this game will become second nature, and in an emergency you will instinctively know where to go.

The "escape cone," as professional drivers call an escape route, is wide and safe on a straight road with flat fields on either side. You can go in almost any direction in an emergency. You can just swing off the road into the flat field on either side. There is nothing to hit. But the cone narrows drastically as traffic moves in, or road obstacles appear. In this case, race drivers often slow down, and so should you.

The escape cone is almost zero if you are going down a road with big trees on either side. Or going over a bridge with walls on each side. Or if you are driving down a street with cars parked bumper to bumper on each side. In these cases, since the escape route is so small, you should compensate by driving slower.

Race drivers also know of the "zone of blindness," and they use it for safety. So can you. They tend to drop back before they pass, because they know that the closer you get to a vehicle in front, the narrower your view of the road ahead becomes. This is the angle of the area blocked from your view by the vehicle in front.

Nobody in his right mind would pull up within a few feet of a semitruck, then swing out into the other lane to pass. Why? Because that close to the truck, you can only see a very small part of the other lane and any oncoming traffic. If you

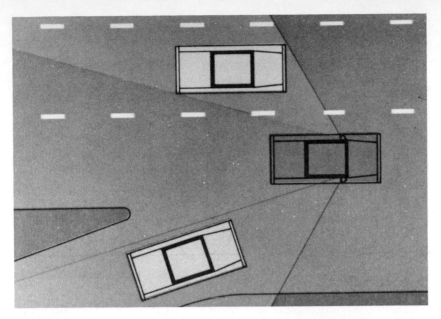

Remember, you can't see other cars moving along in what racing drivers call the "zone of blindess."

drop back a bit, the zone widens and you can see much farther up the road.

The same is true if you pull up too closely behind a car. The angle narrows so much that you can't really see what's coming from the other way. Smart drivers drop back. If you need that extra little bit of space in order to pass, you shouldn't be passing in the first place.

No professional driver would ever move out without fastening his seat belt, though at one time there was some disagreement over this. Rex Mays and Mario Andretti are two of the great names in racing, though from different generations. Mays, who was convinced that seat belts would only trap him in his car in case of an accident, was killed when he was thrown from his racer during a race and hit by another car. Andretti has lived through several crashes that totally disintegrated his much faster cars. About all that was left of the racer was the cockpit section, with a healthy Andretti still strapped inside. He may have bounced around a little and collected a few bruises, but he was alive.

Don't believe those who insist that they don't want to be trapped in a wrecked car by a seat belt. According to the National Safety Council, if everybody belted in every time they got in a car, 22 to 28 lives would be saved. Not 22 to 28 lives every month, not every week, but *every day.* We've all heard at least one horror story about somebody, somewhere, who was trapped by seat belts. But the dead drivers who were *not* wearing them are not around to tell their stories.

Many states have laws about seat belts. You must strap in even if they aren't "comfortable," or even if they do "muss your dress." The experts know that lives are saved by seat belts, in spite of the odd accident in which somebody was trapped by them.

No professional driver would ever take medication before doing his job. The intake of drugs, alcohol, or any other substance that could affect your driving is stupid. These things may make some folks feel better, but they affect reaction times, judgment, and the ability to respond in an emergency.

We all know how many people are killed by drunk driving. Drinking while driving is one of the silliest things you can do. Hey, it isn't just the drunk's life—it's yours and mine, too.

Less obvious is the danger of driving after a big meal. Few highway drivers even think of this. You visit your grandmother, overindulge on her marvelous cooking, then you know how you feel. Stuffed, right? Much of your body's activity at that time is involved in the digestive process so you become less alert, perhaps even dangerously sleepy. A professional race driver *never* has a big meal before a race. For one thing, he doesn't want a full stomach in case he gets hurt, and for another, he knows he won't be quite as sharp with a full stomach. He doesn't dare gorge himself and neither should you before a demanding drive. Have that sumptuous meal *after* the drive, not during or just before. You'll enjoy it more and you won't be risking your life.

Yes, grandmother's food is hard to resist, but you don't have to stuff yourself if you are planning a long drive home just after the visit.

ACCIDENTS DO HAPPEN

And not always to the other guy. We know this, intellectually at least. Most people do not go out on the road expecting an accident. Most of us motor away as confident as we should be, knowing the odds are greatly in our favor, and that in almost every case we will arrive in the condition in which we left.

Fred Stigale is a senior safety engineer with Shell Oil Company. In considering accidents and what to do about them, he talked to a doctor, a group of paramedics, a highway patrolman, and other professionals. "I tried to cover as many 'typical' accident situations as I could. From coming upon a collision to actually being involved in one. I combined the things I knew with what I learned to give advice on how to handle several different situations."

Stigale listed the major concerns and questions about auto accidents.

"What's the most important thing to remember when a serious accident occurs?"

There are three things to remember: 1. Don't panic. You will need all of your wits and calm to handle the situation. 2. Think. Do things in a logical order at an accident scene, and don't do more than you're qualified to do—especially in first aid. 3. Don't try to be a hero. Call for help as quickly as possible.

Let's break this down a bit. Accidents happen. It isn't, hopefully, the end of the world. An accident can be frightening, but panic will only make matters worse. Try to stay as cool and calm as you can under the unpleasant circumstances. You'll need your wits about you when it comes to talking to the police and to the other driver if there is one. How you react now can have a real affect on what happens later, in court, for example.

There is a logical sequence which will be explained on pages 142–43. Do these things in order, one by one, and don't be hurried or misdirected by witnesses or anybody else involved in the accident. One young man was hurrying (but not speeding) home after work. It was raining and there were deep puddles on the street. A driver pulled out of a side street and hit him broadside. Her car was barely damaged but his, because he was moving, was wrecked.

He was heading for a nearby telephone to call the police when another car pulled up. It was a car he had passed, and upon which he had splashed water. The windows had been open and the driver was soaked and irate. "If you call the police, I'll tell them you were speeding!" shouted the wet driver. "I'll tell them you were driving recklessly. I'll fix you!"

So the young driver was cowed. He didn't call the police, but merely allowed the driver who had caused the accident to drive away. He was left with a wrecked car, never thinking

Always carry flares in your car, and know how to use them. First, be sure there is no spilled gasoline. Then place the flares behind the accident, about 15 to 20 paces apart. Angle them toward the side of the road, as far back as you can. The object is to form a no-man's-land behind the accident by guiding approaching traffic around the wreck.

that the irate driver's testimony wouldn't have meant all that much. It wouldn't even have mattered if the authorities *believed* him, since speed had little to do with the fact that the offending driver had pulled out through a stop sign and hit him.

"Being 'involved in an accident' means physical contact involving my car, right?"

Wrong. You are *involved* if you *contribute* in any way to a crash, even if it is by another driver. If you swerve in front of another car, and he crashes to avoid you, you are involved. If two other cars crash because you are breaking a law, you are involved. Not once has your car been touched, but you are required to stop just as though it had been.

The temptation might be just to drive on, and many drivers do that. But the consequences of leaving the scene of an accident are just as severe even though you weren't physically touched in the altercation.

"I am the first to arrive at the scene of a bad accident."

There are five things you should do, and they come straight from the paramedics of the Los Angeles County Fire Department. These people are some of the best-trained emergency workers in the world.

1. Avoid a second collision by not parking behind the wreck, or on the opposite side of the road from a wreck. Pull up several yards *beyond* the accident and turn on your flashers.

One man saw a travel-trailer whip about and finally jackknife up a low highway slope. He stopped his car and ran forward with a fire extinguisher, just in case. He thought he was doing everything just right, but in seconds his car was hit from behind, then another car hit that car, and soon the highway looked like a battle zone. In the original jackknife nobody was hurt and the vehicle was off the roadway. In the resulting crashes several drivers were injured.

2. If it is safe, reduce the chances of fire by turning off the ignitions in the wrecked cars. This is a simple matter under most circumstances, and nobody will fault you for fooling around with the evidence. Especially any injured drivers who might otherwise burn to death.

3. Finally, assist the injured to the extent of your skill. Check to see if everyone is breathing and look for those with severe bleeding. But don't move any of the victims unless it is absolutely necessary. Many traffic accidents inflict neck or spine injuries, and moving the victims could be fatal. An exception to this rule is if the car is burning, or there is some other immediate danger involved. In that case yanking them out will be the lesser of two evils. But remember, "smoke" rising from the scene might be no more than steam from broken radiators, not real smoke from a fire. Be certain before you move anybody.

4. Get help by calling the police, an ambulance, or the fire department. Many drivers have radios in their cars, and some will have stopped at the scene. Although many highway patrols do not monitor it, CB channel 9 has become the emergency channel. There'll be somebody out there who can relay a call for help. If you are busy aiding the injured, ask somebody else to call for help. If you have time, or can get somebody to do it, set out flares or reflectors, but be careful of putting flares near spilled gasoline.

5. Search, or ask somebody else to search, for victims who might have been thrown from the cars involved. It is sad how often a child or baby is thrown from a car into a nearby bush or field and neglected until it is too late. If the people involved in the accident are conscious, ask them if others were in the car with them.

"I'm involved in an accident."

You are legally required to *stop.* You are required to identify yourself, and you should help anybody injured. Stop as near the scene as possible without further endangering traffic. The police won't cite you for "leaving the scene" if you are only moving your car out of the way of other traffic. But carefully note the location of each car for later accident reports.

Give your name, address, and the license number of your car to the other driver, as well as any insurance information the other driver requests. Never leave the scene without identifying yourself. It isn't really fair to use the trick of the driver who backed into another car in a parking lot. He got out of his car, looked around for the other driver, then proceeded to write a note to be left on the windshield. As other witnesses watched his good citizen actions (and thus neglected to take down his license number) he wrote, "Everybody thinks I'm leaving my name and address, but I'm not." He put the note on the windshield and drove away.

You are not required to, and *should not*, discuss any aspects of the accident with the other driver, or to admit fault, even if it is obvious that you are at fault. That is for a court to decide, and you might weaken your position, and that of your insurance company, if you try to be a "good guy" by admitting liability. For example, there could be "contributory negligence" on the part of the other driver. He might have done something, anything, that in some way helped to create the situation, and your insurance investigators will root it out later. Don't be polite by accepting all the blame to pacify the other driver.

When the police arrive, cooperate with them. They'll know what to do. In many states you are required to have proof of insurance. This can be an insurance policy number, or any other proof provided by your company. In some states you will be required to file an accident report form, especially if the accident has resulted in injuries or a certain monetary damage figure. Cooperate, so that you don't get into trouble later with the Department of Motor Vehicles.

"Should I direct traffic around the accident?"

Yes, if you can do it safely until the police arrive. Then they will take over. Position yourself so that you won't get hit by a driver who, since you aren't a real "traffic cop," refuses to cooperate with your signals.

"What are the basic first-aid procedures I should know?"

There are four things you should know and do, and one thing you should not do. Let's look at the first four.

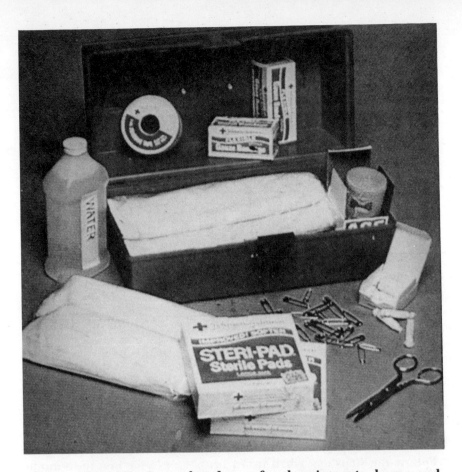

The Accident Kit: Gauze bandages: for dressing cuts, burns and lacerations. Three-inch elastic bandage: for stopping bleeding and wrapping wounds. Heavy-duty feminine napkins: work like gauze to help stop heavy bleeding. Distilled water in plastic bottle: for cooling burns. One-inch adhesive tape: for securing gauze and splints. Safety pins: have multiple uses. Scissors: for cutting gauze, bandages, tape, etc. Ammonia inhalants: to revive a person who has fainted. Folded sheet, double-bed size: can be cut to make slings, wrappings, good for groundcover, etc.

1. If somebody has stopped breathing, his life is threatened. Something must be done *now*. Be sure the back of the tongue is not obstructing the breathing of the victim. Force open his mouth to check for yourself. Then, if the victim is not breathing, lift the jaw forward to help open it. Pinch the nose shut. Take a deep breath and open your mouth wide. Put your mouth over the victim's mouth, make a tight seal, and blow to fill his lungs. Watch for his chest to rise. Listen for air to come out

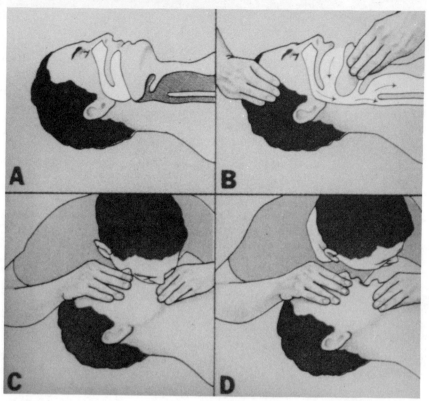

Follow the steps described in #1 on page 145 for mouth-to-mouth resuscitation.

when you back off and watch the chest fall. Repeat these steps over and over, every five seconds, until the victim starts to breathe on his own or until emergency help arrives. For an infant, puff *gently* into the nose and mouth at the same time.

Let's get really serious for a moment. The victim could be bloody, ill, or otherwise unpleasant even to touch. Put your own sensibilities aside. The person you are helping will almost certainly *die* if he stops breathing for more than about four minutes. You are giving him the oxygen he needs. If he doesn't breathe for two to three minutes, he can suffer serious brain damage. Start mouth-to-mouth resuscitation, known as "the kiss of life," immediately. Don't wait.

2. If the victim has an obvious, heavily bleeding injury, press directly against the wound with the cleanest cloth or pad available. This is no time to play doctor and worry about sanitized bandages. Your handkerchief will do, or any clothing part you

can tear off. Hold the injured part up, if possible, and keep pressure on the wound until the bleeding stops. If the cloth or pad becomes soaked, leave it on and apply a fresh pad over it.

If direct pressure doesn't stop the bleeding, try the pressure points in the arms and legs (see page 148). The pressure points in the arms are between the elbow and the shoulder. Reach in from behind, keep your fingers flat so that you don't use just your fingertips against the inside of the arm, and squeeze. The pressure points in the legs are where the leg meets the body, not on the leg itself. Press with the heel of your hand. If the bone isn't broken, press against the bone itself to close off the bleeding vessel. Remember, a person can bleed to death in one minute if a major blood vessel is cut. Stop the bleeding as quickly as possible. Don't wait.

3. A person who is badly hurt (and, occasionally, one who is not hurt at all) can quickly slip into shock, especially if he's bleeding. If the victim looks sweaty, pale, and weak, and has an unusually rapid heartbeat, he is going into shock. Try to get him to lie down and then prop his feet up. Keep him as comfortable as possible by wrapping him in a coat or blanket and remember, words of encouragement can help a lot.

4. If the victim is burned, try to cool the burn by rinsing it with cool, clear water, then cover it with a clean cloth. But don't apply any ointments. Burn victims often are in shock, so treat for shock at the same time.

Here is one thing not to do. If the victim has an eye injury, a foreign object such as glass or wood lodged in the eye, leave it there. Wait for medical help. If the eyes are injured, but there is no foreign object involved, cover both eyes with a cloth or gauze and wait for medical help. A covering will help to reduce movement of the injured eyes.

The American Trauma Society says, "Remember: you always have your most valuable equipment with you—the use of your hands and the breath of life in your lungs."

It is best not to try to move the victim unless absolutely necessary, especially if you suspect broken bones. Try asking the victim to wiggle fingers or toes. If he can't, his neck or back might be broken. Wait for medical help to arrive on the scene.

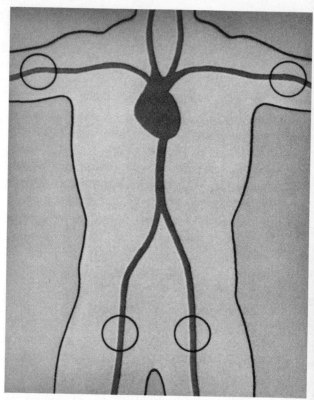

The body's pressure points are circled. Locate them by feeling for a pulse, then follow the directions in the text.

Stopping bleeding with pressure points: A. Arm: Reach in from behind. Keep your fingers flat. Don't use your fingertips. B. The pressure point is where the leg meets the body, not on the leg itself. Press with the heel of your hand. In both cases (if the bone isn't broken), push against the bone and remember to keep pressure directly on the wound with the arm or leg lifted up.

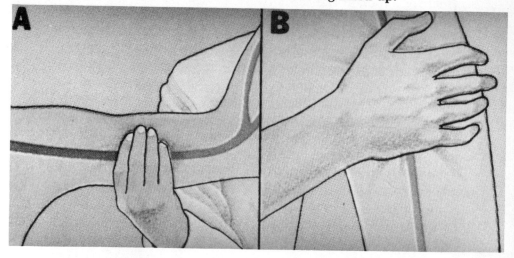

Nobody knows until it happens whether or not he might "freeze" at the scene of an accident and be unable to respond to the injuries. Some paramedics even worry about this. But remember, you have the gift of life to give and that important thought might help you get moving. You aren't trying to be a hero, you are just going to do what you can within your capabilities and knowledge, until trained help arrives.

Now that you can help others, let's help ourselves.

HOLD ON TO YOUR CAR

There were more than a million cars stolen last year. Millions more were vandalized or stripped. You can fight back. And just because your car is nothing special or not very fancy doesn't mean it won't be hit. One former professional car thief said, "I didn't care what kind of car it was, as long as it moved and was easy to steal."

A car doesn't have to be shiny and new to be a target for thieves. Even if your car is ordinary, a professional thief might have his eye on it because the ring he works for has specific

You could come out and find your car missing.

orders for that car, or for car parts from that type of car. The market value of every car is up in this day of higher prices.

But the fact is, most cars are stolen by amateurs. They are stolen because they are easy to steal. If your car is sitting there with the keys in the ignition and the next car in line, even if it is nicer, is locked, guess which car the amateur thief is going to take? The interesting thing is that 80 percent of all the cars stolen last year were unlocked at the time of the theft. Would you believe that 40 percent of them actually had the keys hanging in the ignition? The first thing you can do to hold onto your car is to keep the keys in your pocket unless you are driving it, and to keep it locked when you are not driving it. Amateurs will generally "shop around" for another car to steal even if yours presents only the mildest of difficulties.

Here are some other tips to help protect your car from thieves.

- Roll the windows up tight. Make it as difficult as possible to get a tool in through the window to unlock the door. The longer it takes them, the more likely they are to move on to another car.
- Store spare keys in your wallet and not in the car. Pro thieves know about *all* of the hiding places. You think they don't know about that spot back under the frame where a magnetic keyholder will safely rest? They do, and they chuckle as they reach in and pull out your keys.
- Replace standard door lock buttons with the slim, tapered kind that are almost impossible to pull up with a bent

Replace your regular door-lock buttons with tapered buttons to make it difficult for a thief to get in.

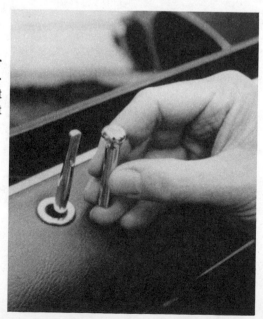

Your car should have three different locks and three different keys.

coat hanger. Foil the amateur "coat hanger" thief, and you've gone a long way toward protecting your car.

- When you park your car in the driveway at home, park it with the nose aiming out into the street so thieves working on the engine can be more easily seen. Engine-parts thieves have been known to wear uniforms from local service stations and garages, hoping not to attract the attention of neighbors.
- Never leave the engine running even if you are going to be away from the car for just a minute, not even in your driveway at home. Did you know that car thieves wait around convenience markets watching for an unattended car with the engine running? They just walk up, get in, and drive away as though they owned the car. Nobody pays enough attention to identify them.
- Install three different locks: one for the doors, one for the ignition and one for the trunk. Then a thief who gets the door key won't be able to start the engine, and if he has the ignition key, he will have to fight the locked door. Also, a parking lot attendant won't be able to get into your trunk with the ignition key or the door key.
- The more difficult you make it to steal your car, even doing little things, the less likely it will be that a thief will take the time and effort. He'll just look elsewhere.
- Don't keep your title or registration in the glove compartment unless your state law requires it. In any case, no state law requires that you keep the ownership papers, the "pink slip," in the car. Keep it in a safe place at home, away from the car.
- Car alarms, while not infallible, do help to protect your car from thieves. And they even bring down insurance rates in some states. But there are four other antitheft

Car alarms are not infallible, but they do help protect your car from thieves.

devices that will stop an amateur altogether and slow down a pro long enough to get him to consider moving on to an easier mark.

- Install a "kill switch." This is a simple, hidden switch in the ignition system that prevents the car from being started until it is switched on. Only you know where the switch is, because you put it there. Of course, car thieves know about kill switches, but knowing the time it might take to search for yours, they'll usually just decide to move on.
- Install a fuel cutoff switch. This is a valve that shuts off the gasoline somewhere between the fuel tank and the carburetor, and though it might be a little more difficult to install, it does foil most thieves. The only trouble is, they can drive away on the fuel in the carburetor. But then, a few blocks down the street, the car will stall and they'll usually leave it there.
- Install an "armored collar." This is a metal shield that locks around the steering column and covers the ignition switch. Most thieves, seeing this device, will move on unless they want your car bad enough to take a chance with heavy destruction.
- Install a "crook lock." This metal bar locks the steering wheel to the brake pedal. It is easy to use and available at most auto parts stores. With it in position, the thief cannot turn the steering wheel or use the brake pedal until he figures a way to break the lock and get it off.

Former FBI special agent Al Brooks, retired head of corporate security for Shell Oil Company, even had a car stolen. "A couple of years ago I returned a rental car and left the keys in the trunk lock as they requested. A month later I had a call: What had I done with the car? Some thief had a pretty clever racket going—until the car rental companies caught on."

Brooks asked a professional car thief how he protected his own car. "The one I interviewed uses tapered door lock buttons, a kill switch, and an alarm."

You can also help to protect your car from parts thieves who don't want the whole car but just the valuable things. Auto strippers can strip a car down to the bare body right where it's parked in about eighteen minutes. They'll get the wheels, radio, battery, doors, front seats, hood, front fenders, and trunk lid in this brief time. To help prevent this, look for a spot on the street (if you must park there) that is well-lit and heavily trafficked at night. Consider special locks for easy-to-steal parts like wheels, gas caps, and seats. A hood lock will help protect the engine and accessories and keep the thief from getting to any alarm devices.

1. Shell hired two experts to show you how fast car strippers can work—whether they do it in your driveway or haul off your car somewhere. 2. Wheels, radio, and battery disappear in 5 minutes, 42 seconds. 3. Doors and front seat gone in 4:02 4. A steal-to-order "nose job" and trunk lid finish the car in 8:47. Total time: 18 minutes, 31 seconds. Can you fight back? See preceding page.

Then write down your license plate number and check your plates now and then. If a thief stole yours to use on a "hot" car, he would probably substitute stolen plates on your car. This could lead to a police cruiser pulling you over and the officers going for their guns.

Here are some tips for when you must leave your car in a parking lot.

- Don't tell the attendant how long you are going to be gone unless he must know. Parking-lot attendants have been known to use a car all day when they know the owner isn't going to return until late afternoon.
- Leave only the ignition key with him (if you must) and never your trunk key. Of course, never leave your ring of keys holding your house key. Home theft rings have worked hand-in-glove with dishonest parking lots, splitting the take, since parking-lot attendants can identify you by your license number then make an impression of your house key.
- Jot down the speedometer and fuel gauge readings on your claim check, in full view of the attendant. Then check the readings when you pick up your car. This will help to prevent any borrowing of your car for a joy ride or for the removal or exchange of parts while you're gone.
- If you wish, and the parking lot has no reason to move your car, you can totally disable it with one simple act. Remove the ignition high-tension lead from the distributor to the coil. It simply unsnaps at each end. Do it with the engine *off* to prevent shock. Any service station can show you how to do it if you plan to leave your car unattended for a longer time.

Valuable items are often left inside a car. Many cars are built with places to hide luggage, packages, and purses, since these are so attractive to thieves. Out-of-state plates are a magnet to thieves, so if you park overnight at a motel or hotel, remove anything of value from inside the car. Mount CB sets, stereo equipment, mobile telephones, and other such equipment out of sight or use easy slide-in, slide-out units so you can take them with you. Or lock them in the trunk.

Here's another trick to thwart thieves. Mount a CB or stereo bracket in plain sight under your dash, then hang ragged an-

Ben Visser's Opel, or at least it *used* to be an Opel.

tenna and power leads alongside the bracket. Why break in, the thief will ask himself, if the good stuff has already been ripped off?

Finally, take a look at your insurance policy to be sure you are protected in case none of this works. Is the coverage full, or is there a "deductible" amount you must pay. Does it cover items stolen *from* the car, or stolen *with* the car? Will it pay for a rental car in case yours is stolen? You can also ask for *stated amount insurance* if you feel your car is worth more than average, or contains special equipment you want covered. It will cost you more but it could be worth it.

LET'S GO BACK TO DRIVING

You've protected lives and your car, now let's save some money on your driving habits. Every test has shown that drivers who are aware of their driving habits and drive to save fuel do succeed. You can drastically improve your mileage, and you don't have to make unreasonable demands on your driving style or hurt your car. But it is possible to get carried away with the matter.

Ben Visser tore his Opel apart, threw away the frame, transmission, springs, shock absorbers, rear axle, window glass, and generator. Then he built a new frame with rear wheels side by side in the center where the trunk used to be. He put loose bearings in the engine. Then he installed the engine sideways

THE ANATOMY OF A CAR

COMPONENTS:

- **(A)** radiator
- **(B)** fuel filter
- **(C)** carburetor
- **(D)** front disc brake
- **(E)** engine
- **(F)** exhaust pipe
- **(G)** parking brake cable
- **(H)** shock absorber
- **(I)** rear drum brake
- **(J)** differential
- **(K)** muffler
- **(L)** fuel tank
- **(M)** rear leaf spring
- **(N)** fuel line
- **(O)** drive shaft
- **(P)** transmission
- **(Q)** master cylinder
- **(R)** fuel pump
- **(S)** voltage regulator
- **(T)** upper control arm
- **(U)** brake lines
- **(V)** front coil spring

THE ANATOMY OF A CAR

SYSTEMS: Power train; Fuel system; Brake system; Suspension system; Exhaust system; Electrical system. COMPONENTS: A) radiator B) fuel filter C) carburetor D) front disc brake E) engine F) exhaust pipe G) parking brake cable H) shock absorber I) rear drum brake J) differential K) muffler L) fuel tank M) rear leaf spring N) fuel line O) drive shaft P) transmission Q) master cylinder R) fuel pump S) voltage regulator T) upper control arm U) brake lines V) front coil spring.

where the back seat was, wrapped it in layers of insulation to hold in the heat, and hooked it to the wheels with an oversized bicycle chain. He put about eight times the normal pressure in new high-pressure airplane tires.

In a highly structured and carefully controlled economy run, he managed to get *376.59 miles per gallon* from his strange vehicle. Also, he didn't just drive it, he *babied* it down the highway. He never drove more than 17 miles per hour and coasted whenever possible. Visser could have driven from New York to Los Angeles on about seven and a quarter gallons of gasoline.

In competitions like the Mobil Economy Run, drivers go to other extremes to improve their mileage.

They get results. One Economy Run driver drove a reporter's everyday car that had been averaging 20 miles per gallon. She squeezed 28.7 miles per gallon in an on-the-spot test, driving over city streets and on higher speed roads.

"But," said pro driver Jean Calvin to the *Los Angeles Times*, "driving for maximum fuel economy is one of the dullest, most exasperating methods of getting from Point A to Point B that exists."

Even in these more standard competitions, drivers often do not drive safely. The car may be in third gear all the time— and the engine may be running only *part* of the time. They start the engine, speed up to an exact speed depending upon their own formula, then shut off the engine and coast. Unsafe, yes, but these tricks cut fuel consumption dramatically. They should *only* be used during competitions, and they are *demanding* and often *dangerous*. They are not typical and often require a full competition team of skilled professional drivers, support groups, and highly modified cars to squeeze every last mile from each drop of fuel.

So how does that help you and me?

Somewhere between these radical gas-saving techniques and the jackrabbit starts and high speeds of drivers totally unconcerned about fuel conservation falls the average fuel-conscious driver who calculates his mileage and has a normal concern for fuel economy. That driver is you or me, and we can find comfortable, easy secrets to nearly *double* our own mileage.

We can do it in our present car using our present gasoline. The larger the car, the more improvement we can expect.

There are three ways to become a real "mileage miser" safely.

1. Buy your car carefully. Luxury accessories such as air conditioners, power steering, V-8 engines, automatic transmissions, and other comfort items can guzzle gas. You'll pay for them now, and you'll pay for them later.

2. Take good care of your car. Proper engine tune, tire pressure, and wheel alignment, plus radial tires and multigrade motor oil can boost mileage substantially.

3. Drive your car correctly. By accelerating smoothly and gently, anticipating stops, and watching your speed, you can add even more miles to each gallon.

Dave Berry, of Shell Oil Company's research and development department, conducted a test. He took twenty-three ordinary drivers and one ordinary car to show how normal car maintenance and informed driving can really save gas. The results were impressive.

Everybody saved gas. On the average, Berry's drivers went 40.4 percent farther on a gallon. You and I can do the same.

Berry tricked them right at the beginning of the test. He sabotaged the car for the first twenty-two miles of the city-street and country-road course. He set the ignition timing back five degrees. He set the engine idle up a bit. He put on bias-ply tires instead of radials and underinflated them five pounds. He misaligned the wheels slightly. Then he filled the crankcase with 30-weight oil instead of better-mileage multigrade oil. He figured most cars on the road have some or all of these handicaps, since none of them were noticeable to the drivers involved.

Then he took careful mileage figures. They still weren't *too* low for a car of that year and make.

But gradually, in test after test, Berry corrected the slight problems. He wanted to show how simple maintenance can make a difference. So he switched from bias-ply to radial tires and inflated them to the proper pressure. Those two simple changes improved gas mileage by 7 percent. Correcting the ignition timing accounted for another 5 percent savings in fuel. Fixing the idle speed, correcting the wheel alignment, and switching to all-season oil pushed the mileage up a total of 14.5 percent.

Tuning up the engine added another 5 percent.

Then Berry worked with his test drivers, acquainting them with four driving tips to save gasoline. Here were his suggestions for driving on the test route.

1. Accelerate gently. You don't have to creep away from a stop, but take it easy. Few driving errors waste more gas than jackrabbit starts.

2. Anticipate stops. Look ahead and take your foot off the gas, allowing your car to use its own weight to coast down to an intersection. But do it safely by keeping an eye on the rear.

3. Don't go too fast or too slow. Most cars get their best mileage around 35 to 50 mph. Berry's drivers never went over 50 mph on the course.

4. Get into high gear as quickly as possible. This slows the engine. If you have an automatic, lift your foot slightly off the accelerator to make it shift earlier.

Berry's drivers added another 8.9 percent to their gasoline savings.

Doesn't all this take a lot of extra time? No. Berry's drivers took thirty-three minutes to cover the twenty-two-mile course in the first runs, before learning the driving tricks. After they began practicing the gas-saving driving tips, they took only six minutes longer to cover the course.

Here's a couple more tips.

- Use the sixty-second rule. If you must wait for sixty seconds or more, shut off the engine.
- There are times when *air* is not free. That is when you don't have enough in your tires, when you are trying to push your way through it at high speeds, and when you make it colder inside your car with an air conditioner.

The *best* way to save fuel is still to drive only when you have to drive. Carpool. Use public transportation. For short trips, use bicycles, or even feet. Nothing cuts a gasoline bill more than leaving the car in the driveway.

Chapter SEVEN

Scheduled Maintenance

Imagine for a moment how the pioneers would have felt if they had seen a modern automobile. There they are, struggling across the vast prairie, facing each dip and rise as a major obstacle to be overcome. A river could be like a solid wall requiring great planning and skill, and a lot of luck, to ford. A covered wagon was a lumbering, generally uncomfortable vehicle that became very dangerous at the first sign of trouble.

St. Louis to California? *Months!*

Just imagine how the grizzled old wagonmaster would have chuckled and shaken his head if you tried to tell him that in only a few dozen years the children of his great-great grandchildren would cross the same prairie in *hours*. They'd do it in an "air conditioned" metal vehicle with a "telephone," "stereophonic sound," "radio," and "television."

An automobile is a fascinating machine. You can get less expensive ones, more expensive ones, and very expensive ones. You can buy a secondhand one or a new one. They come in all sizes, from sporty little two-door high-performance vehicles to huge, four-door sedans. They come in various shapes, from limousines to vans, from sleek, aerodynamic, high-performance machines to family station wagons, with almost anything you might want in between.

You can buy them, rent them, borrow them, sell them, love them, or hate them, but they are a part of our lives. And what we see today is the general shape and size of what we will see well into the future. Auto designers will use the current "five

160

points" method in designing cars—the hip points of the front and rear seat passengers (1 & 2), the center of the wheels front and rear (3 & 4), and the engine location (5)—for years to come, or at least until the shape of people changes. These points must be taken into consideration so the car will fit the human shape and size.

Cars are powered by an internal combustion engine that will, with a number of sophistications, be powering them for years to come. The engine of today is relatively powerful, relatively efficient, relatively clean, and relatively inexpensive. Until somebody invents something that will do all of these things better (and that's what it will take, not just *one* of them), the engine we know will still be around.

HOW THEY WORK

Most automobiles work the same way. You turn the key, the engine starts, you put the transmission in gear, and you drive away. When you get ready to stop, you step on the brakes. When you are finished, you turn off the key and the engine stops. Cars are simple, convenient, trustworthy, and as safe as you allow them to be. A driver doesn't even have to know what makes them go, and many drivers do not. They don't care, just so the car does what it was designed and purchased to do. How many times have you heard it? "I don't really care why it won't run...just *fix* it!"

But there are many drivers who *are* interested in the inner workings of their vehicle. The fact that you are reading this book indicates you have more than a casual interest in your car. Let's take a "white gloves" look at how they work.

HERE'S WHAT HAPPENS

When you turn the key to start the engine, two things occur. The *starter*, a small electric motor driven by the *battery*, engages the *flywheel* of the car's engine (which is attached to the

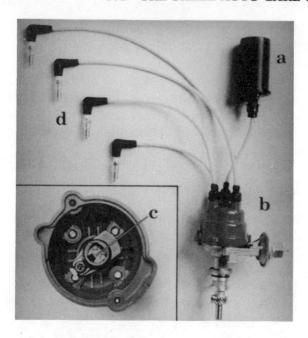

COIL (a) boosts voltage, sends current to DISTRIBUTOR (b). ROTOR (c, inset) sends current to SPARK PLUGS (d) in turn.

end of the *crankshaft*), spins it, and the *pistons* in the engine (which are also attached to the crankshaft by *connecting rods*) begin to move in their *cylinders*. The motion of the pistons sucks a precise mixture of air and gasoline into the cylinders from the *carburetor*. The gasoline has been provided to the carburetor by a *fuel pump*, which begins to work as the crankshaft turns.

Meanwhile, turning the key has activated the *ignition system*. This system, still drawing from the battery, energizes the *coil* which, through the *distributor*, creates a spark in each cylinder at the proper moment. The sparks ignite the fuel mixture in each cylinder just as the pistons have compressed it. The rapidly burning (but *not* exploding) fuel expands, and the expansion of the gases pushes on the piston in each cylinder.

The pistons are forced to move on their own, turning the crank-shaft without the starter, and the engine is running on its own. The starter kicks out, and the engine sits there idling, waiting to be put to work.

The engine has become a self-contained unit ready and wait-ing to move the car. When the engine is running, a complex variety of parts are doing certain jobs inside.

The Fuel Pump

The fuel pump, driven by the spinning crankshaft in the en-gine, continues to suck fuel from the gas tank through the fuel line and provide it to the carburetor. The fuel goes through a filter to remove any dirt or rust before it goes to the carburetor, or *fuel injectors* if the engine uses this system instead of a carburetor. In a fuel injection system, raw fuel in precise amounts is squirted directly into the cylinders.

The Carburetor

The carburetor mixes the right amount of fuel with the right amount of air, which is cleaned by another filter, before send-ing it to the engine. When you "step on the gas" you are telling the carburetor to send more fuel to the cylinders. If too much fuel is sent during the starting procedure, the engine might "flood," but holding the accelerator pedal to the floor will usually correct that condition. Once the engine is started, hold-ing the pedal to the floor will only cause the engine to run faster and faster.

Four Stroke Cycle

Each cylinder on a standard engine is going through four strokes as the engine operates. They are called *intake, compression, power,* and *exhaust.* Let's look at each of the four.

As the piston starts to move away from the spark plug a *camshaft* opens the *intake valve* and the fuel/air mixture is drawn in through a hole (Intake).

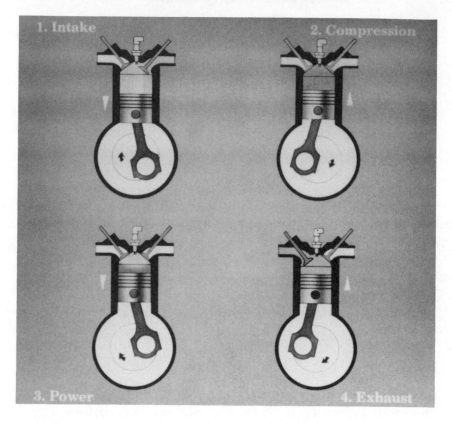

Moved by the crankshaft, the piston starts back the other way. Since it fits inside the cylinder very snugly, and has *piston rings* to further seal it, the mixture of fuel and air is compressed more and more (Compression).

As the fuel/air mixture is fully compressed into the closed end of the cylinder, the spark plug sparks and the fuel is ignited. It burns rapidly, expanding the air in the tight space and forcing the piston back the other way (Power). This power stroke is what moves the car by helping to turn the crankshaft, which is attached to the *transmission*, which is attached to the *drive shaft*, which is attached finally to the *wheels*. The piston rings help to seal the space so that the expanding gases do not leak and cause a loss of power.

Now the piston moves back toward the closed end of the cylinder, this time being shoved by the turning crankshaft, the camshaft opens an *exhaust valve* which opens a hole in that cylinder. The burned gases are pushed out of the cylinder and into the *exhaust system* (Exhaust).

The camshaft is little more than a strong shaft with several eccentric (egg-shaped) lobes, as many lobes as there are intake and exhaust valves. It is driven by the crankshaft, and each time a high point of one of the lobes comes around, it pushes on a valve to open it. The valve closes because of its own heavy spring.

Meanwhile, a *water pump* is forcing coolant around the double-walled engine (unless the engine is air-cooled, with cooling fins). The water pump is also driven by the crankshaft. The coolant picks up heat from around the engine, carries it to the *radiator,* and the rush of air through the radiator cools it to its best operating temperature. A fan also spins to help suck air through the radiator if the car is sitting still. A *thermostat* in the system impedes the flow of coolant so that it doesn't get too cool.

Missing?

If the fuel/air mixture fails to ignite in a cylinder because of a weak spark or some other condition, that cylinder will not provide a power stroke and the engine is said to be "missing." It will lack all of the power it should have. Each piston is important to the efficient operation of the engine. If the engine has four cylinders, all four should be providing power. The same is true of a six-cylinder or eight-cylinder engine.

All of this moving of pistons in their cylinders turns the crankshaft just like the up-and-down motion of your legs on bicycle pedals turns the main sprocket. Your legs go up and down, the pedals go around and around, and the sprocket turns. On a bicycle, of course, the main sprocket drives a chain, which turns the wheel and moves the bike. In an engine, the crankshaft provides the power to move the car.

The Ignition System

Electricity from the battery causes the *spark plugs* to spark. Each spark plug has two electrodes extending into a cylinder. The current must pass from one to the other, and this causes the spark. The problem is, each spark plug must spark at exactly the right instant, and about 20,000 volts is needed to get the current to jump across the gap between the electrodes. The timing and the voltage are produced by the ignition system. A *coil* boosts the voltage from the battery, and a *distributor*, acting like the dealer in a card game, sends the right spark to the right cylinder at the right instant.

If you hear a metallic rattling noise (a "pinging" sound) as you accelerate or go up a steep hill, the spark plugs might be firing too soon. Sluggish performance and poor fuel economy could mean they are firing too late. But this isn't a serious problem. The *timing* should be checked with a timing light. You can do it if you have a timing light, or any service station can do it quickly and easily for a reasonable fee.

The Alternator

The battery doesn't "run down" (lose all of its power) because the *alternator*, driven by a *fan belt*, is constantly recharging it. But too much recharging could hurt the battery, so a *voltage regulator* is in the system to prevent that from happening. If your "ALT" or "GEN" light stays on while you are driving, something is wrong with the charging system. It could be a bad alternator, a loose or broken fan belt, a faulty voltage regulator, or maybe even a loose or broken wire or connection in the circuit. In any case, the battery is not being recharged at all, or not being recharged enough, and although you can still drive, the battery will finally discharge all of its power and the engine won't run.

The Transmission

The *transmission* has different gears for different situations. The faster the engine turns, the more power it makes. So when the transmission is in a "lower" gear, the engine is going faster (to get the car moving, to go up a hill, to haul a heavy load, etc.). A "higher" gear allows the engine to slow down a bit and takes the strain off it for cruising at highway speeds. If you have a manual transmission, you select the gears yourself. If you have an automatic transmission, the gears are selected automatically. In either case, be sure you have the right amount of the right fluid in the transmission, or it will be seriously damaged.

The Brakes

Now that you have the car going, there is something even more important. That is stopping the car.

When you step on the brake pedal, you are activating a *master cylinder* and sending hydraulic fluid through lines to each wheel, where there is a *wheel cylinder*. The pressure of the fluid forces little plungers in the wheel cylinders to move *brake shoes* against the brake drum or to press the *disc brake pads* against the *rotor* on each wheel. The friction created when the stationary shoes or pads rub against the moving drums or rotors stops the car.

Eventually the rubbing of the shoes or discs against the drums or rotors will wear them out and they will have to be replaced. If you begin to hear odd squealing, grinding, or clicking noises when you apply the brakes, it's time for a checkup. A brake job isn't that expenisve, and it is cheap when you consider the alternative.

If your "BRAKE" warning light comes on when you apply the brakes, the brake system could be low on fluid (check the brake-fluid reservoir in or on the master cylinder under the hood) or you could have a leak in a brake line or a wheel cylinder. Have it checked out. Or, you may have forgotten to release your *parking* or *emergency* brake, since most manufacturers also tie this warning light to that system as well.

Steering

When you turn the steering wheel, gears are turned inside a *steering gear box* (or a gear acts against a row of teeth in a "rack and pinion" type of steering system). The gears move rods which are connected to the front wheels.

If you have *power steering* in your car, high-pressure hydraulic fluid is doing the work of turning the wheels when you turn the steering wheel. If you have power steering, the fluid in the *power-steering fluid reservoir* should be checked frequently.

The Suspension System

The *suspension system* is what holds the *car body* on the *frame* and helps the car ride smoothly on a bumpy road. Most modern cars have "independent suspension." Each wheel has its own *springs* and *shock absorber,* so a bump at one wheel is not transmitted to the others or to the body of the car.

Springs in the suspension system support the weight of the car's body on the frame, keeping the body level with the road. They compress and rebound to allow up-and-down wheel movement. *Sway bars* keep the car from leaning too much on road curves. Shock absorbers reduce bouncing. If you notice that your car keeps bouncing after hitting a bump, your shock absorbers are probably worn out.

And that's how a modern car works. Simple, eh?

But later in this chapter, you will find that *keeping* all these parts working smoothly together will require some effort on your part. Not all that much effort, and it can even be interesting and fun, but modern cars do demand certain periodic checks and inspections, and the adding of certain parts and fluid, to keep things running efficiently together.

In fact, for best results, there are certain inspections that should be done every time you get in the car to drive.

FROM THE DRIVER'S SEAT

Most of us can overlook things that are right under our noses. There are three things you can check every time you get in the car, before you drive away. These are easy, simple checks to make and will insure that you get where you are going.

1. Do the dashboard warning lights work? They should all light up when the engine is cranking and the parking brake is on. Common warning lights on modern cars include the alternator light, the brake light, the oil pressure light, and the temperature light. The last one, of course, won't come on until there is an overheating problem.

One poor driver ignored the fact that his oil pressure light didn't come on when he turned on the key. Eventually, he promised himself, he would look into the matter. Meanwhile, his engine seemed to be running just fine. It wasn't. The oil pump was slowly failing, gradually providing less and less oil to the moving parts. Only when the engine ground itself to a stop from lack of lubrication did the driver learn that a simple, ten-cent light bulb had burned out. A one-hundred-dollar oil pump repair job turned into a thousand-dollar engine rebuild because of a ten-cent bulb, and a driver's failure to heed a common warning.

Many automobiles have gauges for heat and oil pressure instead of a simple warning light. Some drivers prefer to know exact readings, and for them the gauges are better. Otherwise, the warning lights will do the job just fine. If something is wrong, they'll tell you. If everything is OK, they won't flash on (except when you first turn on the key in the case of the very important oil pressure light).

2. Does your horn honk? This is easy to check and then when you need it, it will be there. Funny thing about horns, though. They are regional. Anybody who has been to New York City knows how important a horn is on a car. But if you travel in certain other big cities, Los Angeles for example, you seldom hear a horn blow. And if you do, you think the driver is an impatient bore. It all depends on the city and the driving style of its drivers.

One thing is certain—when you need your horn, you really need it, so check it out frequently.

3. What about the outside lights? Get a helper to check headlights (high and low), emergency flashers, side markers, parking lights, license plate light, taillights, brake lights, backup lights (shift into reverse with the ignition key on for this test), and turn signals. Most cars need the key on for the last one as well.

WEEKLY INSPECTIONS AND MAINTENANCE

There are some slightly more complicated weekly checks every driver should perform to keep the car running as smoothly and efficiently as possible. If you do them weekly, you can be almost certain that your car will get you where you are going safely and on time.

1. Check engine oil once each week or every time you add fuel, whichever is most often. This is not a difficult job. With the engine off, pull out the dipstick (be careful, it could be hot), wipe it with a clean rag or a paper towel from the station, then shove it back in. This puts the end of the dipstick down into the oil in the pan at the bottom of the engine. The end of the dipstick dips into the oil reservoir. It is marked with graduations, usually "full" and "add."

If the oil level is between the two, you may drive on, but if the oil level is below the *add* mark, then add a quart of oil by removing the oil cap and dumping it in. Try to avoid spilling any oil on the engine. A clean engine is a more efficient engine and besides, the smell of oil from a spill may not be pleasant to some of your passengers. Wait a minute, then check it again to be sure the oil level is now correct. Nothing will destroy an engine quicker than running it without enough oil.

Some oils have been advertised as being so good that an engine using that brand can run on for some miles even after the oil has drained out. Don't you believe it. An engine must have oil all the time or it will quickly damage itself, and ultimately destroy itself.

Do not overfill an engine, either. Too much oil can also harm a modern engine, if for no other reason than the oil inside begins to froth and is less efficient as a lubricant. That's why you don't add a quart if the level is between the two marks. The two marks are generally "one quart" apart.

It is best, but not necessary, to check the oil level in an engine when it is cold or has had time to sit for awhile. At a gas stop, fill your fuel tank first, then check the oil. This gives any oil in the upper part of the engine time to drain down into the oil pan making the reading more accurate.

There is another reason why the oil should be checked frequently. Notice the color and quality of the oil on the dipstick. Fresh oil is clear with a yellowish tint. Black oil that is gritty or sludgy can mean that something is seriously wrong with the engine, or that it is long past time to get the oil and oil filter changed. Ask a mechanic to take a look. Oil that is milky brown or gray (and not black, which is normal with modern oils) can mean that there is a problem in the cooling system. Water might be leaking into the oil system, and this is serious. Oil with a noticeable smell of gasoline is a sign of a fuel system leak, or some other carburetion problem.

It is possible, for example, that the engine is running much too "rich" (with too much gasoline for the amount of air) and part of the extra fuel is running down into the oil pan instead of being burned. It is also possible that some part in the emission control system has malfunctioned.

Adding oil when the oil level on the dipstick is down is not enough. Engine oil must be changed on a regular schedule (check your owner's manual). There are additives in oil that are expended during use and must be replaced by dumping out the old oil and replacing it with fresh oil. If your car is used severely, for heavy-duty work or trailer towing, or driven stop-and-go consistently, oil should be changed even more frequently. If the oil on your dipstick is gritty then the oil should have been changed a month ago. There will be more about oil changing later in this chapter.

Oil comes in a variety of prices and types. The better types are "multigrade" and more expensive. Let's take a look at the code numbers and what they mean.

At fifty-five miles per hour, each piston in your car is moving up and down inside its cylinder about thirty-five times *per second.* Each one is moving at a blinding blur, so fast that it would be impossible to see as more than a solid wall of piston. This amazingly quick movement creates power, and it also creates heat. Piston temperatures can reach four hundred degrees Fahrenheit, not to mention the over two-thousand-degree heat in the combustion chamber of a modern engine.

Connecting-rod and crankshaft bearing pressures usually exceed one thousand pounds per square inch. Oil is the only thing inside that is keeping the parts from grinding themselves to death against each other. A very thin film of oil, much thinner than this page, holds the parts ever so slightly away from each other, so they don't rub against each other and deteriorate.

Modern motor oil is a precisely manufactured liquid formulated by skilled petroleum chemists to do the amazing job it does. There are two things on the lid or side of a can of motor oil that indicate which type it is and the service it will give. The "SAE" number reveals the "viscosity," or thickening of the oil. The higher the number, the thicker the oil. The lower the number, the thinner the oil. Some oils are as thick as honey (a high SAE number) and some are as thin as water, or kerosene, which is an oil (a low SAE number).

The API Service letters on a container of modern motor oil are a service classification code. Oils that have "SE" on them, as most service station oils do, are suitable for most cars. Some oils, for example, would not be suitable for use in an automobile engine. Sewing-machine oil would quickly break down. Kerosene would be too watery and wouldn't provide the film needed between parts. An oil as thick as honey wouldn't flow through the tiny passages oil must travel to get to the parts needing lubrication.

Oil is numbered according to how thick it is. Chances are, the oil you are considering will have either a single number (30W) or a series of numbers (10W-40, 20W-50, etc.). The one with the single number is a cheaper, single-grade motor oil. It is 30-weight and will remain so, thicker at lower temperatures and thinning out at higher temperatures. It may be too thick at lower temperatures and too thin at higher temperatures for a modern engine.

Modern engines are precise. They run best over the longest period of time with an engine oil that is a bit thinner when cold, for easier starting and warming up, and then doesn't thin out too much at the high temperatures a modern engine generates. A modern engine likes its oil to have lubrication qualities that remain consistent.

The oils with two numbers indicate a multigrade of oil and will cost more. But they are worth the extra expense. A 10W-40 grade of oil will be about 10-weight when it is cold, for easier starting, then will provide high-temperature protection after it has warmed up. Generally speaking, the weather in which you normally drive will determine the multigrade of oil you should consider using. If you consistently drive where the weather is colder, you should choose an oil with lower multigrade numbers (5W-20, 5W-30, 10W-40, etc.). If you drive where the climate is much warmer, go for the higher numbers (20W-40, 20W-50, etc.).

2. Check the radiator coolant level. This is also an easy job, since on most modern cars there is a see-through overflow tank connected to the radiator. When the hood is up, visually check to be sure there is coolant in the tank. The tank will be marked with graduations to show the correct level whether the engine is cold or warm. An engine with an overflow tank operates by pulling coolant from and pumping it back into the tank. The warmer the engine, the more the expanding coolant flows to the tank to be held. As the engine cools down it contracts and some of the coolant is drawn back into the radiator block to keep the cooling system full to the brim.

On an engine without an overflow tank, coolant can be shoved right out onto the street the first time the engine warms up, losing valuable antifreeze. It just runs out through the overflow tube attached to the filler cap on the radiator. Then when the engine cools, air comes in. The level of the coolant in the radiator finally stabilizes much lower than it could be with a tank, so you are losing cooling efficiency.

If the level is low, coolant can be added directly into the overflow tank rather than in the radiator itself. This is much safer, too. There is no pressure in the coolant tank, but plenty of pressure in the radiator, especially if it is hot. Coolant added to the overflow tank will be drawn into the engine as it is needed.

If you have no overflow tank on your car, you can check the coolant level by removing the radiator cap. But *never when the engine is hot!* There is pressure in the cooling system, and a hot engine will have even more than normal. It is possible to get scalded by hot coolant if you remove the cap under these conditions. If the radiator is too hot to touch, it is too hot to open.

Once the cap is off, you should be able to see clean, clear coolant in the top of the radiator. If not, add some, but only to a normally warm or cool engine, never to a blistering hot engine. If the engine has "boiled over" allow it to cool down a bit first. If you are in a hurry, you can cool down an engine by flushing cool water over the outside of the radiator with the engine running.

Today's engines run hot. They need the cooling and anti-corrosion properties of a coolant/antifreeze solution. Water alone simply doesn't do the job. So whenever you add more coolant to an engine (perhaps it has boiled over and lost some of its coolant, or perhaps a hose has developed a leak and coolant has been dumped out) add antifreeze as well. Yes, an engine should have about half antifreeze even in a warm climate that never gets down to freezing. Antifreeze has antirust and anticorrosion qualities, as well as one other important quality. Adding about a 50-50 mixture of water and antifreeze raises the boiling point of the solution. Your engine won't boil over at 212 degrees, the normal boiling point. It will be able to get hotter than that and still not boil away coolant.

While you're at it, visually check the top and bottom radiator hoses for cracks, leaks, and bulges. Especially around the hose clamps. Do the same for the heater hoses, the smaller hoses that carry hot water to the heater core inside the passenger compartment of the car. Also, when the engine is cool, squeeze the hoses. They should be flexible, not stiff. It's good insurance to replace the hoses every two years.

3. Check tire pressures and add air if necessary. The "footprints" of your tires, those four small spots that actually touch the surface of the road, are your only real connection with the street. No matter how everything else is, these four spots are where you get rideability and control. Proper air pressure is very important for tire life, and for safety.

Remember this. A tire that is only 25 percent low, hardly enough to notice, can lose one fifth of its useful life. On top of that, underinflated tires waste gasoline. Checking tire pressure is usually a free service at full-serve gasoline stations.

First you must determine what the recommended pressure is for your tires. You'll find the numbers printed on a sticker in your glove compartment, on your door jamb, or in your owner's manual. Notice that the pressure might be different for front and rear tires, and notice that these figures may not exactly agree with the numbers on the tires.

Keep a good tire pressure gauge in your car, perhaps in the glove compartment. You can buy tire gauges for a couple of dollars, or you can get an accurate one. You can even get one that attaches directly to the valve stem. What should you get?

A good one, even if it costs a few dollars more. The cheap ones aren't accurate, and the ones that attach to the tire valve stems are not only inaccurate as a general rule, but add weight to that point on the wheel and could unbalance the tire.

Unfortunately, in this modern day of self service, fewer and fewer gasoline stations are offering an accurate gauge with their air—if they offer air at all. Customers at the self-serve islands tend to batter the gauges, drive over them, and otherwise abuse them. This affects their accuracy. There are stations that are discontinuing air, with or without gauges, unless you go to full-serve. Some states are now passing laws that require service stations to provide free air, to combat a rash of coin-operated air pumps. If you have found the station you prefer, it will probably offer free air. But you can only trust your own pressure gauge.

Recommended tire pressures are for *cold* tires, when your car hasn't been driven for a few hours. So it is best to check the pressure with your own personal gauge before you drive away from home. Or before you have driven more than a mile or so. If you check your tires when they are hot, they will be over the recommended pressure. But don't release any air to bring them into the proper range. The increase is caused by the heat of operation and is allowed for in the manufacturer's recommendations.

For a long trip, increase the pressure in your tires by two to four pounds (when they are cold), but never go over the tire pressure number on the side of the tire.

When you check the tire pressure, visually inspect the tread wear. A worn-out tread *edge* can indicate that you have been running the tire without enough air. This cuts down on gas mileage, increases tire wear, and even improves the chance of a blowout. A worn-out tread *center* generally means you have been driving on overinflated tires.

A bald spot or "cupping" is usually caused by an out-of-balance wheel or a weak shock absorber. Wheel misalignment can cause one edge of the tread to wear faster. Take a look at the tread wear indicators on your tires. These will appear as bands across the tread, and they show up when the tread gets down to the last sixteenth of an inch. When they show across two or more grooves, the tire can be dangerous and should be replaced. This is a law in many states.

Visually inspect the rest of the tire as you check the pressure.

A. Bald spots or "cupping," usually caused by out-of-balance wheels or weak shocks. B. Tread wear indicator showing across two or more grooves means tires should be replaced. It's the law in most states. C. If the center of the tread wears faster than the edges, overinflation is the cause. D. When the edges wear faster than the center, it's probably due to underinflation or hard cornering. E. Wheel misalignment can cause one edge of the tread to wear faster.

Look for cuts in the side, tears in the tread, and other signs of dangerous wear. Replace any missing valve caps, and while you're at it, rub a little spit across the top of each valve stem. A slow leak will immediately show up as a bubble. Any tire with a blister or bump needs to be replaced immediately. It is a real danger and should not be driven upon for even one mile. The tire's internal structure has begun to rupture because of an impact, and the tire could blow out suddenly.

Keep in mind that a radial tire will tend to "bulge" out at the bottom a little more than a bias-ply tire. This is a normal condition and doesn't necessarily mean that the tire is low on air. But many knowledgeable owners are fooled by this "radial bulge," assuming the bulge is because the tire is radial and not because it is underinflated. Check with an accurate tire pressure gauge to be sure.

4. Check windshield-washer fluid level. There is a reservoir under the hood to store the water for the windshield washer. Although water is all that is required, most drivers add a windshield-washer solvent to the tank. This inexpensive solvent will help to dissolve road grime on the window, but won't hurt the paint on the car if it splashes back as you are driving.

If the level is low, add water and solvent. When you most need the windshield washer is when it will spit a few drops and run dry if you don't keep an eye on it and keep it full.

Windshield-washer hoses tend to dry out and crack because they are used infrequently and yet are always exposed to the heat of the engine. They are easy to replace or, if the leak is right at the connection, to cut off and reattach. To replace a windshield-washer hose, just unsnap the old one, then, before you remove it, route the new one along the same path and in the same clips. Windshield-washer hoses can be bought at many service stations and most auto parts stores.

A needle wiggled into the nozzle that squirts the cleaner will unplug any clogs. A clogged nozzle allows no washer fluid through at all, or misdirects the washer fluid to the wrong part of the windshield. But do the job carefully. You don't want to spread the opening in the nozzle's soft metal, or change its direction.

MONTHLY INSPECTIONS AND MAINTENANCE

1. Check the battery fluid level and general battery condition. If your battery is not one of the "maintenance free" models, which have sealed cells, pull off the caps and look inside. The fluid level should be up to the bottom of the filler neck for each cell. Remember, there is corrosive *acid* inside the battery. It can be harmful to skin, clothing, and automobile paint. It can be a serious danger to eyes. When the level is correct, the fluid will touch the filler neck and "pucker" a little. If it's too low, add some distilled water or, in an emergency, regular tap water.

Don't smoke during this operation. Batteries can give off explosive hydrogen vapors.

Every battery should have clean, uncorroded terminals with tightly fitting cables that are clean and unfrayed. It is amazing how many drivers will "click" and "click" the starter and finally buy a new battery when the only problem was corroded or loosely fitting battery terminal connectors. The battery was just fine, but the connections weren't being made. Corrosion will appear as a light-colored puffy powder or paste on the terminals. This can be easily cleaned with a thick mixture of water and baking soda. Just pour it on, smear it around in the corrosion, wait a few minutes, then hose it off.

But be careful. This chemical mixture will discolor a concrete driveway. Spread some newspapers around to absorb the mixture as it washes off the battery. When the terminals are clean, try to turn them on the posts with hand pressure. They should be snug. If they turn, remove them, clean them and the posts until they are bright, then firmly reattach them.

Careful drivers inspect the battery at each gasoline stop, especially on a trip where you could get stalled on a faraway road.

If everything else is OK and you still suspect that your battery is low, it can be checked at any service station. Or you can use a "trickle charger" in your own garage to keep it up to par. This is especially helpful to a battery on a car that is not driven often. Hook on alligator clamps, red on the plus side and black on the ground, minus side, then plug in the charger. The battery will be fed a light voltage to bring it up, and keep it up, to specifications. A modern trickle charger can be left hooked up to the battery for any period of time. It won't put too much charge in the battery. Be sure you set the charger correctly, six volts for a six-volt battery, and twelve for a twelve-volt battery.

2. Check the air filter. There is a can atop the carburetor, the lid of which is usually attached by a finger-operated wing nut. Inside the can is the air filter and through it must pass thousands and thousands of gallons of air as the engine is operated. All of the air that goes into the engine is filtered by this unit. Eventually the filter will be saturated. After that, dirt or dust can quickly clog the tiny passages in the carburetor; it also gets into the crank case and causes engine wear.

Checking the filter is easy. Just unscrew the wing nut or other connector on top of the can, lift off the lid, lift out the filter, and look at it. Hold it up to a light. You should be able to see light through the filter element. If you cannot, the filter is probably clogged. It will help temporarily to tap the filter on a hard surface, shaking free some of the dirt. You'll see a ring of dirt on a clean surface if you drop the filter a few inches on one of its two flat sides.

You can then reinstall the filter and drive on, but as soon as possible buy a replacement at your service station (they'll install it for the price of the filter) or auto parts store.

3. Check the brake-fluid level. Whether or not your brake

warning light is on, it is a good idea to check the fluid level every month. You know it is low, regardless of the light, if you have to push the brake pedal almost to the floor to get the car to stop, or if you have to pump the brakes to make them work.

Some foreign cars have a see-through reservoir for brake fluid, so it's easy to take a look. On an American car, clean off the reservoir lid first, then unsnap or unscrew the lid and lift it off. The brake fluid should be within a quarter inch of the top of the reservoir. Don't disturb the wires. They are there to activate the brake warning system.

If you need to add fluid, it might be a good idea to get it done at a service station. They'll put in the right type, but even more important, there may be a reason why the fluid was low in the first place. There could be a leak in the system, and this could be a very serious problem. They can quickly check things out just to reassure you.

4. Check the power-steering fluid. If the power-steering fluid is allowed to get too low in its reservoir, the unit itself could begin to fail. You could begin to hear an ominous grinding sound every time you turn the steering wheel, since the fluid in the power-steering unit does more than turn the front wheels. It also lubricates the unit.

The reservoir will have a dipstick attached to its cap. With the engine off (since the power-steering unit is often close to the fan belts and fan blades) remove the cap, wipe the dipstick clean, reinsert it, then pull it out again and check the fluid level. You can buy power-steering fluid at your service station (they'll add it for the price of the fluid) or at your auto parts store. Your owner's manual will tell you what type of fluid to use. In an emergency you can use automatic-transmission fluid, but it is best to use what is recommended.

5. Check the automatic-transmission fluid. This is one of the checks that is most often neglected, yet inside a modern automatic transmission are hundreds of parts doing their job in a bath of oil they must have in order to continue. What's worse, automatic-transmission repairs can be among the most expensive of all service work. Yet this check is almost as simple as checking your engine oil.

A modern automatic transmission should operate for the life of the car if service and maintenance is performed, oil is kept at the right level (not too low and not too high), and oil and filter are changed when necessary. Transmission fluid should be checked after the car has been driven for five miles or more. This circulates the oil in the transmission. But it should not be checked after a long, hot drive. In this case, the oil will have become hot enough to expand, and will give a false reading.

Transmissions have dipsticks just like the engine. They are usually located more to the rear of the engine and often on the passenger side of the car. The check should be done with the engine *running*, the transmission in "park" and the car on a level surface. Pull out the dipstick, wipe it with a clean cloth, stick it back in all the way, then pull it out and look at the level. The stick will be marked. Don't add fluid unless the level is below the add mark. Look at the fluid itself. It should be clean and a clear red in color. Cloudy brownish or amber fluid or a fluid that smells "burned" indicates that it is time to get the fluid changed or worse, so pay attention. You will have to get the problem fixed sooner or later, and sooner means it will be less costly in almost every case.

After you have added automatic-transmission fluid (if you need it) through the pipe that holds the dipstick, check again to be sure the level is where it should be.

6. Check the drive belts for condition and tension. Without drive belts, the car won't go very far. It can overheat for one thing, and generally none of the accessory items (power steering, air conditioning, etc.) will operate. Checking them is easy. With the engine off, just look at them for wear, cracks, fraying, chunks missing, and general deterioration. Twist each one over to check the underside for signs of wear or too much shininess, indicating a glaze on an old, worn-out belt. Replace any worn belts, or ask your service station or garage to do it for you.

Press your thumb down on each belt in the middle between the pulleys. They shouldn't give more than about a half an inch. If they do, they are too loose and should be tightened. This is not a difficult job.

With each belt there will be an "idler" pulley or an engine accessory unit (alternator, etc.) that can be moved to increase the tension in the belt. Just loosen the nut that holds the idler, pry the idler back a little, and retighten the nut. On most cars, the main fan belt is tensioned by the alternator. So just loosen the nut and bolt that helps hold the alternator in place, pry back on the alternator (tightening the belt), and retighten the nut.

Many people use a full-service station rather than a self-serve, and pay the extra in gasoline cost, to get many of these weekly and monthly checks done free. Most of them are a part of the routine inspections given cars in a full-service station. A full-service station also generally has a service bay with a lift, and a mechanic on duty who can give you advice as well as do tune-ups and work on air conditioners, front-end alignment, and brakes.

A final word on visual inspections. White smoke from a cold engine is normal. But white smoke from a warm engine can indicate trouble in the engine, perhaps a cracked cylinder head, cracked block, or a blown head gasket. Blue smoke from the exhaust means the engine is burning too much oil. It can indicate a problem with valves or rings. Black smoke looks most ominous of all, but it generally means you need something as simple as a tune-up.

Even though it is colorless and odorless, carbon monoxide can indirectly indicate its presence when it is leaking into the driving compartment. If you find yourself becoming drowsy or developing headaches whenever you drive the car, have a mechanic check for leaks in the exhaust system. These fumes can be lethal, so don't ignore the problem.

Chapter **EIGHT**

More Maintenance

Weekly and monthly checks are reasonably routine. They are fairly easy jobs almost anybody can do, and they can add immeasurably to the life of your car. Many car parts will last the life of the car with this kind of easy maintenance. But there is more to this than money, or money lost in unnecessary repairs.

Imagine yourself out on a country road at midnight, in midwinter with the temperature hovering near zero, in strange territory, and in a hurry to get home because your family will worry if you are late, or, in the same situation, you're on the way to a very important meeting, one that might cost you your job if you miss it. Imagine that you begin to hear strange noises from your car.

Imagine that the noises increase. You really begin to worry. The car isn't acting right at all. Then suddenly, the car goes slower and slower and, with a gasp, stops dead.

That's when it will happen, you know. Very few breakdowns caused by neglect of routine maintenance ever happen in the driveway, or at the island of your local, trusted service station. They almost always happen at the worst possible time, in the worst possible location, when you are in the greatest hurry, when the situation is truly critical.

Worse yet, imagine your wife or husband or another loved one stranded in the family car, away from home and friends, threatened by weather, unfamiliar surroundings, a lack of knowledge of what to do—and even lurking strangers watching the situation and waiting to see what might happen next. A breakdown in a car can be more than inconvenient, it can be dangerous.

The problem can seem almost impossible to solve, too.

One man was moving his family from a midwestern state to California. They were on a shoestring budget, so they decided to haul their belongings in a rental trailer. They had a *lot* of belongings—furniture, records, books, stereo equipment— really heavy stuff. Still, they planned to get some enjoyment from the trip, to do some sightseeing along the way, so they decided to take a side trip to Hoover Dam. The car had been no trouble at all, and though the trailer was heavy, it wasn't *that* heavy. They arrived at the dam on Saturday afternoon, in midsummer, during the height of the tourist season.

It was true that at the last gas stop the attendant had checked the transmission fluid, and suggested a change of trans oil and filter.

"That trannie is working *very* hard," the young mechanic had warned. "The oil looks *beat!*"

Sure...sure, the man thought. And a transmission service will lead to a transmission repair or rebuild. He knew about roadside stations and how they can get into your wallet. OK, so the transmission is working hard. It was doing the job just fine. Yes, the temperature was very warm there in Nevada. But they were only a day from California and their new home. They'd make it in good shape.

"Won't take but a half hour or so," the young man at the station had promised.

No way! They had driven on from the station with the helpful mechanic, though they noticed him shaking his head sadly as they drove away.

They'd "saved" thirty bucks or so, at least.

They were crossing the dam when it happened. They were in a long line of traffic from both ways on a two-lane road. As they reached the center of the dam, the engine began to boil over. Well, thought the man, even that isn't too serious. He had an emergency water jug in the trunk. He ignored the honking from other cars, opened the trunk, pulled out the water, and raised the hood. Soon the engine cooled down enough to get the radiator cap off, so he started the engine and began to pour the water in. No problem. He'd held up some traffic, but the engine was cooling down in good shape. He'd be on his way in no time.

No such luck. It was the transmission heating up the engine as it ground out the last of its tortured life. It had overheated so much that parts were melted inside, though he didn't know that yet. He knew he had a real problem when he shifted into "drive" and pushed on the gas pedal.

Nothing. The car didn't move at all.

The thirty dollars he had saved turned into a hundred-dollar towing charge, dozens of irate motorists, and a several-hundred-dollar transmission rebuild in a strange garage. Plus an extra three days in a motel in Boulder City while they waited for the work to be done.

The transmission was at the point of failure, and the young mechanic recognized the fact. He had tried to tell them, but they ignored him. If the man had paid attention or taken the trouble to do the most routine maintenance on his car, it might not have happened.

Weekly and monthly maintenance checks and corrections, and even an extra few dollars spent on the road if the car is working hard, could have prevented what turned into a real problem. The monthly checks are easy, even enjoyable to accomplish. Most drivers get a good feeling from knowing that their car is in shape for anything.

There are other car maintenance jobs that are a bit more involved, requiring a little more time and effort, but they are needed less frequently than the routine matters.

In the long run, you'll probably spend less money too. According to a comparison study of a well-maintained vehicle versus a poorly maintained one, researched by technical service consultant Joe Alacchi of the National Automotive Fleet Association, proper maintenance will save more than three thousand dollars in overall expenses.

"The fuel bill alone," said Alacchi in *Fleet Maintenance Newsletter,* "will run about 8.5 cents per mile on a maintained car, versus 9.1 cents per mile on a poorly maintained car—a savings of about .6 cents a mile." The study is based upon figures from the Department of Transportation, the American Automobile Association, the Internal Revenue Service, Runzheimer & Company, and Alacchi's personal observations over the past three years.

It reveals the acquisition costs, operating costs, resale value, and net costs for a car in service for two years and/or 60,000 miles.

"If you were to eliminate a regular and recommended preventive maintenance program," explains Alacchi, "you may save on tune-ups, oil changes, and car washes, but you will be spending more for fuel. An untuned car will burn more fuel. You can also wind up with increased expenses for a transmission overhaul and replacement of springs and other suspension parts due to a lack of periodic suspension and transmission service."

Ball joints on front-wheel-drive cars, CV joints, and entire drive axles can cost $400 or more each.

"It is also likely that there will be a high-ticket repair bill for some heavy engine work. Just a valve job will run about $500," warns Alacchi in the *Los Angeles Times*. When you add the acquisition cost with the operating cost of a well-maintained car, the total cost, according to the study, is $18,780. On a nonmaintained car, the total cost is $19,970, or about twelve hundred dollars more.

Trade-in? The nonmaintained car will be worth much less.

"The reason for the difference," noted Alacchi, "is because the dealer will probably have to spend at least $2,000 to recondition the car or he will forego any profit and wholesale it."

Maybe you've tried to trade in or sell a "dog" of a car. You know what Alacchi is talking about. The dealer will usually look, chuckle, then hit you with a price about half of what you were expecting.

QUARTERLY CHECKS

Changing the Engine Oil and Filter.

Engine oil is the lifeblood of the engine. Without it, the engine won't run. It will grind itself to pieces without the microthin layer of oil between moving parts. Oil works in an interesting way between two moving parts. Try to visualize the thin film of oil between a shaft and a bearing in your engine. The oil has run off when the engine is not running so that in the morning, before you start the engine, the shaft is actually resting directly on the metal of the bearing. Only a very thin residual film of oil is left between the two.

When you start the engine, oil is made available to the shaft and the bearing, and the spinning shaft draws the oil in. The shaft is actually shoved away from the bearing by the layer of oil. As the engine runs, the two metal parts are separated. They are apart, not touching. That's why it's a good idea to allow the engine to idle for just a few seconds (you don't have to wait for the engine to "warm up") before driving away. This gives the oil time to be drawn into the areas where it is needed.

Here's another interesting fact. The oil tends to retard movement where it contacts the bearing and where it contacts the shaft. The movement between the two, the "slippery" effect, is near the center of the film of oil.

You can be religious about adding oil to your engine whenever the dipstick indicates that the level is low, but that's not enough. The oil in any engine must be changed periodically, and the job is not that difficult. It isn't that oil wears out in the traditional sense. Oil can be used up, it can be burned or otherwise expelled through the exhaust system, but the "oil" part of the oil doesn't ever wear out.

What happens is that the *additives* in the oil do their job until they can do it no more. Modern oil is not merely oil alone. Into the oil of every company are added synthetic materials to retard foaming, to make the oil flow freely at low temperatures without becoming too thin at high temperatures, to protect engine parts from corrosion, to suspend impurities until they are removed by draining the oil, and to give each brand other special properties that a particular company can advertise.

Eventually these materials are used up or worn out, and the oil will no longer do the job it must do in a modern, high-tolerance, high-compression car engine.

What about the *extra* engine additives you can buy in a can and add to your car's crankcase? They are all heavily advertised, especially around the theme of auto racing. They claim to prolong the life of your engine—or even internally rebuild an engine that is worn out. They'll spruce up your valves, free up your piston rings, jazz up your oil pump, and put a coating on your cylinder walls that will add wonderful extra life to your engine.

Maybe they'll help your engine. But for an engine that has been running well, burning only a mild amount of oil, and which has enjoyed regular changes of good oil throughout its life, there is probably no need to spend extra money on extra additives. For new engines just beginning what will hopefully be a long and productive life using a good multigrade oil, save your money. For an older, gummed-up engine that has received poor service, extra additives *could* be worth the money.

Some mechanics, however, will tell you that adding life-prolonging oil products to an old engine will do little more than give it a good internal cleaning. But the cleaning might remove built-up carbon deposits that are helping to keep the engine sealed inside. Remove the carbon, sludge, and gum deposits and you could lose some of the compression of the engine. Give it a try if you wish, but be aware that this could happen.

Sooner or later, the old oil must be drained out of every engine and replaced with fresh, new oil. At the same time, the old, dirty oil filter should be replaced with a new one. This should be done on a time or mileage schedule which you can find in your owner's manual or by asking any service station mechanic to look up in his manuals.

One driver, a man who paid little attention to his car, had no idea that the oil had to be changed periodically. He hadn't changed his oil in *years*. When a mechanic finally convinced him to have the job done, the oil was so thick and sludgy that nothing came out when the drain plug was removed. Nothing at all. The mechanic had to stick a screwdriver up into the pan and wiggle it to get the gooey mess to finally begin to ooze out.

Here's what the manual, or the mechanic, will probably say. An engine can be severely damaged when oil is run too long and allowed to "break down." Appearances can be deceiving, though, particularly with modern detergent oils. You can waste money needlessly by changing oil just because it begins to *look* dirty. Modern detergent oils keep small particles in suspension. So the oil may look dirty, but it's still doing a good job. Oil should be changed according to mileage and degree of use, not according to what it looks like on the dipstick.

Most manufacturers recommend changes from between five thousand to seventy-five hundred miles. Can you go up to seventy-five hundred miles on a change without hurting your engine? You can under *ideal* conditions, otherwise you should change sooner. Here is what mechanics consider to be ideal conditions.

1. The engine is operated for reasonably long periods whenever it is operated at all. You don't just drive the car back and forth to the store, you drive it for at least twenty miles every time you drive it at all.

2. The engine is operated at between 180 degrees and 200 degrees, or even higher, when it is operated. Of course you don't have the time or inclination to dip a thermometer into the radiator every time you drive, but the point of this is the same as above. The engine has time to get completely warmed up every time it is driven, and the thermostat is operating properly to keep it warm.

3. The engine is in good mechanical condition. You should know whether it is or not, but if you don't, any clicking, knocking, grinding and clanking will tell you that it is not.

4. The oil filter is clean and efficient, and changed with each oil change. If it is changed every time the oil is changed, it will be clean and efficient.

5. The crankcase ventilation system is functioning properly. Any service station mechanic can check it out quickly. It is merely a matter of checking to see if all hoses are connected, all valves are operating, and all air pumps and filters are clean and working.

6. The engine is operated at moderate to high speeds. You don't poke around the supermarket parking lot without ever taking the car out on the street.

7. The air filter is efficient, and changed according to conditions. If you change it every time you get an oil change and filter, it will be clean and efficient, but this costs extra money.

8. The carburetor is in good mechanical condition and correctly adjusted. If you are getting good mileage from the car, and the engine runs smoothly and efficiently, the carburetor is probably working well.

9. The engine is operated under *clean* conditions. Where do you live? Is it dirty, dusty, sandy? Or is the air clean and clear and the car never driven in dirty areas?

An engine driven under the above conditions should require an oil and filter change only at the high range of the manufacturer's recommendations, to be found in your owner's manual or at any service station in their books.

Engines that are started and stopped often, idled frequently, driven short distances and seldom really warmed up, or that are operated under dirty or dusty conditions or allowed to get out of tune, need oil and filter changes much more frequently. Possibly even more often than the lower limit of the manufacturer's recommendations. That hurts the old pocketbook, of course, but if you want your engine to last as long as it could, do it.

The job is not difficult, but you might get your hands dirty. In any case, it should be done with planning. Here's how.

1. Change the oil when the engine is *warm*. Cold oil is full of soot, acids, and other suspended matter that will cling to engine parts. The old oil is still doing its job in holding this debris in suspension. The residue will contaminate the new oil you are adding and you'll end up with half a job. You can tell this is true by feeling the old oil. Take a sample from the dipstick, or from the oil draining out, and rub it between your fingers. You'll see how dirty and perhaps even gritty it really is.

2. Place the car on a level surface, set the brake, and put the transmission in "park," or in first gear if it is a manual unit. This is assuming you do not have a lift to raise the car, which is the easiest way. The brake and the gear settings have nothing to do with the oil, but it will keep the car from moving during the job.

3. Put a ten-quart drain pan under the engine drain plug at the rear of the oil pan. You know what this is for, so be sure the pan is in the right location or you'll have old oil all over the place.

4. Crawl under the car (unless it is on a lift) and use a wrench to remove the drain plug. Then get out of the way, because the oil is going to come out in a solid stream. It will take a few

minutes for the last of the dirty oil to drain out of the engine, but you can use this time to change the filter.

5. Wipe off your hands, then, using a round oil-filter wrench (a couple of bucks), put the strap around the filter and start unscrewing it. Turn it to the left to loosen it. You can finish the job by hand once the filter has been loosened. But remember, the old filter is full of old oil. Be careful how you tilt it or you'll have more oil splashing around.

6. Unpack the new filter of the correct type and size, smear a little of the old oil (you'll have plenty of *that* around by now) on the rubber gasket at the fitting surface, then hand screw the new filter in place. Doing this by hand is easier and will assure that you won't strip the threads. Tighten the filter firmly using a cap type filter wrench if necessary, but don't overtighten. Oil filters do not need to be force-tightened, since there is no strain on their threads. You just don't want it leaking or falling off on the street.

7. When no more old oil is dripping from the drain, put the drain plug back in and tighten it securely with a wrench. Once again, don't overtighten it since this could damage the threads in the pan or deform the gasket and cause leaks. Another thing you don't want is to have your new oil dripping out slowly. The stuff is expensive but what's worse, the engine could be damaged before you realize you're losing oil.

8. Add the correct amount of fresh oil of the proper type and grade. Check the owner's manual, and don't forget that the filter will hold some oil. Then, when the job is done, check the dipstick to be sure the oil level is correct. Go ahead and start the engine.

9. Idle the engine to allow the new oil to circulate. Watch the oil pressure gauge for a normal reading or the oil pressure indicator light to be sure it doesn't come on to reveal a lack of pressure. Look under the car and under the hood to check the oil-filter seal and the drain plug to be sure no oil is dripping.

10. Shut down the engine and once again check the oil level on the dipstick for proper level. It should read at the full mark. If it doesn't, give the oil a little time to drain back into the pan. Check it a third time. Still low? Maybe you forgot the oil the filter will hold. Add more oil until the reading is correct, possibly even another full quart.

That's all there is to it, and you have done a better job than most service stations will do. By draining the engine completely and only when the engine is warm, you have not only saved money but you have probably extended the life of your engine by allowing all the old contaminants to drain out.

Disposing of the old oil might be your only problem. You can't merely flush it down your drain (there are laws against this in most states). But you could try taking it to your service station for disposal. They might not welcome you with open arms, but most stations have an oil recycling system and they will allow you to pour your old oil in there.

If you have to add a quart between changes, don't panic. This is normal. Engines burn a little oil, and many manuals even admit this. Just keep an eye on your dipstick when you check the oil level and add a quart when the level is below the add mark.

"Engines run better when they are a quart low," you might have heard your Saturday-morning-mechanic buddy say. Don't believe it.

It is an old wives' tale that an engine runs better a quart low. The oil level marks on the dipstick would be changed if that were true. Remember that a quart low on oil means that about a fifth or even a quarter of the total amount of the oil is gone— 20 percent or more. You have that much less oil to help absorb heat, and that much less to provide helpful additives found in all modern motor oils. Keep the engine oil level at the correct line on the dipstick.

Don't add too much oil in the mistaken impression that if the right amount is good, more will be better. In fact, after a long drive the oil on the dipstick might read slightly below the add mark. If you wait a few minutes for the oil to drain down from the engine into the crankcase, it might read above the add mark. So don't add oil.

Brake System Checks and Adjustments.

You probably don't think of men like Sir Isaac Newton, mathematician Daniel Bernoulli, and philosopher Blaise Pascal when you are slamming on the brakes to miss a child, but the car wouldn't stop without their work. Newton formulated the laws of motion, which apply to liquids like brake fluid as well as to solids, Bernoulli did pioneer work with hydraulics, and Pascal first figured out the master-slave cylinder relationship.

Still, it is doubtful that Newton ever said to Bernoulli, "Hey, guy, let's do something that will help the people of the future stop their cars."

In fact, Newton probably never even spoke to Bernoulli, and if he did, Bernoulli would have said, "Are you sure you're feeling all right, Isaac?"

Still, the work of these men made brake systems possible. Then through many more years, devoted auto engineers put it all together and more to come up with modern brake systems that stop a car as quickly as possible. They rarely fail. You could probably use some other system than hydraulics to make brake shoes and pads move in wheels. You could do it mechanically, electronically, or with belts, pulleys, wires, cables, levers, rheostats, or magnets. But of all the ways to do it, hydraulic pressure seems to be the best in this day and age. Here is how brakes work, and what you can do quarterly to keep them working.

Liquid, unlike air, is noncompressible. Imagine for a moment a very simple hydraulic system: a tube with a plug at each end. Call one of the plugs the master cylinder, the other the slave (wheel) cylinder. If the tube was full of air you could push the master plug back and forth all day, and the slave plug wouldn't move because the air would merely compress inside. You'd have to give a real shove to the one before the other would pop out. But put a *liquid* in the tube and every time you shove on the master plug, the slave plug is going to move the same amount. The liquid won't compress. It acts as a solid link between the two. It is like a steel rod.

Expanding the simple experiment one step, let's double the size of the plug in the slave end of the tube. Now you will get twice the force when you press on the master plug (but only half the movement). That is how brakes work in your car. You step on the brake pedal and a piston moves in the master cylinder. This forces a fluid in the system to move, shoving against pistons in the wheel (slave) cylinders. They move and in so doing move brake shoes against drums, or brake pads against rotors. This creates a friction that stops the car. It is simple and efficient, providing the system is free of leaks and compressible air, and as long as the brake shoes or pads don't wear out.

Generally speaking, if your brakes stop working efficiently, get them to a brake mechanic. This is not something upon which to gamble. Your car engine can stop running and it usually means inconvenience. If your brakes stop working, it can mean *death*.

Still, there are some things you can do to keep your system operating efficiently. Brakes, especially brake shoes, get out of adjustment, even on cars with an "automatic" brake shoe adjuster. Such adjusters work every time the car is backed up and the brakes are applied. They work through a lever and star wheel system to move the brake shoes closer to the drums.

You can turn the same star wheel on a nonadjusting system by removing a small rubber plug on the back side of the wheel, sticking a screwdriver or adjusting tool in, and levering the star wheel one way or another. It will "click" with each move. If you do this with the wheel raised so that you can turn it, you can move the shoes very close to the drums and this will give you less brake pedal movement when you step on the brakes. Very simply, the pedal won't move as close to the floor because the piston in the master cylinder won't be able to move the slave piston as far before the shoes contact the drums. So click the star wheel until the wheel won't turn, then back it off a click or two.

Naturally when the shoes or pads are worn down until they make a noise that sounds like metal against metal, it is time for a complete brake job, a replacement of the shoes or pads and a general going over of the other components.

Checking the parking brake is another simple operation that you should do every three months unless, of course, you are having a problem with the brake. Then it should be adjusted when the problem develops.

1. With an automatic transmission, set the parking brake then put the car in gear. Normally a car will creep forward in gear with the brakes off. The parking brake should hold it in position.

2. With a manual transmission, set the parking brake, put the car in first gear, then slowly let out the clutch. The engine

Disc brakes, different from drum brakes, "grab" the rotor to stop the car, as shown here. Imagine the rotor to be a dinner plate and your index finger and thumb to be the brake pad in the calibur. Imagine the dinner plate spinning, while you pinch the edge of the plate between your thumb and finger. The harder you pinch, the quicker the plate will stop spinning.

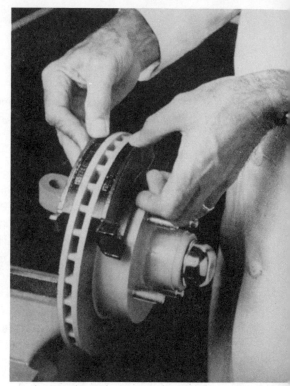

should die before the car moves forward, if your foot remains off the accelerator.

3. The parking brake should hold a car on a hill when it is parked. If you are really planning to park on a hill, though, you would also have the transmission in park (or in gear in a manual), the front wheels turned into the curb on a downhill grade or away from the curb on an uphill grade, and perhaps even a block under the wheels. Do all of these things unless you are specifically testing the parking brake.

Parking brakes are adjusted by several means, though adjusting the brake shoes or pads often adjusts the parking brake as well. The parking brake, though, is a mechanical system and usually has another means of shortening the cable between the parking-brake handle and the rear brakes. This could be a screw or even a simple turnbuckle adjustment.

Your service station will probably do the job for little or nothing as a goodwill gesture for a good customer. Or you can easily locate the means by which your own particular parking brake is adjusted. Go ahead and adjust it, but be sure you don't make it too tight or the drums or discs will "drag" when you are driving, and this will wear out the brakes very quickly as well as cost you in fuel mileage.

Washing, Waxing, and Cleaning.

There are real dollars-and-cents reasons to keep your car clean and protected besides the pride of driving a car that looks new. A quarterly cleaning and shining program will cut down on repairs and add significantly to the value of the car at trade-in time. To keep a car gleaming and rust-free is not that difficult. It can even be fun on a Saturday afternoon.

Remember the television commercial on car wax where the guy is spending a great deal of time to get the car as shiny and perfect as possible? In the background can be seen a pretty girl in short shorts. Finally the job is done and he looks at it with pride as the girl congratulates him.

Then she says, "And when are you going to do your *own* car?"

The camera pans over and it turns out that his car, a decrepit-looking little machine, is in the next driveway.

Well, so much for him and keeping his car clean.

1. Washing a car not only keeps it looking good, it also removes corrosives such as road salt and tar that can cause serious damage to the finish. It is also a step that must be taken before you put on a coat of protective wax. Commercial car washes make their profit on speed and volume, which means that your car gets a superficial wash that removes surface dirt but skips over some of the most harmful dirt. Generally the underside of the car is not washed at all. Even if you stand over the attendant at the end of the line, you will probably get a quickie job, nothing like you could do yourself at home with a few extra minutes.

Even more serious is some of the cleaners used by commercial car washes. You are subjecting your car to high-pressure water, hot steam, and high-strength detergents. No car finish is going to last forever under such treatment. So wash it yourself, and don't make the mistake of commercial car washes. Use a bucket of cool water and wipe off the surface with a large, soft sponge. If your car is really dirty, you can add a mild soap that is made especially for car washing.

Road tar? Dried bugs? Don't use kerosene or gasoline. They'll dull the finish. Specks of road tar should be removed with a tar cleaner and bug spots can be removed with household baking soda. When completely dissolved, baking soda doesn't have abrasive qualities, yet it will quickly soften bug spots. But remember this: Both tar remover and baking soda will remove auto wax, so don't use them unless you plan to wax your car after the wash.

Rinse your car with clean, cool water, using the soft sponge gently. Do it in a shady spot or the water will dry too quickly on the hot metal and leave spots. Then wipe your car clean and dry with a good quality chamois or a soft cotton terry cloth towel.

2. Waxing is a little more difficult than washing, but extra time and elbow grease here will protect your car's finish over the long haul. Most cars today are painted with an acrylic

Washing and waxing a car is easy, and it helps to hold its value.

lacquer that should be waxed soon after you buy the car and at least every three months thereafter. Never wax your car unless it has been thoroughly washed, and take with a grain of salt the wax manufacturer's promise that using their wax will also clean and remove tar and bug spots. Wash the car first.

Generally, there are two wax types: liquid and paste. You'll get what you pay for and whatever you are willing to put into the job. Liquid waxes are easier to use, but this means a thinner coat of wax on the car surface. Paste waxes take a little more time and effort to use but give a thicker, more protective coating that will last longer.

There is no need to rub with modern waxes. Apply them in a circular motion according to the direction on the can, making sure you cover the entire area. After the wax has dried, use an old terry cloth towel or an old piece of carpet to polish the surface.

Be very careful of power buffing. If not done just right, you will get circular whorls in the finish, but you won't know it at the time. Besides, you are removing more of the protective coating with a power buffer. Hand polishing is a job that will pay off with a better appearance if you don't mind doing the extra work.

3. Chrome cleaning is also easy, and there is nothing that will make a car look newer and better-kept than sparkling chrome. Chrome cleaners do a fine job, but remember that they are strong and take everything off right down to the bare chrome. Cleaned chrome will rust faster than chrome that has never been washed at all. Be careful that none of the chrome cleaner gets on painted surfaces, then be sure to wax the chrome after you have cleaned it. Here, a liquid cleaner wax will do the job just fine if chrome cleaner is not available, or if you want to skip a step.

Never clean aluminum with chrome cleaner unless the package says you can do it without harm to the metal. Shiny aluminum surfaces can be dulled by the wrong chrome cleaner. With aluminum, it is probably best to just wash it with the same solution you are using on the car's body, then wax it with a wax that contains no abrasives. Look at the directions before you start to be sure the material will work on aluminum.

4. A clean and sparkling engine is a pleasure to behold. Besides, a dirty engine can be a dangerous engine. A minor fuel leak, for example, can result in a fire if there is a spare spark or too much heat around. But with the good engine degreasers on the market today, you don't have to pay for an expensive steamcleaning. There are, however, some precautions.

Remove the battery cables since most degreasers are flammable. Then remove the air cleaner and plug up the carburetor throat and any hoses that attach to the air cleaner. Cover the alternator and distributor cap by wrapping them in a plastic bag and securing it with a rubber band or some tape.

Using a putty knife, scrape away any collected grime or caked oil, then, with the engine warm, spray on the engine degreaser. Let it stand for a few minutes for the solvents to do their job, then spray it off with a garden hose. Be sure you are parked where the runoff won't do any damage. It turns into a soapy substance that won't do grass or plants any good at all.

After the degreasing, be sure to oil the carburetor linkage, the shift linkages, the handbrake cable, and any other working parts that might have been degreased along with the engine. Degreasing sprays remove all lubrication, not just the dirty oil and grease you want to go away.

5. The real enemies of your windshield are windshield wipers, especially when they get old and rough and dirty and brittle. They can even scratch the glass. Here are some tips to help prevent glass damage. Be sure your windshield-washer reservoir is full and with the correct mixture of cleaning compound. This compound won't normally hurt the glass or the paint surface of your car, but the reservoir should be kept full. If water evaporates from the tank, the mixture can become too strong.

The nozzles throwing the spray on the windshield should be aimed correctly. Sometimes they will only wet the bottom half of the windshield so the dry, brittle wipers are scraping away at the upper half and perhaps leaving scratches. You can take a pin and clean out the holes of the nozzles to get the spray going full blast, and, in some cases, you can re-aim them by slight bending.

Wiper blades as well as windshields will last longer if you

don't use the wipers dry. If a light mist begins, don't turn on the wipers until the windshield is wet, then turn them on at the slowest speed. You'll double the life of your wipers and take better care of your windshield.

Old wiper blades can be salvaged for awhile by lightly sand-papering them. This might extend their life by several months by removing the very top layer of brittle rubber. But wind-shield-wiper refill blades are cheap and readily available at your service station or auto parts store. They snap out and snap in easily, so when you really need them to work at their best, they will.

6. When you think about rubber and vinyl on your car, you might think of tires and little more. Yet modern cars are loaded with rubber and vinyl and these parts must be cared for. Trunk lids and doors and windows have rubber or vinyl gaskets, and these deteriorate. Vinyl tops are becoming popular again, and you know what a car looks like with a deteriorated top.

But these items are difficult to clean with soap and water. One of the best things to use on gaskets is good old talcum powder. If you rub it onto trunk, door, and window gaskets, you'll delay aging and cracking and you keep them from stick-ing, too. You can keep the powder from washing away and further protect the gaskets if you mix up a paste of talcum and glycerine, then paint it on.

There are also some excellent spray products for use on rubber and vinyl around a car, or, for that matter, around a home. Just spray the stuff on then wipe it off. It will extend the life of rubber and vinyl products and also improve their appearance. If everybody used this stuff on their vinyl seats, for example, you would rarely see ugly cracks and dried-out spots.

There are good commercial vinyl-top cleaners to remove grime and oxidation, but be sure to wax the vinyl after you have cleaned it. Use a black wax for a black top, and a neutral wax for white or colored tops. There are even special vinyl-top waxes if you want to use them.

Car care such as this will not only improve the appearance of your car but will extend its life—and make it much safer and more pleasant to operate. Not only that, but it can be fun—so give it a try.

Chapter NINE

Semiannual Checks

It'll happen to every one of us sooner or later. You take your car in for a tune-up and as you drive away you realize that it is running worse than it was when you brought it in. If it had been missing a little, now it is bucking and jumping down the street. Before, the car was just a little difficult to start. Now you have to grind and grind on the starter to get it going. And talk about dieseling—it won't shut down at all when you turn off the key.

If only you had done it yourself. Nobody, you decide, could have done it any more incompletely than that. Not even you.

Well here's the good news. Doing a tune-up is a job many weekend mechanics tackle with enjoyment and efficiency.

One young potential mechanic acquired a car that was barely running. In fact, he talked the price down by an extra two hundred dollars because of the sound of the sputtering, missing engine. The previous owner was ashamed of the car and unsure of just what was wrong.

"I can *fix* that," he insisted to himself.

With the help of his father, who took a "white gloves" role in the matter, the young driver tuned up the car. He changed the plugs, put in new points and condenser, changed the fuel and air filters, and adjusted the timing (with a borrowed timing light). All of this took an hour of his time. When he hit the starter, the car's engine roared to life. It sat there purring, idling more smoothly than it had in years. The car, which had barely started before and tended to lurch along the street, was ready to *go!*

What the young mechanic did, anybody can do.

The matter could appear more serious, of course. It could even *be* more serious, but consider the following cases.

A driver recently got a $500 estimate on a job that a neighbor then fixed for free. It seems the car wouldn't start so the driver, a nonmechanical person, called a garage. They came out and looked over the situation.

"Well," said the gruff young man driving the tow truck, "I figure about five hundred bucks to put her back in shape... but that includes the towing charge."

Fortunately (at least at the moment), the driver didn't have that much cash available, so she called a friendly neighbor to come and help her.

"I have no idea what's wrong," she said, near tears, "but they said it would cost *five hundred dollars*. I don't *have* five hundred dollars!"

The neighbor, a Saturday morning mechanic, arrived, then took a moment to raise the hood.

"Just take it easy for a minute," he soothed. "I'll have a look."

He did, and noticed that the air cannister in the emissions system had come loose, and was upside down. He turned it back over, refastened it, and the car started. It's been running fine ever since.

It's hard to say whether or not the mechanic who answered the call noticed the cannister, but he was the one who made the estimate. Perhaps he noticed it, or perhaps he merely gave a high estimate to cover every possible problem. The bottom line is that you and I need to have the knowledge to notice such things, as this lucky driver's neighbor did. Also realize that if a garage has given you an inflated estimate to cover hidden matters, they will tend to work their way up toward it even if the problem turns out to be minor.

Another driver noticed a sudden loss of oil pressure while on the way home. He did the best thing possible: he pulled off and parked the car. A car's engine won't operate long without oil pressure. This driver had at least a little mechanical knowledge. He took the time to raise the hood. The problem was obvious. The oil filter had come loose and fallen off. Although he had some choice thoughts for the service station attendant who had last changed his oil (who possibly faced a legal situation as well), his luck couldn't have been better. He had pulled over directly in front of an auto parts store. He went in.

"Make and model?" asked the clerk.

He gave them the information, then spent six bucks for a new filter and a couple more for some oil, just in case. Easily and quickly he installed the new filter and added some oil to make up for what had been lost. His hands were barely soiled as he drove away with the car healthier than it had been before the problem.

One couple spent over eight hundred dollars on rental cars while "waiting for a part to come in" on a warranty job at the dealership where the car had been purchased. That was the story the dealer gave them while the car was parked in the dealership's back lot. Actually, the part was readily available at any auto parts store, but the dealer had to go through his own channels to make his usual profit on "factory service" and markup on the part. Because of this, he had to stall the couple for the two weeks the car was down.

"It'll be ready tomorrow, for sure!" he'd say.

So they waited till the next day.

"Well, the part finally arrived. You can pick up the car this afternoon," promised the dealer's service manager.

At last. But when they went in, the car was not ready yet. It was still sitting out in the lot. Hadn't even been moved.

But the service manager had a good explanation. "Sorry, my parts man screwed up the records. We'll get it handled tomorrow, for certain."

When the part eventually arrived two weeks after the deal was struck, it took half an hour to put on the car. Sure, the car ran fine after the part was finally installed, but what about the several hundred dollars spent on rentals, and the inconvenience of running back and forth?

Meanwhile, the couple had probably not checked on "factory service" from the dealer. Very likely, any dealer in that chain could have done the job under the warranty—if they could move the car.

THE SOLUTION

The answer to all this frustration and possible shadiness?

Have an idea of what needs to be done and how to do it, then *do-it-yourself!*

The couple could have done it themselves, and for a modest amount of money, if they had only known. Cars of the future, as you have read, will probably "tell" us in some way if a problem is developing. And owner's manuals will probably tell us exactly what to do about it—if the car doesn't just go ahead and do it all by itself. Until then, it isn't that complicated to tackle some of the more difficult jobs. As you do so, you will learn more and more about your car. You won't be stopped by the need for a simple tune-up, or stalled by a flip-flopped emissions control cannister or a lost oil filter—or a delayed part, if that is the case.

There are several interesting and pleasant jobs for the weekend mechanic that will have a real affect on your car's performance. At the same time, if you do the job yourself, you'll save a bundle. Does your engine need a tune-up? Probably so. If it has been six months since the last one, it probably will need one. How's your headlight aim, your body-door locks, hinges, and linkages, your disc brake pads and your tires?

So your car is running just fine. But is it running as *efficiently* as it should? Sometimes that is hard to tell from the driver's seat.

Remember Dave Berry's experiment? He sabotaged a car before he asked twenty-three ordinary drivers to try it on a course of city streets and highways. Then, one by one, he "unsabotaged" the timing, the tires, the oil, and other parts. He corrected them. Yes, mileage improved dramatically each time, but the point is, the drivers didn't even realize anything was wrong.

That could be true with your car.

Let's take another quick look at a car's ignition system. The engine needs a spark to ignite a fuel mixture in the cylinders one by one. The spark needs to be there at the exact instant to do the job right, and the spark must be pushed across the electrodes in the spark plug (to make the spark) by a very high voltage. Electricity flows easily in wires, but when there is a break in the wire, such as the tiny space between the electrodes, it takes much more voltage to push it across. When it jumps across, it sparks.

Still, a car has only 12 volts in its battery to provide the electricity in the system. So the ignition system does the job of raising the voltage and getting it where it's needed. When the system does it right, the car runs smoothly, but if there is a problem, it will run less efficiently or not at all.

When you turn the key to start, you complete two circuits. The first is from the battery to the "solenoid," which operates the starter motor. This small electric motor, driven by the car battery, engages the flywheel of the engine and turns it. This is what the old-timers did with a hand crank.

The second circuit allows current to flow from the battery through a coil of wire, where it is strengthened, to the distributor. From the distributor it goes to individual spark plugs as it is needed. Most modern cars have an electronic device rather than the traditional points and condenser in the distributor.

With the starter turning the crankshaft and moving the pistons in their cylinders and sparking the spark plugs, the engine begins to run. The starter motor disengages since the engine is running on its own, and you are ready to drive away.

An engine in proper tune provides all these actions at the right moment.

How can you tell if you need a tune-up? First, keep a running check on your gasoline mileage. Figure your average mileage for every three tankfuls. When this average has dropped by over 15 percent, chances are you need a tune-up (or some other work). Other symptoms of an out-of-tune engine are (1) too fast an idle when warm, (2) stalling, (3) low power, (4) rough idle, (5) knocking or pinging, (6) hard starting, (7) misfiring, (8) hesitation, (9) rough running, (10) run-on or "dieseling" (engine runs when the key is off), and even (11) black exhaust smoke.

Watch for any of these changes in how your engine runs. Any one of them can indicate a need for a tune-up.

But here's the big question. "Can I really do my own tune-up?"

The answer is yes, if you have only a little mechanical aptitude and can identify and handle the following items:

Compression gauge
PCV air filter
Dwell/tachometer
Timing light
Distributor cap, condenser, and breaker points (if needed
  on your car)

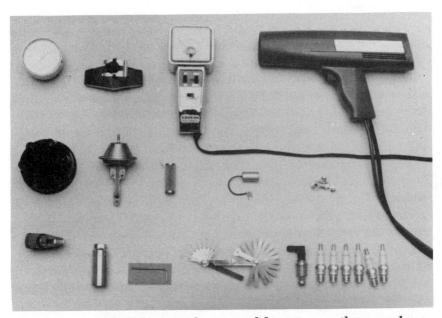

If you know what these tools are and how to use them, and can identify the parts most commonly used, you might be able to do your own tune-ups. 1) Compression tester. 2) PCV air filter. 3) Dwell/tachometer. 4) Timing light. 5) Distributor cap. 6) Vacuum advance unit. 7) Fuel filter. 8) Condenser. 9) Breaker points. 10) Distributor rotor. 11) Spark plug socket. 12) Allen wrench. 13) Feeler gauge. 14) PCV valve. 15) Spark plugs.

Fuel filter
Spark plugs and socket wrench
Feeler gauge
PCV valve
The repair manual for your car, showing engine and spark-
    plug specifications.

Tune-up

Let's *do* it. It isn't difficult, and it can be fun. Your reward, besides saving about fifty dollars, will be a peppier, more economical, more reliable engine. If you don't have a repair manual for your car, you can probably get one at the local library, bookstore, or auto parts store. Owning one will make this and other jobs on the car much more easy and efficient. Read all the way through the tune-up chapter to determine ahead of time what's required for your car and the tools you will need. If a special tool is required, it is quite likely you can borrow or rent it if it isn't already in your toolbox.

We'll start with the easy jobs. Every job you do will help, in case you decide you are getting in too deep or lose interest. Meanwhile, if you don't intend to do the job yourself, degrease your engine with a spray while it is warm to make the job easier for your mechanic. Don't breathe the fumes. If you do intend to go on, prepare yourself. Wear cotton gloves or rub soap under your nails. Any grime will wash away much easier when you are finished. Work slowly and carefully, and watch out for any sharp edges that might cut your hands. Engines have all kinds of attachments and angles that seem to jump out and bite when you least expect it. If you find a nut or bolt that won't come loose, don't fight it. Spray it with a shot of penetrating oil. Let it soak for awhile, then go at it again. Keep your nose out of the way. A nut that suddenly comes loose can send a ratchet handle flying. Use a caged safety light to brighten the dark areas so you can see what you're doing, and it isn't a bad idea to have a fire extinguisher close at hand. You're working around gasoline, where a loose connection can quickly start to drip. Wear safety glasses or goggles for these same reasons, and if the car must be jacked up, use safety stands and not milk cartons or concrete blocks, which can collapse at the worst possible time.

None of this is to indicate that the job is very difficult, but only to help make the job easier and safer.

Before you install any part, take a look to see how the old part was fitted. It doesn't hurt to make a diagram if you think you might forget. Then compare the new part with the old part to be sure they are exactly the same.

Some weekend mechanics even attach numbered tabs to wires and components to be sure that everything goes back in the same place, and in the same order, as before.

Before you do anything else on the job itself, check the compression in each cylinder with the compression gauge. This is done by removing the spark plugs.

First, remove the wires to the top of the spark plugs by grasping the rubber boot at the spark-plug end and twisting as you pull. Keep track of which wire goes where. Then use the spark-plug wrench to unscrew the old plugs. It is best to blow out the recesses first so no dirt falls down into the cylinders through the open spark-plug hole.

Now screw in the compression gauge, or if the gauge has a rubber cone end, hold it into each spark plug hole in each cylinder in turn as the engine is cranked over. If you don't have a "remote starter switch" to do this, ask a friend to crawl into the driver's seat and hit the starter while holding the accelerator pedal down. Take a reading from each "hole" and write it down.

The engine won't start with the plugs removed, and your readings will tell you how much pressure you are getting from each cylinder. Why are you doing this job? The key here is that you want the readings close to the specifications in the manual, and you don't want one or more of the cylinders to be much different from the others (which could indicate valve or ring problems).

If you run into a problem with this job (perhaps one cylinder reads a much lower pressure than the others), you might want to take the car into a service station or garage for a "leak down" test. This test is inexpensive and will indicate whether or not you are losing compression through misadjusted or damaged valves or worn piston rings.

Throw the old spark plugs away. Screw in and finger-tighten the new plugs after you have gapped the electrodes to the specifications in your owner's manual. You'll need an inexpensive gauge for this job, and you'll accomplish it by slightly moving the outer electrode and not the inner one.

Then use a torque wrench to tighten each plug down properly. Torque specifications will be in the manual. If you don't have a torque wrench, tighten them as tight as you can by hand, then tighten them one more quarter turn with the spark-plug wrench. Snap the wires back on, the correct wire to the correct plug.

What would happen if you got the wrong wire on a couple of plugs? Those plugs would spark at the wrong time, when the piston is in the wrong place in its cylinder. The engine will run roughly and could even be harmed by mixing up the spark-plug wires.

With this job done, you have gone a long way toward improving the operation and efficiency of the engine. One old Chevie convertible was running *terribly*. It huffed and puffed and stalled and was a real consternation to its owner—until she changed the spark plugs. That was *all* and suddenly the old car purred like a kitten. Spark plugs are a key element in the car's ignition system. Sure, you can clean the old ones and regap them, but spark plugs are not expensive and if you use regular gasoline should be replaced every six months or so. With lead-free gas, spark plugs usually last at least 30,000 miles.

Yes, there's more to an engine tune. Points and condenser are a little more complicated, but your car might not even need them if it has an electronic ignition system. In these cars, everything is done electronically inside or outside the distributor. If there is a problem with the electronics, it is best to take the car to a garage for service. They'll probably just replace the "black box" electronic module rather than try to repair it. Unfortunately, these things can cost a hundred bucks or so.

The points and condenser inside the distributor of a non-electronic ignition system, though not as efficient or long-lasting, can be replaced routinely by weekend mechanics. There are two clips that hold the cap of the distributor to its body. Just leave the wires on where they are plugged into the top of the cap. Unsnap the clips with a flip of a screwdriver and lift the cap off. It'll look like an octopus with all the wire "arms" still attached. Inspect it for dirt, cracks, or other signs of wear.

The cap is not expensive, but if you replace it be sure you get the same type and be sure all the wires are plugged into the right sockets.

Next will be the rotor, and it will lift off. Check it for signs of wear or cracking. It, too, is inexpensive and can be easily replaced. Under the rotor you'll see the points and condenser. Generally, two screws hold the points in place, then there will be one for adjusting the distance between the two points. Another screw will hold the condenser down. Unscrew them, and lift the points and condenser out, noting the routing of the wire from the condenser.

The new points you have purchased will come as a single unit. Put the points unit into the exact place the old one was, and then put the new condenser in the place of the old one. Route the condenser wire along the same path as the old one and tighten it down.

The only tricky part of this job is to get the points set the right distance apart, but you can do it. Crank the engine (it won't start because the cap is off the distributor) until the points are as wide apart as they can get. You'll see the cam follower on the points assembly riding up on the bumps of the shaft in the center of the distributor (and a drop of high-quality grease where the follower rides on the shaft won't hurt). The points will open and close and open and close as the engine is cranked.

Once you have them at their most open point, use a screwdriver on the adjusting screw and a feeler gauge, of the thickness directed by the specifications manual, to open or close the points to the right setting. Tighten down the final screw on the points and you have it. It's a good idea to crank some more and measure again to be sure the points have held their setting. Put the distributor rotor back on, then the cap, and snap the clips. Reinstall the coil wire, and the engine should start.

You've completed the two major chores in a tune-up.

But there are more tasks before you button things down.

Engine idle speed and engine timing are important in a tune-up. The idle speed is a simple setting, usually a screw on the linkage at the base of the carburetor. Check your owner's manual for the proper speed, and if you don't have a tachometer, *listen* for what seems right. Many cars now have a tachometer on the dash, making the job very easy.

But first, let's check the timing. Then you can get a friend to sit in the driver's seat and watch the engine speed as you adjust the idle speed.

Engine timing is set with a timing light. Look down by the front pulley on your engine and you will see an indicator pointer. On the flywheel will be a series of marks. Your manual will tell you where the pointer should be. Check it by hooking up the timing light to ground and the distributor (check the directions with the light) and, with the engine running, point it down at the pointer. The light will flash off and on very rapidly and the flywheel will appear to have stopped. You'll be able to see where the pointer is on the scale.

If it doesn't read at the mark where the spec manual says it should, you can reset it. There is a clamp holding the distributor in place. With the clamp loosened the distributor can be turned one way or the other. Turning the distributor changes the instant when the spark is sent to the plugs. Turn the distributor as you watch the pointer under the timing light, and you can set it wherever you want it.

When you have it just right, tighten the clamp, recheck the setting with the light, then put away the timing light. Store it in a clean place, in a box where it won't be banged around by other tools.

A tune-up should also include checking the spark-plug wires and the high-tension wire from the coil to the distributor for cracking or peeling. These wires come in sets for your make and model. If one is bad, change them all. The ignition-wire set is not expensive and can make a real difference in how an engine runs.

The PCV system carries unburned gases from the crankcase back into the air intake system to be burned. Plugged or disconnected tubes can affect the operation of the engine. Be sure all tubes are connected and that the PCV valve clicks when you remove it and shake it. Look over all the vacuum hoses to be sure they're sound and solidly plugged into their nipples. One of the hoses will go to a nipple at the bottom of the distributor if your car has a vacuum advance. Be sure this one is in place, and that it has no cracks or leaks.

Headlights

How many times have you driven down the highway at night and been blinded by an oncoming car's headlights?

You flick your lights from dim to bright and dim again, but get no response. It happens, and it might not be that the other guy is a clod who simply refuses to dim his lights. He might think he is doing you a favor by not flicking his own lights. Or the guy answers your flick of the lights with one of his own, and then you realize in the blinding glare that he *did* have his low beams on.

In fact, other drivers might be muttering to themselves about you.

Headlight aim can get out of adjustment, and should be checked every six months. You can probably tell from the driver's seat that your high beams are too high and that your low beams reach out too far in front of the car. Low beams should light the road ahead and slightly to the right. High beams should light the road well ahead of the car.

Headlight adjustment should be done by an expert with the proper equipment. But you can adjust your lights if you know they are wrong by driving up to within about ten feet of a garage door, turning your lights on, then noting where the centers of the beams hit. Switch from high to low and it should be obvious if there is a misadjustment.

Changing the aim of your headlights is simple. You'll probably have to remove the decorative rim around the lights, but *don't* remove the screws holding the bulb in place. There is an adjustment screw or screws (usually mounted on springs) that will change the aim of the light without loosening it in its holding ring. Make these adjustments carefully. They will only be rough adjustments at best, but if somebody is constantly flickering lights at you at night even though you have your low beams on, consider lowering your own lights a bit.

Lubricate Locks, Springs, Linkages, and Body

There are dozens of places on the body of a car that require, but seldom get, periodic lubrication. These areas will eventually begin to protest if they need oil. Worse, they will quit working as they should. Doors, hood latches, striker plates, hinges, and other moving parts should be oiled or greased every six months.

As a general rule, use oil on rotating parts. Motor oil will do the job well, except in door locks where the oil might freeze. For locks, a shot of graphite lubricant, applied sparingly, will keep the mechanism working summer and winter and won't stain the inside of the door or run down the paint on the outside.

Grease should be used on sliding or rubbing parts, such as striker plates.

The hood linkage is often ignored, yet a couple of drops of oil or a little grease (oil on pivots, grease on sliding arms) will keep it operating smoothly.

Be sparing with lubricants, starting at one end of the car and working to the other so that you don't miss anything. Too much lubricant can eventually work out onto the finish or into somebody's clothes.

Then, if you really want to do a job, "Get out and get under," as they used to say. Only this time it won't be for a hasty repair, but for a complete lubrication.

For years, Detroit has tried to convince us that a modern car doesn't need a chassis lube as often as we might feel good about. In fact, they have invented "permanent lube" connections and joints. Meanwhile, we find that linkages are wearing out prematurely, and squeaks are developing in suspension and other parts.

Many smart drivers are getting back to the old way of doing things. A quick chassis lube at a service station takes only a few minutes, if your car can handle it. That's where the problem might develop. Some modern cars, in the spirit of permanent lubrication, have no grease nipples.

Don't despair. There's an answer to this problem. Just take your car to your service station or garage and ask the mechanic to install grease nipples in the same threads where the permanently lubricated plug is located. Then give each a shot of grease. You'll be amazed at how much fresh, clean grease your car's joints really need. Many of the creaks and groans you have become accustomed to will be gone. And at the same time you'll be prolonging the life of balls, joints, and linkages.

Once the nipples are installed, you can take over the grease job yourself. That's where the "get out and get under" comes in. For a few dollars you can buy a hand-operated grease gun which uses convenient grease cylinders. Before you pull the trigger, wipe the nipple clean to remove dirt and old grease. Service station attendants, incidentally, may not do this even though the abrasive dirt can eventually work into the joint and result in a hefty repair bill.

After the nipples are clean, force new grease in until the rubber grease retaining pockets begin to bulge slightly, or until grease begins to ooze out of the joint. The whole thing takes only a few minutes (you can locate the joints in your car service manual) and you will be sure the job is done right.

Rotate Tires

How do you get the most safe mileage from your tires? It's fairly simple. Keep an eye on inflation, on tire condition, and on wheel alignment. See to it that tires are repaired in the event of damage. Finally, pay attention to your driving habits.

Also, though there is some disagreement on this point, rotate your tires periodically.

Why disagreement?

Some experts say that tire rotation tends to mask alignment problems. What they are saying is that by leaving the tires alone, you will finally begin to see tire-wear patterns that indicate misalignment. Still, rotation can add thousands of miles to the life of a tire providing there is no alignment problem.

The solution to this problem is simple. Rotate your tires on schedule and keep an eye on the alignment in the meantime. Don't use your tires as a gauge for misalignment. Have the alignment checked once every year or so, or when you have noticed a problem in steering (or when you have hit a pothole or a curb soundly). Most service stations or garages can handle this easily and the fee is nominal.

Remember this: Radial tires are rotated differently from bias-ply tires. Bias tires can be rotated *across* the car, radials should remain on the *same side* of the car.

Here's how to rotate the tires.

1. Bias-ply. As a general rule, right rear goes to left front.

Left rear goes to right front. Right front goes to right rear. Left front goes to left rear. If you want to work the spare tire into the rotation to keep the wear even on all five tires, enter it at any point along the way, and follow the same pattern.

2. Radial tires. Right rear goes to right front. Left rear goes to left front. Right front goes to right rear. Left front goes to left rear. Work the spare into the pattern if you wish, but once it is in, keep it on the same side of the car.

While we're at it, here are a few more tire-care tips.

- Have a periodic check of tires, brakes, wheel balance, and wheel alignment. Any mechanic or tire store will be glad to look over the system, often at no charge, in the hope of selling something to you.
- Have a wheel alignment check after a wheel hits a curb or chuckhole in the road. Any service station or garage can do it inexpensively, unless you need parts or adjustments. If you need something, it won't cost as much as the new tires will eventually cost because they've worn out too soon.
- Maintain correct tire pressure at all times. Do it with your own personal tire pressure gauge, not the one at the service station or garage.
- Maintain an even driving pace, with smooth starts and stops. You know how to drive for fuel economy. Do the same for tire economy.
- Check regularly to be sure you have valve caps on each stem. Most service stations have a drawer full and most of them will give you one free if you lose one.
- Stack stored tires neatly on a clean, oil-free floor, away from electric motors or generators. These devices generate a rubber-damaging gas that can, over the long haul, hurt the rubber in stored tires.
- Store specialty tires (snow tires, etc.) in a cool, clean, dry, sunless area away from air currents and electric motors or generators.
- Drive extra carefully on rough roads. A rough surface can beat up a good tire.
- Avoid squealing around corners. That's your expensive rubber you're leaving behind on the street.
- Avoid riding on the edge of pavements or tracks. This kind of driving can really damage tires.

Inspect Disc-brake Pads

You don't need a mechanic or special measuring devices to check your disc-brake pads. Unlike the shoes in a drum-brake system, which are out of sight inside the drums, disc-brake rotors and pads are out in the open. They are just behind the wheels so they can be kept cooler by airflow, and this makes them much less prone to "fade." They are fairly easy to see. Your car might have disc brakes only on the front wheels, which do most of the work of braking, or it might have "four-wheel disc brakes."

If you don't know how they work, spin a plate then pinch the edge between two fingers to stop the spin. The plate is the rotor attached to the wheel, and your fingers are the disc pads. Not only do disc brakes run cooler, but they are able to withstand much more heat than drum brakes.

At a race at Ascot Speedway in Los Angeles, one racer's disc brakes heated up so much that the rotor, and eventually the whole center of the wheel, became red hot. Racing fans in the grandstands were fascinated by the sight of the blistering wheel. Yet the brakes still worked. Modern disc-brake pads are saturated with copper and other metals. The pads will still grab onto the rotor at extreme temperatures, with little or no fade.

The best time to look over disc-brake pads is when the car is up on a hoist, but if you don't mind crawling under (or better yet, removing a wheel) you can look at them anytime.

It will be obvious to you if the pads are worn down to where the metal of the pad is getting near the metal of the rotor. Never allow metal to grind against metal or you will have an unnecessary, and expensive, rotor repair.

Disc-brake pads ride almost against the rotor, even when the brakes are not being applied. This helps to keep them clean, to help them self-adjust, and to keep them slightly warm, since they tend to lose some of their efficiency when they are cold. In fact some people, and many dogs and other animals, can hear the first signs of brake failure as the pads wear down. A high-pitched squeal is the first sign. If your dog appears upset in your car, and no cats are around, take a look at the brake pads.

Check the rotors at the same time. The rotor (the "disc" of

a disc-brake system) should be smooth, or reasonably smooth. Pits and other damage should be lathed out. You can tell if a rotor needs work by scraping your fingernail across its surface. If your nail snags in any ridges, grooves, or pits, ask your mechanic to resurface them on a lathe. A little roughness, though, won't matter, since the discs will have rubbed themselves to fit the brakes and will still work very well.

You might get an argument about this from a brake mechanic, but use your judgment. A disc rotor doesn't have to be mirror-smooth, in spite of what they may tell you. But it should be a certain *thickness*. Too much wear and they can break under pressure of braking.

Inspect and Replace Windshield Wiper Blades

There is nothing worse on a windshield than an old, hardened, and brittle wiper blade. Worse, a bad wiper blade is a safety hazard. Yet wiper blades are one of the forgotten items on a car. You only remember them when it rains, and by then it might be too late. Check them every six months, and replace them if you are in doubt. They are cheap and easy to snap out and snap in. Your service station will do it for the price of the new blades.

As suggested previously, you can extend the life of wiper blades by scraping the edge with sandpaper. This will scrape away the hardened part and get the blade back to rubber. It may not be perfect, but at least you won't be scoring your windows.

Check Differential Fluid Level

Many drivers don't even know where the differential *is*, let alone how to check it for fluid level. Yet this is another of the neglected items on a car, a neglect that can cost big bucks if something goes wrong.

On a standard, front-engine car, the power must get from the engine to the rear, driving wheels. Most of us know that the power comes off the rear of the crankshaft of the engine. It goes from there to a transmission, either automatic or manual. From the transmission it goes to a drive shaft, connected at each end and sometimes in the middle by universal joints that can bend and turn at the same time.

Incidentally, U-joints need attention too. Some of them have grease nipples that should be attended to at every lubrication. Others have "permanently lubricated" joints. These joints are tough, but they can fail.

One driver was hauling a heavy trailer behind his car when he began to hear the "clunk...clank...clunk" of a failing U-joint. He was still fifty miles from home, it was late at night, so he decided to go for it—in spite of one last, long hill he had to climb.

Carefully, slowly, attempting to put no more strain than necessary on the joint, he drove home. The next morning, when he took the car to the garage, the joints were disassembled. The bearings were pure *dust*. They were gone. Yet the joint had held to get him home. They're solid.

Let's get back to the drive train and the differential. Where does the power go from the rear end of the drive shaft?

It must go out to each wheel. This means the power must change its direction, and that's where the differential comes in. Look at your rear axle. There is a lump in the center, where the drive shaft is attached. Inside this housing is a set of gears that takes the power from the drive shaft and sends it out to each wheel. These gears must operate in a bath of oil. Without the proper amount of oil, the differential will fail. This is a *costly* failure indeed.

Checking the oil level is fairly easy, although you will have it much easier if the car is on a lift. Otherwise, it is get out and get under once again.

Somewhere on the housing, usually on the back side halfway between the top and bottom, is a grease plug. Remove the plug with a wrench and see what happens. Oil might ooze out and drip down the outside of the housing. Good. Put the lug back in and the job is done. There is enough oil in the differential.

If oil does not ooze out, stick a finger into the hole and wiggle it toward the bottom of the housing. If you get oil on the end of your finger, you are probably still in good shape. But if you can't touch the oil inside, add enough differential lubricant to bring the level up to the edge of the hole. Pour it right through the hole, using a funnel to maintain neatness, or use an oil gun. In this case, as with most other components, it isn't like it used to be with the old Tin Lizzie. Then, you just poured in any oil. Nowadays, there is a special oil for each application. So there is a special oil for differentials, and it should be used. It costs a little more, but it'll be worth it.

Chapter TEN

Annual Checks

Of all the cars in the world, which do you suppose are the most perfectly maintained and tuned?

Taxicabs? Well, cabs are well cared for as a general rule. They often work twenty-four hours every day. They work hard, in all weather, under all road conditions. They must be ready at a moment's notice to go around the block or across a city or state. Time is money to the owners, and a cab in the garage is a liability. A cab must be on the street, hauling fares, to earn its keep.

Regular maintenance is routine with a taxicab.

Still, they often run slightly out of tune, or out of alignment or balance, or with less than perfect tires, brakes, suspension systems, or exhaust systems. They *have* to. So they probably are not the most perfectly maintained vehicles.

What about a chauffeur-driven limousine?

Money is generally no object with these vehicles. Their owners want them running right, and *now*. They are willing to foot the bill for routine maintenance and repairs.

You've heard it before in the movies. "Jeeves, get the limo repainted. There's a spot on the fender."

Limousines are among the most cared-for cars in the world. But there are vehicles that are even more pampered.

Classic cars? Those jewels from the past that owners restore to as near perfection as possible?

Heavy construction machines that do gargantuan work to

repay owners for the immense investments that have been made?

Your car or mine, if we really *love* the machine?

In every one of these cases, the machines involved get loving care. But there is a class of vehicle that gets even better care. It is hauled to its job in a fancy trailer, protected by locked doors, and never touched by anybody but highly skilled technicians. It is cleaned and waxed with the greatest affection. It often has a name and is frequently photographed.

When it is ready, finally ready, it has been inspected by X-ray and by eagle-eyed technical people. It does its job before thousands of spectators and often millions more on television. If it succeeds, it is depicted in newspapers around the world. Often, when its job is done, it is retired to a museum where it can be viewed by people for years to come.

Because of the precision construction and lavish care given this class of vehicle, it costs its owners far more than any other type of car.

By now you have probably guessed that this type of car begins its active workday with the words, "Gentlemen, start your engines!" And you may also have realized that this type of car, in spite of all this, sometimes ends its workday as a pile of junk.

The most lavishly cared-for car in the world is the big-time auto-racing car. Indy cars, stock cars, dragsters, any of the machines from the top associations, where prize money can run into the millions of dollars, are "hang the expense" vehicles. Oil is changed not semiannually, or monthly, or weekly, or even *daily*, but generally after each run of the engine.

Spark plugs? They're changed so routinely that most do not get more than a few miles of operation.

What about *engines*? The same. A big-time racing mechanic often has a truckload of engines from which to choose. The slightest problem can easily result in a decision to change an engine. If the problem develops during a race, they might change the engine in the pits, hoping to get back into the competition before it's too late. One crew changed an entire engine and rushed the car back into the race in less than twenty minutes.

The routine maintenance procedures described in this book are much like the maintenance procedures used in the garages

at Indianapolis. The only difference is, at Indy they are accomplished many times more often. Why? Because the most
skilled mechanics in the world know that these routine procedures are what make a car go the distance under the most
difficult conditions.

You and I might not be professional race car mechanics, but
we can use the same techniques to keep our own vehicles
operating efficiently and safely. We can do it with confidence
if we take our time, if we remain cool, calm, and collected.
An automobile is a machine; complex, yes, but still a machine
that works in a certain, technical, understood way.

One racing mechanic was asked by a friend to check out a
boat engine. The engine had been operating beneath its ability.
It had been misfiring at higher speeds and generally lagging.
An inspection by the owner had uncovered no major faults,
still the engine was not performing up to standard.

"Let's take her out a few hundred yards," said the friendly
mechanic, "and I'll check things out."

Remember, this is a mechanic who must perform in the heat
of battle. This is a mechanic who can't be ruffled, who must
make instant decisions and take immediate corrective action
to hold his job. His car must win, or he must find a new car.

So the two eased out of the harbor in the cabin cruiser. A
couple of hundred yards offshore the mechanic spoke. "OK,
shut 'er down."

The owner, noting the distance to shore and the heavy break-
ers on the beach, mildly protested. "Ah...we aren't very far
out. We...that is...well, I usually don't shut down the engine
this close in. I mean, what if it won't *start* again?"

"Hey, do I look worried? Shut 'er down," replied the mechanic.

So the boat engine was shut down and the mechanic went
to work. Since he was down in the bilge and the owner was
on the bridge, the owner could only watch as the boat drifted
closer and closer to the huge waves building up to break on
the beach. Finally, he could stand it no more. He left the bridge,
hurried through the galley, and ducked his head into the engine
room.

"How are you...Oh, my *heavens!*" he said.

There sat the mechanic, happily surrounded by ignition parts.

"I think I found the problem," he said, holding up a distributor.

"But ... but ..." the owner could only garble, "we're nearly *ashore!*"

The mechanic looked up calmly. "OK, I know where we are. How much time do I have?"

"We ... you ..." stammered the owner, looking out the galley window at the onrushing shoreline and gesturing. But by then the mechanic was calmly reinstalling parts. Carefully, item by item, he worked.

"Better get back up on the bridge," he said quietly. "You'll be needed there in another minute."

The frantic owner rushed to the bridge and very soon, though it seemed like an eternity to the owner, the mechanic appeared. "Go ahead, hit it," he ordered.

The owner punched the starter, the engine roared to life, and with a twist of the wheel he avoided the first of the building waves. Soon the boat was safely offshore again, the engine rumbling smoothly and the unruffled mechanic enjoying the ride. The engine was operating more beautifully than it had in months.

The moral? Working on an engine is no time for panic. The more you need the car, the more self-assured you must be. Don't hurry any of these jobs. It'll all work out.

THE MORE COMPLICATED JOBS

When you begin the more involved, annual checks that help to keep your car running efficiently, keep the racing mechanic in mind. Be cool, calm, and collected. Think about what you are doing before you do it. Don't be hurried and never, never panic. Yes, these take even more effort, but they can be done by the weekend mechanic who enjoys his car and wants it to be reliable.

Besides, you have worked your way up to this. You know far more about your car than even you might realize. You are ready.

Overheating

One of the most common problems of a modern car, for one reason or another, is overheating. An auto engine needs a certain amount of heat to run efficiently, but too much heat is even more serious than not enough heat. If dirt is the number-one enemy of a modern engine, too much or too little heat is certainly number two.

There are air-cooled engines, but most modern engines are temperature-controlled by a coolant which circulates around the hot parts and then through a radiator where heat is removed. Then the cooled-down coolant returns to pick up more heat. It is an endless cycle when it is working right. If the engine isn't warm enough, a thermostat in the system slows down the flow of coolant. If the engine is too warm, the thermostat opens to allow the coolant to run to the radiator and back much faster.

Remember the man who was driving along without a care in the world when his heat gauge began to climb? Instead of immediately pulling off and locating the problem, he drove on.

"No real problem," he decided. "I'll just keep an eye on it. If it gets too hot, I'll pull off and have it checked."

The result was a seriously overheated engine and a $300 repair bill for a new head gasket. It could have been worse, much worse. He could have "frozen" the engine, scored the cylinders, warped the head, or done some other very expensive damage.

You'll recall that he had dumped his coolant out through a broken heater hose, and that his heat-sensing mechanism was reading hot *air* and not hot coolant. So of course it didn't go up all the way and he thought he was safe for the moment.

Overheating breaks down the additives in oil, burns away insulation, grinds parts together, even fuses metal. The problem can be compounded by modern emissions control devices that tend to recirculate hot gases. The problem can be further complicated by the extra compression and extreme tolerances of modern high-performance engines. They generate tremendous heat, and this heat must be dissipated. When everything is working correctly, heat is no problem. Modern engines are designed to run at the correct temperature.

But even with an expensive new ultramodern engine, designed by skilled engineers with loving care and attention to every detail, the owner's manual might suggest that on a hot day, on a stop-and-go drive, when the engine doesn't have the opportunity to cool itself, you might just give some consideration to shutting down the air conditioner. You don't *have* to, of course, but you might think about it. The manufacturer knows what might happen.

Here's a couple of simple tricks to keep an engine cooler.

1. If you have padded insulation under the hood, you might want to remove it. It absorbs heat and holds it under the hood. Worse, as it ages, it can come apart and bits of it can be sucked into the air cleaner.

One of the reasons it is there other than to deaden engine noise is because of the great heat of the engine and the possibility of paint damage on the hood. Keep the cooling system in good shape, and rip out the insulation if you live where it is always hot or gets very hot during certain months.

2. What you want is a surface that bounces away heat and still helps deaden any noise. Paint the underside of the hood with normal undercoating and you'll reduce the strain on your cooling system.

The best way to assure a correct temperature in a modern engine is to keep the cooling system in good repair. Auto cooling systems are efficient, but they do require at least annual attention. Otherwise, you're going to have troubles ranging from moderate overheating (which will cause long-range damage to the engine) to one of those spectacular moments of gushing steam that always seem to happen at the most inconvenient moment. You can see these unfortunate motorists every summer day alongside every roadway in the country.

Keeping Your Cooling System Working

There are two ways to keep the system working as efficiently as possible.

1. *Inspection*

The parts of your cooling system that are most likely to fail are the hoses, the radiator, the radiator cap, the drive belts, and the water pump. A single ten-minute inspection will tell you if any of these are about to go.

Start with the radiator hoses. Squeeze them along their entire length and look closely for signs of wear. If a hose shows tiny cracks or if it feels spongy, replace it.

One young motorist simply couldn't figure out why his engine was constantly overheating. Oh, he knew he was losing coolant, but he couldn't find from where. By day's end, every day of driving, his radiator was low on coolant and his engine was overheated.

He finally turned to a mechanic friend who applied every test. Could the coolant be leaking into the engine and burning away in the exhaust? No. Was a hose leaking? Apparently not. The hoses weren't new by any stretch of the imagination, but they felt reasonably firm.

Eventually he discovered the problem. As the engine heated, a failing radiator hose, by then quite warm, was allowing a thin stream of coolant out. Under the pressure of the system, the coolant was hitting the exhaust manifold and turning to steam. So the tiny thread of coolant was gradually emptying the system. When cooled down, the hose worked just fine.

With a change of hose, the problem was solved.

Don't forget the lower radiator hose. This hose contains a coil spring to keep it from collapsing under the suction of returning coolant, so it will feel more firm even if it is old and worn. Most motorists know that the upper hose may need replacing long before the lower hose. Yet a lower hose can just as quickly cause an overheating problem. If it collapses while the engine is running, the flow of coolant will be shut off.

If it leaks, it isn't as obvious as an upper-hose leak. If the lower hose feels spongy, the spring may have lost its tension and the hose may be partially collapsing and restricting the flow of coolant. Yes, the lower hose generally lasts at least three times longer than the upper hose, since it is not subjected to as much pressure and heat as the upper hose. The lower hose is full of water if everything is working right. But it can give you problems that are just as serious.

The best advice? Replace *both* hoses if one needs changing. It'll cost twice as much, but think of the peace of mind.

While you're inspecting the hoses, look carefully around the hose clamps for any sign of leaking. Look for a whitened area or rust. This might be solved by tightening the hose clamps. Look again a day or so later to be sure the hose is no longer leaking.

Replacing a hose is not difficult. Modern hoses are made for the car. They are bent to shape and should fit in simply. On many modern cars, the job can be done from the topside of the engine. All you need is a blade-type screwdriver to loosen the hose clamps, or a pair of pliers to open the spring of a spring-type hose clamp while you wiggle it back from the junction. And by the way, you might want to get rid of this type and install the screw-type hose clamp if you get into the job. They are more efficient and easier to work with.

So work the hose clamp loose and then push it back onto the hose. Twist off the old hose at each end. After you have removed the old hose, use a stiff wire brush to clean the connection, then slide the new hose on. A little vaseline or other petroleum jelly will help to slide the new hose onto the nipple. Be careful your new hose isn't touching the engine, the fan, fan belts, or any other moving part. Both the hose and the engine vibrate, so be sure there is space between them.

When you install the new hose clamps, put them at least one-eighth inch from the end of the hose then tighten them down securely. The pressure in a modern engine can blow a hose right off its pipe, so the clamps must be firmly in place. When you put the clamps back on, you'll again learn why you might want to avoid wire-loop hose clamps. The flat ones cost very little, are easy to install, and are much more efficient.

Don't forget to check the heater hoses. These are the hoses that take hot coolant from the radiator and carry it to the heater core inside the car. If one of them fails, it is just as serious as a leaking radiator hose. There also may be a bypass hose between the water pump and the block. It doesn't often fail, but if it does it is just as serious as any other hose.

If any one of these smaller hoses fail, replace them all. You have had the warning that they are old and weak.

Drive belts are also important for engine cooling. They should be inspected regularly, and if you see signs of wear, damage, or glaze, replace them immediately. A drive belt can even "chunk" and show sections missing. More about replacing drive belts on pages 255–56.

Look over the radiator during your inspection, and at the same time take a moment to clean out dead bugs and other debris that has collected over the past year. This debris will cut down on the air flow through the radiator and heat up the engine. Use a garden hose from the engine side of the radiator to blast the debris out toward the front.

Look for signs of leaks in the radiator, usually indicated by a whitish deposit. A pinhole leak can indicate that the radiator is failing and is due for repair or replacement (although radiator "stop leak" will work in an emergency, until you get to your home station or garage). A radiator shop will clean and repair the inside of the radiator and while the job is not inexpensive, it is much less expensive than a new radiator—or a new engine because the old one was ruined by overheating.

Finally, take your car to a service station for a pressure check of the system. They may do it for nothing. They'll connect a pressure tester to the radiator after removing the cap, then pump until a dial indicates the capacity marked on the cap. If you have a leaking gasket or hose, you'll see fluid oozing out. If within a few minutes the pressure drops, you've got a leak, possibly even inside the engine.

To check the water pump, shut off the engine and run your hand around the pump (generally behind the fan). If there's a leak, you'll feel it because your hand will get wet. Weekend mechanics can replace the pump, but it is an involved job that could include removing the radiator. You'll probably find it easier and more convenient to take the car to a mechanic for this job. But if you want to tackle the job, it will be explained in the next chapter.

You can test the thermostat, though it is a bit more involved. It is possible that a car can continually overheat (or run too cold) and still have a perfectly functioning radiator and no leaks in the system. This can happen because the thermostat, which controls the flow of coolant in the system, is not working correctly. The thermostat actually blocks the flow of water from the engine to the radiator until the engine is warm, then it opens and allows a flow to the radiator to keep the engine from getting too hot. Every thermostat has a heat-range rating, from perhaps 175 to 180 degrees on older cars up to 195 to 200 degrees on new cars. Your owner's manual will tell you the range of your thermostat.

First, get a thermometer that will cover the heat range of your thermostat, then drive your car for about ten minutes to warm it up. Turn it off, then remove the radiator cap—carefully!—and put the thermometer in the coolant in the filler neck. Then start the engine and watch the thermometer as the engine idles. The thermometer reading should drop to or slightly below the thermostat temperature rating. If the reading is substantially above or below the manual's thermostat temperature rating, you should replace the unit or have it replaced.

Replacing the thermostat is easy. Drain off enough of the coolant (save it if it is new and you want to reuse it) by opening the drain cock at the bottom of the radiator. The system doesn't have to be completely drained for this job. Then remove the upper radiator hose where it goes into the top of the engine. Unbolt the thermostat housing and remove the old thermostat from its seat. It'll just lift out, though you might use the blade of your screwdriver to help it a little. Discard it.

Carefully and throughly clean the mating surfaces, one on the engine block and the other on the thermostat housing. Put the new, correctly rated thermostat in place in the cavity, then install a new housing gasket using some gasket seal. The old gasket was probably ruined removing the thermostat housing and in any case it has probably deteriorated.

Place the thermostat housing in place and tighten down the bolts, then reinstall the upper radiator hose. Put the coolant back into the radiator as you idle the engine.

See, it was an easy, no panic operation.

2. *Draining and cleaning the radiator.*

One of the big lies of modern automotive lore is that "permanent" antifreezes are truly permanent. No antifreeze protects against rust and corrosion forever. Modern antifreezes do contain rust and corrosion inhibitors, but after a year or so they are used up. Enough acid can build up in the system to cause serious damage. Accumulated rust can clog up the passages in the radiator and cause overheating.

Yes, antifreeze is added to the system to keep the coolant from freezing. Why? Because if coolant freezes inside the engine block, it can expand and crack the metal of the block. That's why manufacturers put "freeze plugs" in a block. They are supposed to pop out and relieve the pressure of the expanding ice if the coolant freezes inside the block. But if the coolant is trapped in a cavity away from the freeze plugs, damage can be done. So antifreeze is added to lower the freezing-point temperature of the coolant. The coolant (water plus antifreeze) thus will not freeze solid even at temperatures far below the normal thirty-two-degree freezing point of water alone, depending upon how much antifreeze is added.

But antifreeze does something else as a side benefit (beyond providing the great benefit of the additives that help prevent rust and corrosion). It *raises* the *boiling point* of the mixture. Water boils at 212 degrees, but with antifreeze added, it won't boil until heated to a much higher temperature. Coolant is lost when it boils away. If it can't boil, it won't be lost and the engine will be protected even though it is very hot.

Even if you live in a warm state in the middle of summer, add the correct proportion of antifreeze. You stand less chance of boiling away the coolant on a very hot day, something that can happen to a modern, high-powered engine under normal operating conditions if only water is present in the radiator. All cooling systems should have antifreeze regardless of weather.

To drain the old stuff and put in the new is not a difficult job, but get your supplies first because you won't be able to drive the car in the middle of this operation. You'll need new antifreeze (half as much as the total capacity of the radiator— check your owner's manual), a can of fast-flush radiator cleaner, and a garden hose attached to a water faucet, plus a place for old coolant to drain.

Warm the engine, turn it off, then turn on your heater. Open the drain cock at the bottom of the radiator and any drain cocks on the engine itself (if there are any). When the coolant has fully drained from the entire system, close the drain cocks and fill the system with water from the garden hose. Add a can of fast-flush radiator cleaner, following the directions on the can. This usually means running the engine as warm as possible (with the heater on to include its passages in the cleaning). You can force the engine to run warmer than usual by placing a cardboard or newspaper over the front of the radiator. The draw of the fan will usually hold it in place, and with the airflow blocked the engine will warm up quickly. Keep an eye on it so that it doesn't get too warm.

The extra heat combined with the radiator cleaner circulating inside will cut some of the scale that has developed in the system. The directions on the can will often suggest that the engine be run warm for at least a half hour to give the cleaner a chance to work. When the time comes according to the directions, shut down the engine and once again open the drain cocks and allow the mixture to drain out. Take the garden hose and, with the drain cock open, add water to the filler neck of the radiator as water drains out the bottom. Start the engine and allow the fresh water to circulate, rinsing out every passage in the radiator, engine, and heater. Be sure to keep water flowing into the top. Don't let the water level drop, or the engine will overheat.

You'll know when the job is done because the water out the bottom will appear perfectly clean. Allow the system to drain completely once again. You are ready to fill that bright, clean cooling system with new coolant. Close the drain cocks at the bottom of the radiator and any on the engine block, then fill the system first with the correct amount of antifreeze. Top it off with water. Figure it half and half but follow the directions on the antifreeze containers to protect your radiator against the lowest possible temperatures you might expect in your region.

When you get the radiator filled to the neck, replace the radiator cap, then add antifreeze (if you have any left over) and water to the overflow tank up to the bottom line. If you don't have any antifreeze left, use water alone in the overflow tank. As the engine heats the coolant, it will expand and fill to the top line. That's all there is to it. You will have spent about ten dollars and your cooling system should be good for another six months at least, probably much longer.

In many more cases than you might imagine, pesky overheating problems were solved by the simple procedure of cleaning the cooling system. And what's more, the new antifreeze will protect the system from rust and corrosion.

Check and Refill Air Conditioner

Air conditioner blowing hot? Or at least only as cold as the air outside the car? Nine times out of ten the problem is a lack of freon gas, which tends to gradually leak from even a well-operating air conditioner over a period of time.

There is a way to make your freon gas last as long as possible. Operate the air conditioner, even in the middle of winter, for at least a few minutes every week. This will circulate the lubricants in the system and help to keep the seals pliable and secure.

The air conditioner in your car works on the same principle as the refrigerator in your house. When a liquid is converted to a gas, it picks up heat from its surroundings. When it returns to a liquid state, it gives up that heat. The active ingredient in the system, freon, is a gas part of the time and a liquid part of the time. It circulates as a liquid and picks up heat from inside the car. It becomes a vapor as it flows through the evaporator, then a compressor pumps it to a condenser, where the heat is discharged and the vapor is turned back to a liquid. A fan blows the cooled air into the car and the hot air outside the car.

The moisture from the hot air is discharged outside the car, and is sometimes mistaken for a leak in the cooling system. The only liquid you should ever see dripping from a car is the moisture from the evaporator of the air-conditioning system. The system is closed, so the refrigerant circulates back to pick up more heat from inside the car.

All problems with air conditioning are not necessarily with the flow of the refrigerant. If you are having a problem, first check the drive belts for looseness, fraying, glazing, or any other sign of wear. The belt driving the compressor must be tight enough to operate the compressor without slipping on the compressor pulley.

The air-conditioner clutch should be checked if you are having a problem with the system. Ask somebody to sit inside your car and, with the engine running, switch the air conditioner on and off several times. You should see and hear the clutch that drives the compressor clicking on and off. If it doesn't, the problem could be with the clutch or the sensing device that switches it off and on.

Check all the hoses for any obvious leaks. One of these hoses is a high-pressure unit, so it will probably be the one with the problem. The other hose is a return hose that operates under much lower pressure. Check the condenser screen for debris— dirt, leaves, dead bugs, etc. Cooling efficiency will be lost if the condenser radiator is clogged and the refrigerant cannot be cooled down.

In the condenser unit of most air-conditioning systems is a "sight glass." This is a little window into the system to tell you if you have air bubbles, indicating a need for more refrigerant. If you see bubbles rushing past the window after the air conditioning unit has been operating for more than ten or fifteen minutes, it's probably time for a recharge.

You can do-it-yourself with a kit or ask your service station to do it for you. Chances are a recharge will bring your air-conditioning unit back up to par. A kit includes a hose with a fitting that attaches to your filler nipple and a pressurized can or two of freon. The job is not difficult, though you are working with pressurized gases so care should be exercised.

Attach the filler hose to the nipple on the air conditioner (after removing the protective cap), then attach the can to the filler hose. With the air conditioner operating, on most cars, hold the can upside down above the hose and allow the contents to be taken into the system. However, follow the directions in the owner's manual. You can tell when the can is empty because the freon gas is a liquid in the can and it will be obvious when it is gone. As explained, it is a liquid in part of the air-conditioning system and a gas in other parts.

Operate the air conditioner for a few minutes, then check the sight glass. No more bubbles? Good, the system is ready to provide you cold air for months. A few bubbles still visible? Add more freon from another can. Be sure to put the protective cap back on the filler nipple of the air-conditioning system when the job is done.

Replace Fuel Filter

One motorhome owner was going crazy. The engine was missing, though with no apparent pattern. Sometimes the engine would cough and miss on a hill, the next time on a level road. Sometimes it would miss on acceleration, and then the next time under no load at all. There was no rhyme or reason to the malfunction.

The problem seemed to be in the ignition system, so he replaced the spark plugs (with no improvement), then he tuned the engine. Still no improvement. He checked with mechanic friends and they suggested various remedies, but the problem persisted. One mechanic was certain it was the ignition wires (and it could have been), but it wasn't.

Nobody, including the owner, thought of the poor little fuel filter. This inconspicuous device filters out any dirt in the fuel before it reaches the delicate carburetor. Eventually it gets full of dirt and begins to restrict the flow of fuel.

Finally one service manager mentioned it, assuming it had been changed with each service. It hadn't been, yet changing a fuel filter is easy. You'll find yours in the fuel line under the hood near the carburetor. You can get a replacement at a service station or auto parts store. Loosen the fasteners, take out the old one (be careful you don't spill the small amount of fuel inside onto something hot), then put the new one in the same way. Watch for the direction of fuel flow, often indicated by an arrow on the filter.

Make a new fuel filter part of your regular annual maintenance program even if the engine seems to be running smoothly. There is dirt in the filter for sure, and you never know when it might finally clog up and stop the flow of gasoline. The motorhome owner changed his fuel filter at a cost of less than eight dollars, and the problem was solved.

Repack Wheel Bearings

Click...grind...growl...click. Is your car speaking to you from the front wheels? Then it's too late for a repacking. Front wheel bearings are another of the forgotten components in a car. They should be cleaned and lubricated every year and though it is a rather dirty job, perhaps best left to a mechanic, it can be done by the weekend mechanic.

The wheel bearing is between the wheel and the axle. It is the bearing that allows the wheel to turn on the stationary axle.

The rear wheel bearings are lubricated by oil from the differential, but the front bearings need attention annually. Old-time mechanics, experts who will perhaps always shy away from "new-fangled" devices, have a trick to determine if a wheel bearing is beginning to fail. You'll see them put the car up on a rack, get the wheel spinning (either by hand with the front wheel or by putting the car in gear and idling the engine for a rear wheel), then get out a metal rod such as a lug wrench.

They'll put one end of the rod up against the back of the wheel or axle as near to the bearing as possible. They'll hold the other end cupped around their ear. A failing bearing will give off a sound that is carried through the metal rod to the experienced ear of the mechanic. He'll be able to hear the failure long before it becomes a problem on the road.

You can hear the same slight grinding sound, and you can change a wheel bearing. Here's how.

Remove the wheel and tire, then pop off the grease cap at the end of the axle. A nut with a cotter key will be evident. Pull the key, remove the nut, and the drum or rotor (the brake system) will come off to reveal the front wheel bearing.

Bearings should be washed in clean solvent and then re-greased with a pressure wheel-bearing greaser that forces grease into the bearing. Otherwise, the job must be done by hand, and you must be certain that grease is packed into and between each roller. Bearings with end shields or seals should not be washed in solvent, since there is no way to replenish the grease.

Blow dry bearings by air after their solvent bath, but do not air spin them. Air spinning can generate rpm speeds far beyond the design limits of the bearing and cause premature failure after the bearing is reinstalled in the wheel.

Lubricate Exhaust Manifold Heat Valve

There is a butterfly valve on the exhaust manifold that should be working freely. You can check it every oil change by reaching down and jiggling it. If it is jammed (and every year in any case), free it up by working it back and forth while applying special exhaust manifold heat valve lubricant (generally in a spray can) or a mixture of graphite and kerosene. The valve should move freely.

SOME TROUBLESHOOTING TIPS

Engine Noises

Engine noises are good indicators of problem areas. Many times the first indication of a developing problem in an engine will be a noise. A malfunction inside an engine is usually cause for taking the car to a mechanic, unless you are skilled at tearing down engines. Still, it is helpful to know what's going on up front, what's happening inside your engine, and what might be needed to correct it.

Mechanics have sophisticated tools and gauges to determine many inner engine problems, but there is an easier way. Get yourself a sounding stick similar to the one described in the wheel-bearing section on pages 233–34. Any stick about three feet long (a broom handle or a hollow tube) can be used. This stick can be used in place of a mechanic's stethoscope. If you love engines, you'll find the procedure fascinating.

Here's how.

With the engine running (be *careful* of moving parts) place one end of the stick on or near an area where you suspect a noise. Cup the other end around your ear and listen. The stick tends to dampen noise from around the area and transmit the suspected sound directly to your ear. Moving the stick from place to place around the engine will help you to hear sounds coming from particular locations inside the engine.

A mechanic's stethoscope does the job in the same way, but brings the sound more clearly to the ear.

Let's diagnose.

The main bearings are the units that go around the crankshaft to support it inside the engine block. The crankshaft spins in those bearings, so they are very important to the operation of the engine. They are lubricated by the oil in the oil pan of the engine. If the bearing doesn't get enough oil, or if it is worn down, it is heading for a failure.

By placing one end of the sounding stick down near the bottom of the engine, but not on the oil pan, you will be able to hear any noises from the main bearings. What you do *not* want to hear is a dull thudding noise. Correct use of the sounding stick will pinpoint a single worn and failing bearing.

Main bearing "knock" can be narrowed down even more by shoring out the spark plugs in the cylinders adjacent to the bearing. When the cylinder nearest the bearing you suspect is shorted out, that cylinder will no longer provide a power stroke and the noise from the failing bearing will diminish because the load on the bearing has been reduced.

If you hear such a sound, the bearing, and all other main bearings of course, will have to be replaced. This will require an engine teardown, an expensive job but better than a ruined engine.

Rod bearings go around the crankshaft journals inside the crankshaft end of the connecting rods. If a rod bearing is failing, considerable damage can be done to the engine. Rod-bearing knocks are similar to main-bearing knocks, but lighter and more metallic, as heard through the sounding stick.

You can isolate a particular bearing in the same way, by shorting out the spark plugs nearest to where you suspect the problem. With the spark shorted out the pressure on that bearing is reduced, and the noise will diminish.

Most commonly heard when the engine is idling is a piston pin noise. The piston pin goes through the top of the connecting rod and out through each side of the piston. The pin holds the piston to the top of the rod in each cylinder and allows the rod to move one way then the other as the piston goes up and down in the cylinder.

A pin noise is sharper yet, a metallic double knock or click. It is often caused by a broken pin retainer, which allows the pin to move back and forth and come into contact with the cylinder wall. In the case of a piston pin, the greatest noise will come with the cylinder shorted out, not working. This is a good way to tell the difference between a piston pin noise and a rod or crankshaft noise.

Piston slap, too much clearance between the piston and the cylinder wall, can also be heard by a sounding stick. If you suspect this condition, you can check it further by removing the spark plug from that cylinder. Add some engine oil directly into the cylinder, crank it over a few times with the coil wire removed so the engine won't start, then fire it up. The piston in that cylinder should run much more quietly for several minutes until the oil is all scraped away and the slap begins again.

Here are some other piston-associated noises. If you hear them, you are probably heading for an engine teardown and rebuild.

- Broken piston. A jagged rattling and an engine that doesn't run well.
- Broken piston ring. The same.

- Carbon deposit on the top of the piston striking the cylinder head with a sharp click at the top of the piston's stroke.
- Out-of-round or tapered cylinder bore caused by wear and tear that has ground away the material of the cylinder wall. You'll hear a "slapping" sound.

Valve-Train Noises

This assembly includes the valves, valve springs, retainers, rocker arms, pushrods, tappets (lifters), and camshaft. The camshaft is connected to the crankshaft by a chain or belt drive, or in some high-performance engines, by a gear train. The camshaft rotates at one half the speed of the crankshaft, and as it spins it opens and closes the intake and exhaust valves in the cylinders of the engine. The eccentric lobes on the cam push the tappets moving them up and down, and they push against the valves through the other parts (pushrods, rocker arms), opening and closing them in the correct sequence.

Noises here are usually less serious, though adjustments could be needed. If the noise is very serious, it still won't usually require a complete engine teardown.

The most common cause of noise in the valve train is incorrect adjustment and too much clearance between the many components. Adjustment of these clearances is usually done during routine engine work, so if you hear slight noises from this area it is usually just a matter of readjusting the valve clearances.

The sound of out-of-adjustment valves is a regular clicking. Since the valves are operating at one half the speed of the engine, the noise will generally be less than other noises if only one valve is out of adjustment.

Finding the specific valve is easy. All you need is a leaf-type feeler gauge. Remove the valve cover from the engine, but not before you have checked the shop manual to see what else must be done before a valve cover comes off. Sometimes other accessories must be removed or loosened. Also remember that you should have a new valve cover gasket available to complete the job.

Start the engine. Select the correct size feeler gauge and insert it between the valve stem and the rocker arm. They'll be moving, of course, so this might take a bit of doing until you get accustomed to the job. If the problem is excessive clearance, the noise will stop for that valve. If you can't get the feeler gauge in, go on to the next valve for now. You'll locate the noisy valve soon.

The shop manual or even your owner's manual will give instructions on adjusting the valve clearance, but it is usually just a matter of holding one nut while turning another with two wrenches. One nut adjusts the clearance, the other locks in the adjustment.

Hydraulic lifters (tappets) can make noise, but this isn't too serious either. The lifter is there to cushion the shock of the opening and closing of the valve, reducing the shock to the valve train. They use oil inside as a self-adjusting medium. If they become noisy, the problem can be lack of oil in the lifter or a plugged oil hole. You can find the offender.

With the valve cover off, start the engine then place a finger on each rocker arm in turn with the engine idling. If the hydraulic lifter is not functioning properly, you will feel a sharp, distinct mechanical shock (not electrical) as the valve activates. Refer to your shop manual or owner's manual for adjusting tips.

Valves can stick at some point during their travel, and the sound will be similar to a misadjusted valve. To check, drive the car at high speed for awhile, then quickly stop and allow the engine to idle. If there is a sticky valve, the clicking will be much louder at first and will diminish as the engine cools down. The noise may be accompanied by a jerky or rough engine idle. When running this test, the roughness should disappear along with the noise.

Here are some other valve train noises.

- Not enough oil reaching the valve components can cause a grinding noise. You can see if oil is coming to the valve train by looking at it with the valve cover off and the engine idling.
- Worn or scored parts, or broken or weak valve springs can cause a "clicking" sound.

Other Engine Noises

1. Preignition.

You've heard this pinging sound before, especially when you drive off too fast, climb a hill, or otherwise put your engine under an extra strain when it is hot. One cause of this is the ignition of fuel (caused by a particle of carbon or metal in the combustion chamber glowing red hot) before it is ignited by the spark plug. This is happening before the cylinder reaches the top of its travel and creates very high pressure inside the cylinder.

Preignition can also be caused by the timing being out of adjustment, by using gas too low in octane rating for your engine, or even by lugging the engine down in the wrong gear of the transmission.

If carbon "hot spots" are the cause of preignition, the top of the engine must be disassembled and the carbon removed. Otherwise, check the timing, or increase the octane rating of your fuel.

2. Excessive Endplay of Crankshaft.

If the crankshaft is moving fore and aft, a sharp click or rattle can be heard. To check, run the engine at idle while engaging and disengaging the clutch (transmission in neutral) several times. You should hear the noise each time you activate the clutch. Unfortunately, this will require an engine teardown to correct.

3. Loose Flywheel Noise.

The flywheel is attached to the back end of the crankshaft. A strong clicking sound can be heard if it works loose. All other things being equal, this isn't too difficult to correct. To check it out, start the engine with the transmission in neutral, then run it up to about twenty miles per hour. Turn off the ignition switch, but just at the moment when the engine is about to stop, switch it on again. Repeat this process several times. If the flywheel is loose, you will hear the clicking sound each time you switch on the ignition.

4. External Equipment Noise.

There are many accessories attached to the engine that can make noise resembling internal noises. Alternators can squeak, water pumps can whistle, power-steering units can growl, air-conditioning compressors can hiss, and fuel pumps can click. All of them can worry the driver who doesn't know what's going on. Most are easy to check by merely disabling them temporarily, removing them from the loop.

For example, if you suspect the air-conditioning compressor is making a noise that sounds like a bad bearing in the engine, remove the drive belt operating the compressor. If the noise goes away, you have isolated the problem.

Oil Pressure Problems

Oil, under pressure, is critical to the operation of any auto engine. Without oil at the correct pressure, engine parts will heat up and quickly wear out. They can even break and destroy the engine, or melt, or weld themselves together. Oil is picked up from the oil pan by a pickup tube from the oil pump. It passes through the pump, which is operated by the engine, then goes through the oil filter and finally through many oil holes and passageways inside the engine block and heads. Eventually, after it has bathed the parts where it is needed, it runs back down into the oil pan to be recirculated. Oil is in constant circulation while the engine is running.

Engines have a gauge on the dash, or at least a light, to indicate pressure in the system. The light, of course, comes on if the pressure drops to a dangerous point. Oil pressure must be within the operating range of that engine, not too high, and certainly not too low.

Here are some areas where problems can develop.

1. Lack of Oil.

Low oil pressure will be indicated if there isn't enough oil in the system. Check this by looking at the dipstick. If the engine needs oil, add it.

2. Oil too thin.

The owner's manual will indicate the weight of oil that should be used. If the oil is too thin, low pressure can be indicated. If the oil in the engine has been thinned out by water or gasoline, the engine will be harmed. In fact, there is a serious problem with any engine that allows water or fuel into the oil pan. If you see drops of water on the dipstick, or if the oil smells strongly of gasoline, the engine should be torn down to locate the problem.

3. Oil Intake Screen Clogged.

At the end of the pickup tube is a screen to filter out any large particles before the oil is pumped into the system. If the screen becomes clogged, oil will not move freely and low oil pressure will result. On most engines, the screen can be reached by removing the oil pan. Cleaning and reinstallation is simple.

4. Worn Bearings.

As bearings wear they become thinner. As they become thinner, there is more space for oil to fill, and pressure can be reduced because a larger volume is needed to fill the extra space.

Oil Loss Problems

Excessive oil consumption can result from something as obvious as an external oil leak. There are many gaskets and places where two parts of the engine are joined. There are oil seals around moving parts that leave the engine, such as the crankshaft ends. They can leak oil.

The most common places for oil leaks are around the oil filter, around the valve-cover and oil-pan gaskets, and around the oil drain plug in the bottom of the oil pan. Large amounts of fresh oil on the underside or running down the sides of the engine means a serious oil leak. This costs money, besides lowering the oil supply in the engine. Check for loose bolts, an oil filter that isn't secured, or broken gaskets.

The crankcase ventilation system can cause oil leaks by forcing "blow by" into the crankcase and forcing oil out. This PCV system is an arrangement of hoses and valves that directs crankcase vapor and pressure back into the intake manifold so they can be reburned. The check valve in the PCV system is a simple one-way valve used to prevent the reverse flow of gases. If it becomes plugged with dirt and sludge, it won't work. The pressure in the crankcase cannot be relieved, and oil can be forced out.

You can easily check the PCV valve. Locate the hose leading from the valve cover or the side of the crankcase to the base of the carburetor. At some point along this line you will find the PCV valve. Start the engine and allow it to warm up, then pinch the hose shut with a pair of pliers. Use flat-jawed pliers or you can damage the hose.

If the PCV system is working, the engine's idle speed will drop between 50 and 100 rpm. This is a drop in rpm that you will easily notice. It can be removed and cleaned very easily and the system should work again.

It is a good idea to merely replace the PCV valve with every tune-up.

If the PCV valve is badly clogged, it's a good idea to check the hose as well. It might be full of dirt and sludge.

The vacuum booster pump that operates equipment like the windshield wipers on many cars can suck oil vapor from the crankcase if the diaphragm inside is ruptured. The oil vapors or sent to the intake manifold area, and oil consumption will seem higher than it should be. Check this by turning on the windshield wipers. If they work, the diaphragm is in good shape. But if they stop when you accelerate the engine, the diaphragm probably needs to be replaced.

Internal oil consumption is usually the result of bad rings or bad valve guides. Both these parts act as internal oil seals and if they wear, oil consumption will increase. When oil is burned in the engine this is usually evident as a blue, smoky exhaust.

If this condition becomes serious enough, the engine will need to be torn down and rebuilt.

Chapter ELEVEN

Unscheduled Maintenance

By now your car should go any distance on any vacation you wish anywhere in the country. With no nagging worries about whether or not you're going to make it to your destination.

Air conditioning okay?

Check

New tapes for the cassette?

Check.

Cruise control working?

Check.

Power seats? Power windows? Credit cards?

Check. Check. Check.

These are your major worries, if you have any worries, and not whether the engine is going to give up the ghost, or the suspension is going to fail, or the tires are going to blow out.

It wasn't that way in the old days. Disposable diapers, collapsible strollers, and fast-food franchises weren't even sketches on the drawing board when Joseph M. Murdoch piled his family into a Packard touring car in 1908 and drove from Pasadena, California, to New York City. Only ten years before, the automobile, now a symbol of the American way of life, was so new that it was displayed as an oddity in traveling circuses. But the Murdochs were brave.

According to the Motor Vehicle Manufacturers Association,

243

Murdoch and his wife and three children became the first family to make the 3,674-mile cross-country journey. It may have been interesting, even fun, but it was a long, *long* journey in those days. It took the Murdochs thirty-two days, five hours, and thirty-five minutes, with Sundays off for resting—which they no doubt needed.

There were no interstate highways, no motels, no souvenir stands selling pink plastic wallets emblazoned with Mount Rushmore. What's more, the Murdochs took along a mechanic and a professional tour guide to ease the trip.

The broad vistas of the unspoiled American continent were their reward, and they enjoyed it. Still, the Murdochs were not the first to recognize the thrill of seeing the country by automobile.

"The finest sight I ever hope to see," said Walter Sebree in 1904 when he drove 400 miles in five days over Oregon's Blue Mountains. Sebree wrote in *Motor Age* magazine, "The best part of the trip was from LaGrande to Pendleton over the mountains.

"There were stumps in the road, and some places hardly any road, but we succeeded in averaging 12 miles an hour the whole distance. From the top of the mountains, some 7000 feet above Pendleton, we could look out for 100 miles and see nothing but wheat. The whole landscape was made up of different shades of yellow."

Two years later, another automobile enthusiast plunked down $1,500—a good piece of change in those days—for a twenty-horsepower, two-cylinder touring car which he promptly dubbed the "Get There." Lee Meriwether then described "the adventures of an average man with a motor car," as he related his 1200-mile journey from St. Louis to New York.

The "Get There" got him there, Meriwether reported, with only seven flat tires along the way. The first flat took three hours to repair and the seventh just thirty minutes, he wrote in *Outlook* magazine. "That is the difference between knowing and not knowing a lug from a valve-stem," he said.

The Southwest was untamed territory full of wild glories for the motorist in the early 1900s. This was a land untouched by freeways carrying station wagons, motorhomes and pop-up campers. This was a day of no bumper-to-bumper traffic and no road shoulders littered with broken beer bottles, candy wrappers, and paper cups.

"From Taos, New Mexico, we pushed through sand for many miles," Philip Delaney recalled in his article, "Frontiering in an Automobile," for *Outing* magazine. "The only living thing we saw was a gray coyote. But the desert was clean and sunny. At last we reached harder soil and green things growing. Indians greeted us on the way."

Delaney predicted that his trip "is only the beginning of automobile exploring and frontiering in the old West."

How right he was, though as late as 1940 there were few broad interstate highways crisscrossing the United States. A journey across the country meant hundreds of miles of two-lane "country" roads, with roadside gasoline stations at intersections and small towns with traffic signals. Traveling, or "frontiering in an automobile" as Delaney called it, was still a rugged pursuit, though the reliability of cars, tires, and accessories had vastly improved.

One man made frequent trips over a period of many years from Biloxi, on the Gulf Coast of Mississippi, to northern Ohio. The first of those journeys took days, then as the years passed the time dropped to a day, and finally to only a number of hours as automobiles and highways improved.

Today, traveling by automobile is a pleasure. Millions of Americans will vacation in an automobile this year. Estimates from the Motor Vehicle Manufacturers Association are that 1.4 *trillion-plus* miles will be added to odometers in city-to-city travels.

Camping along the way, in everything from spartan vans and station wagons to fancy motorhomes with all the comforts, will be common. Travelers will stop in rustic roadside rest stops and luxury campgrounds, as traveling continues to be a popular pastime for modern-day motorists.

They'll also be buying, renting, and borrowing dozens of different types of recreational vehicles. Many will be as fancy as the one Charles Lindbergh borrowed from Henry Ford. But they'll probably be returned sooner. Ford had built a show-piece vehicle for display purposes. He called it the "Stage Coach Trailer." It had electric lights, a stove, an ice box, a toilet, convertible beds, and closets.

Lindbergh borrowed it for a camping trip in 1942. He was obviously delighted with the new-fangled recreational vehicle. He didn't return it until 1957.

Can you guess where the word "automobile" comes from? The word was first used in France in the late 1880s. It comes from the Greek word *auto*, meaning "self," and the French word *mobile*, meaning "moving." Today, more than twenty-five million American families, or more than two-fifths of the nation's car-owning families, own more than one automobile.

The typical American-made car weighs about 3,345 pounds. This total includes 2,098 pounds of steel, 468 pounds of iron, 173 pounds of rubber, 90 pounds of glass, 21 pounds of plastics, and 10 pounds of paint and other protective coatings.

About four out of every five American adults are licensed drivers who drive an average of 9000 miles per year.

BACK TO BUSINESS

OK, let's get serious about this car maintenance stuff. If you have come this far and haven't skinned too many knuckles or endured too many sutures, you're ready for the big time. There are many jobs on a car that are often automatically left to skilled mechanics. But by now, you are becoming a skilled mechanic yourself.

These are jobs that require more time and, in most cases, more skill with tools and supplies. But they can be done by the skilled weekend mechanic to the tune of many dollars saved. These are the jobs for which the labor charge often exceeds the charge for parts. Yet these are not really difficult jobs, though they do take time and planning. And they might require that you buy some supplies before you start.

Think about it. When many drivers hear that their shocks are shot, or their muffler is on its last muffle, or when they see a dent in their fender or a burn in their upholstery, they usually think of how much a mechanic is going to charge to fix things, then they put off the job. Their horn won't stop blowing, or won't honk at all, or their carburetor gums up, and they call a garage. When they see a fan belt going to pot, they look at all the pulleys and decide to wait till tomorrow. Clutch slipping? They call a mechanic.

But not you.

After reading this chapter, you should be able to handle these chores and more all by yourself.

Replacing Shock Absorbers

Car bouncing after every bump? The job of the shocks is not so much to soften the ride as to react with the springs to dampen any bounce. The car's body rests on the frame through the springs. The shocks are not there to carry the weight of the body, but to dampen the action of the springs. The movement of a piston in the oil-filled cylinder of a shock absorber is carefully controlled by valves and holes inside the chamber.

It is possible, with a combination of shocks that are worn out and a rough railroad crossing, to set up a bounce that can result in the wheels leaving the ground. You can guess the amount of control you have over the car in this situation.

How do you know the condition of your shocks? Try this.

Put your hands flat on the fenders, one fender at a time, and set up a bouncing motion. The car should bounce up after each push down. That's normal. But the moment you stop pushing, the car should stop bouncing, with perhaps one last little motion to stabilize itself. If it does, the shock on that corner of the car is working as it should. Try each corner and if you get the same result, don't worry, your shocks are healthy.

But if the car bounces one or more times after you have stopped pushing it, they are weak and need replacing. Not only are they dangerous, but they are costing you in extra tire wear. You can also take a look at each shock at each corner of the car. Put the car in park or in gear, set the parking brake, and stick your head down under each fender. If you see signs of leakage (shock absorbers are full of oil, even air-type shocks), the seals are gone and the shocks should be replaced.

You can also drive on a smooth road at about ten miles per hour, then repeatedly tap the brakes. If you set up a rocking motion in which the front dips and the rear rises, the shocks are defective.

Shock absorbers are complicated devices, but they are not that difficult to replace.

First, get the replacement shocks from your service station or auto parts store. They come in a variety of prices and qualities. For this chapter, let's ignore the air-type shocks or the shocks with coil springs around them to help support the load, though you might consider them if you carry extra loads in your car. The air-type shock absorber can be pumped up with air to help raise the body higher off the ground, the coil-spring type carries part of the load, but they do the same job of dampening the action of the springs as the car rolls down the road. All shock absorbers are replaced in the same manner (though the air-type does have extra air hoses connecting each shock to an air nipple for adjusting the pressure inside).

It is always better to buy quality shock absorbers, something your car probably didn't come with when it was brand new. Manufacturers have a habit of installing just enough shock absorber to do the job and little more. The heavy-duty type will probably work well as a replacement for the average car with a suspension in otherwise good condition.

If you think these units don't work hard at what they do— stopping the motion of the springs by turning the energy into heat (the oil inside gets very hot) and dissipating it—look at an off-road racer. This is a vehicle that is subjected to rough roads, or no roads at all, with the body constantly moving and jerking on the springs. These cars use two shocks, or even *four* shocks, at each corner. Even then some of them have been known to overheat to the extent of *melting*. Shock absorbers on a car are working hard and working constantly to keep the ride smooth and level.

You can improve on the original when you install new shock absorbers, and it's a good idea. You'll notice when you go shopping for shocks that you will be offered a choice. There will be several that will be the right size for your car, but each will be of different quality. Buy the good ones.

Installing them will require that the car be up on blocks, or better yet, on a hoist. But that isn't all. You'll need another way to lift the wheels as you work on each corner, to compress the spring and take the strain off the shock on that corner so that you can remove and replace it. At a garage they hoist the car on its frame, then jack the axles up with a separate jack to lift the springs. With the strain off the shocks they'll be in a "neutral" situation, not stretched or compressed.

Remove the upper bolts, washers, and rubber bushings from the shaft that usually projects up into the upper fender area in the engine compartment. With most shocks you will use one wrench on the specially shaped stud while you use another wrench to remove the nut. You may not need any nut-loosening "liquid wrench" for this connection, but you might need it on the bottom, where the joint has been exposed to more weather and dirt. The bottom of a shock is connected with a bolt through rubber bushings and this alignment job is where you'll need the flexibility of moving the axle up and down. You can also extend and compress the shock itself to help with the alignment. Shock absorbers react to slow movements easily but the oil and seals inside work to dampen any quick movements. So you can slowly compress or expand them with muscle power. It isn't difficult at all.

Align each shock absorber, one at a time. Make sure the upper bolt is back in its seat through new grommets and washers, then shove the lower bolt through new washers and bushings to hold it in place, and you have it. Once the top and bottom nuts are secure, the job is done. Be sure you don't tighten them so much that the washers are squeezing the bushings to the point that they protrude beyond the exterior circumference of the washers.

Remove the axle jack and go to the next wheel.

Only one shock bad? It is best to replace shocks in pairs, even though only one appears to be weak. Generally, the other one on the other side of the car, front or rear, is on the ragged edge and will probably fail soon anyhow.

Replacing the Battery

You come out in the morning and hit the starter. You get a click, or a slow grind that finally just stops. Where do you go? The battery, and sooner or later the old bus is going to need a new battery. This is another place where you get what you pay for. Batteries come in several price ranges. The more it costs, as a general rule, the better it is and the more dependable service it will give. Better batteries will be more powerful and give you more "cold cranking power" for starting the car under adverse weather conditions, or when the engine is flooded or somewhat out of tune.

Cheap batteries will work, but they won't work nearly as long and they won't work nearly as well.

How do you know if you need a new one? One good indication, but not the only one, is when the car responds with a click when you try to start it. There can be other problems, but this is a good indication that the battery has provided the last of its power. A car's battery, though, does not *make* electric power to operate the car, it only *stores* it and provides it as needed. The electric power is made by the car's alternator and regulated by its voltage regulator. So at least at this point, the problem could be elsewhere.

As a first step, check the electrolyte level in the cells, unless the battery is sealed. A battery won't accept a charge if the level, which should be easily visible at the bottom of the filler tubes, is low. If it is low, add water, distilled if possible (though ordinary tap water will work in a modern battery if distilled water is not available). If the water level is below the top of the plates, permanent damage has occurred. Next, try cleaning and tightening the battery terminals. Do this just as you learned earlier in this book on pages 177–78. Take each terminal connector off its post, clean both the post and the connector, then reconnect each one. Always remove the ground cable first and install it last.

With a voltage tester, you can check the output of the alternator to be sure electricity is being fed to the battery. One indication of a failure here, or with the battery, is that the red "charging" light comes on when the engine is running, or the ammeter drops into the "discharge" range. If the voltage regulator is shot, you will also get an indication on the meter or light. But voltage regulators, especially the modern electronic ones, are usually reliable. Generally speaking, the battery (or the battery terminals) are at fault.

Replacing a battery is almost as simple as changing the batteries in your flashlight, though the job requires a little more muscle. Remove the terminals, the ground terminal $(-)$ first and then the positive terminal $(+)$ next. Once they are off, the danger from sparks is greatly reduced. A word of caution. When you remove the ground cable, place it where the terminal clamp doesn't touch any other grounded point on the car. If it does, you can still get a strong spark until the positive terminal is removed. Some batteries have their terminals on the side (as is the case with most modern "no maintenance" batteries), but most have them on the top.

Battery terminal bolts can seem to be welded to the clamps, so work gently. A battery can be ruined with a cracked case or a broken post if you lay on too much muscle doing this simple job. Once the bolts are loosened, a screwdriver can be used to gently pry the clamp apart enough to lift it off the post.

Batteries are held in their pan in a variety of ways, but most often it will be a metal collar around the top of the battery held in place by long bolts which are attached to the bottom of the pan and extend above the top harness. Though the battery is heavy, it must be held in place securely or it might bounce when the car is in motion. Remove the upper bolts and the metal collar, the lift the battery from its pan. Watch how you lift it. More mechanics' backs have "gone out" lifting the dead weight of a heavy battery from an engine compartment than for any other reason.

Place the new battery into the pan with the positive and negative posts in the same locations as the old ones. If you have purchased the right one, it will fit exactly. Attach and tighten the hold-down bolts, working them together rather than tightening one all the way down then going to the other. You want the upper metal collar to fit evenly around the top of the new battery with equal pressure all the way around.

Then set the clean, bright battery-post clamps down on bright posts, positive to positive first, then negative to negative. Tighten, but do not overtighten, since the risk still exists of damaging the posts or case with too much tightening.

Replacing the Muffler

Car sound like a tractor, or semitruck? Getting evil looks from pedestrians when you pass through a neighborhood? Nurses throwing bedpans at you as you drive through a hospital zone? Receiving more than casual interest from police? Your muffler is probably shot and you must face the problem of replacing it. Take a look at it to be certain, since this is not a pleasant, easy, intellectual job. The problem could even be in your exhaust pipe, or your tail pipe, or (and we all hope not) in the exhaust header from the engine.

This latter part is difficult to remove.

You can trace down the leak in the exhaust system, though, and it will probably be the muffler, the thinnest and weakest point.

Replacing it can be more a matter of brawn than brain. Mufflers, and exhaust systems in general, can weld themselves into a single unit, yet you must remove one part of this unit and replace it. It is a dirty job, but it can be done. The first step is to buy a new muffler. You'll need to know the model and year of your car. The muffler will be available at any auto parts store, and with it looking so bright and new the job might appear to be simple. You could be lucky. It might be.

Mufflers also come in a variety of qualities, exhaust sounds, and guarantees. Get a standard muffler unless you are into heavy exhaust noises that make your car sound like a race car.

Raise the car up as high as you can, on a hoist if possible, then loosen the clamps holding the old muffler in place. They might come loose easily, especially if you spray them with penetrating oil and allow them to soak a little. But they may not. If you must, chisel them off and replace them with new clamps. You might even have to chisel the old muffler off, but fortunately the muffler parts are thinner than the pipes on either end, so a chisel will probably cut the right stuff.

Be careful of dirt and grit falling into your eyes if you are working with the car on a hoist. The insides of a used muffler and tailpipe are dirty with old carbon and other by-products of burning fuel. Eye protection is recommended for all auto repair and service, but it is a must when doing this sort of work.

You'll have to wrestle the new muffler into place and tighten the clamps to hold it. Mufflers only go in one way, so follow the directions or the arrows indicating the flow of gases. Once it is in and secure, the job is done and the car should sound brand new. It'll also be much safer to drive, since gases from a leaking muffler can enter the driving compartment and create a hazardous situation.

Replacing the Fuel Pump

The gasoline from the tank must be moved to the carburetor, where it is mixed with air and sent to the intake manifold. It is moved by a mechanical fuel pump, unless you have an electric fuel pump, which is either very routine (if the pump is out in the open) or very difficult (if the pump is inside the fuel tank) to replace. The mechanical fuel pump generally sticks out on one side of the front of the engine.

You can check the operation of your fuel pump by removing the fuel line where it enters the carburetor. Aim the end of the fuel line into a container then have a friend start the engine on the gasoline remaining in the carburetor float bowl. A healthy pump should deliver a stream of gasoline amounting to about a pint in thirty seconds on a V-8, or forty-five seconds on a four- or six-cylinder car. This while the engine is idling.

No squirting gasoline? Before you tear into the fuel pump, check for a clogged fuel filter between the pump and the gas tank. Also look for a restricted fuel line or, on an electric fuel pump, a problem with the circuitry.

In all cases, be very careful of fuel squirting out on hot engine parts.

Most mechanical fuel pumps work by an arm that rides on an eccentric cam on the camshaft inside the engine. As the arm moves in and out, the diaphragm in the pump sucks in fuel from the tank and shoves it onto the carburetor. When the arm is in, the diaphragm is flexed downward and fuel is drawn from the tank. A spring in the pump shoves the arm outward and the fuel is pumped up to the carburetor.

The exact mechanical way your pump works isn't too important, since almost all fuel pumps are sealed. If they fail, you replace them. Replacing just the diaphragm isn't logical or efficient. If no fuel squirts, the pump is probably bad, most often caused by a ruptured diaphragm. Replacing a fuel pump is not all that difficult, since it is bolted to the side of the engine and only a few things need to be removed.

Remove the fuel lines from the intake and exit sides of the pump. You'll need two wrenches for this job, one for the nut on the pump and the other for the hex nut on the end of the fuel line. Then locate and remove the two (or possibly more) bolts holding the pump to the side of the engine block. The pump can then be easily lifted off.

The new pump goes on the same way the old one came off. Be sure the matching surfaces are clean of any dirt, oil, or grit, and be sure the gasket between the pump and the block is flat and properly located. Then install and tighten the bolts holding the pump to the block. Remember that the activating arm must be located correctly, riding on the cam inside the block. If the arm is below or behind the cam, it won't follow and the pump won't operate. If the pump goes into place easily, you can be confident that the arm is in the right place.

On many General Motors engines, particularly Chevrolet, there is a plunger between the arm and the cam. The cam pushes on the plunger, which pushes on the fuel pump arm. When you remove the old pump, the plunger drops down and there is very little room in this area for fingers. Try greasing the plunger with some heavy grease, lifting it into position, and installing the pump. The grease may hold the plunger in position until the pump arm is in place. Or you can try holding it with wire while you get the pump in place then pulling the wire out before you tighten things.

Tighten the holding bolts evenly, now one and then the other, and reattach the two fuel lines, one from the fuel tank and the other to the carburetor.

Replacing the Water Pump

This job is a bit more complicated, especially in a modern car where there isn't much room to work between the front of the engine, where the water pump is located, and the backside of the radiator. How do you know the pump is bad and needs replacing?

Don't believe it when a "mechanic" tells you that because your fan is freewheeling the water pump is shot. The one has nothing to do with the other, except that the fan is often attached to the front of the water-pump shaft. Most modern fans have a clutch that allows them to freewheel when the car is moving forward. This gives the engine just as much cooling since the air is flowing through the radiator and saves horsepower that might have been used to turn the fan.

If the engine has been overheating and you have been losing water around the pump bearing, it's time for a change.

The problem might be in that you must remove the radiator before you can work on the pump with any convenience at all. Once you can get to it (use a socket wrench with no extension at all and work from above) it isn't that difficult to remove the bolts holding the pump to the front of the engine block. Flip the fan belt off the pulley before you start. If the fan is attached to the front of the pump, remove it first. Prepare for some coolant splashing around, since you will be breaking the seal between the pump and the block. Better yet, drain the system before you start, and save the coolant if it is new and you plan to reuse it.

You'll see a matching surface on the pump and the engine block with a gasket between. Clean the surfaces then mount the gasket on the engine block with some gasket seal. Finally, hold the new pump in place while you install the bolts, tightening them finger-tight first, then the same way you tighten a wheel, alternately.

Remount the fan, reinstall the pulley, and check it for proper tension. You're back in business.

Replacing Drive Belts

Most engines have two, three, or four drive belts wrapped around various pulleys of different sizes on different accessories. Belts drive the alternator, the water pump/fan, power-steering pump, air-conditioner compressor, and antipollution air pump.

Obviously, if a drive belt has broken it must be replaced. But belts can deteriorate from use, from poor adjustment, or from oil or road debris splashed up into the engine compartment. If you see signs of deterioration, it's time to replace the belt. Twist the belts and look at the undersides. If they appear glazed, it's time to replace them.

Before you begin, be sure you have the right new belt ready for installation. Your old belt might have cogs or ribs. The width of the belt must be the same as well or it won't fit properly into the V-groove of the pulley. The power comes from the sides of the pulley to the sides of the belt, so it must fit into the pulley groove not too deeply, nor too shallow.

To remove a belt, you must release the tension on it. The usual way to tension a belt is by moving one of the accessories that that belt drives. This is done by adjusting a bolt in an elongated slot in the accessory bracket. As a general rule, slacken this bolt and one other mounting bolt and the accessory will move. Or there might be an idler pulley just for tensioning the belt. Loosen it and the belt will slacken for removal.

To install the new belt, fit it around the pulleys. On some engines it is possible to put the belt on the wrong pulleys, since there may be extras (especially around the front of the crankshaft).

Once the belt is on, it must be retensioned. With the elongated slot-type of tensioning, use a prybar to move the accessory back into position then tighten the holding nut bolt. Finally, tighten the other accessory holding nut. On some cars there is a hole in the accessory's mounting bracket for the purpose of prying it to tighten the drive belt.

Remember that drive belts, especially new ones, tend to stretch when they are put into service. But most of this stretch occurs in the first few minutes of driving. So take a brief test drive, then recheck the tension of the belts you have changed. If you don't have a gauge for checking the tension, press down on the belt with your finger halfway between the pulleys. You want no more than a half inch of give in the belt.

Automatic Choke Service

An automatic choke that sticks open will make a car hard to start, especially in cold weather. A choke that sticks closed will cause extra gasoline to be pumped through and result in significant loss of fuel mileage.

To check your choke, and this is best done when the temperature is lower than fifty degrees, remove the air cleaner. Look at the choke plate in the throat of the carburetor. The choke plate should cover the top of the carburetor barrel. If it does not, floor the gas pedal and the choke plate should snap shut.

If this doesn't happen, reach in and move the choke plate by hand. If it seems sticky and won't move freely, the choke should be cleaned.

If the choke plate did snap shut completely, put the air cleaner back on and drive the car around the block a couple of times to warm the engine. Then remove the air cleaner again. The choke plate should now be vertical, completely open. If it didn't move, or moved only partially, try moving it by hand, looking for stickiness of motion.

A sticking choke or dirty carburetor can cause hard starting, rough running, stalling, and poor fuel economy. Carburetor cleaning sprays may solve the problem, and they're easy to use. Just follow the directions on the can.

If the choke has an external diaphragm, watch the link to that diaphragm as somebody else starts the engine. If the diaphragm doesn't pull the link, check for a good hose connection. If that seems secure, unscrew and replace the diaphragm.

If the diaphragm moves the link but not enough to fully open the choke on a warm engine, an adjustment of the linkage might correct the problem.

Ordinarily, the choke will be sticking because it is dirty. With a can of choke cleaner spray the plate, its shaft, and the entire external linkage that moves when you operate the choke plate by hand. You can get some at your service station or auto parts store. This solvent and lubricant should free up the choke plate and linkage.

Carburetor Service

Most modern carburetors will work for years without problems. The best rule is: Leave it alone. But there is an exception to this. Clean the carburetor periodically (and of course replace fuel and air filters regularly).

There are gasoline additives on the market that are said to clean the inside of the carburetor, and they might work. You merely pour a can of the stuff into your fuel tank and drive normally. Yet there is a better way, though it takes a little more effort, to clean your carburetor.

First, spray the outside after removing the air cleaner. Spray inside the barrel. Use a carburetor cleaner, or even a choke cleaner, for this job. Hit the linkages with the same aerosol solvent. You are, hopefully, saving a full professional carburetor teardown and rebuild, and if you do this often enough (every 30,000 miles or so) you might save it for the life of the carburetor.

But there's more. Disconnect the fuel line at the carburetor and plug it up with a stopper. Then attach a suitable fitting and a hose from an on-the-car cleaning kit. Attach the can of pure solvent to the other end of the hose, hold the can upright, and run the engine at idle until the contents of the can are gone. If the carb has not been cleaned in years, run two cans through it.

If the engine won't run on the solvent, try mixing it 50-50 with gasoline. After this two-pronged job, the carburetor should be clean as a pin inside and outside and ready for many more thousands of miles of efficiency.

Horn Problems

Automobile horns either won't blow, or they blow all the time, or they blow with a weak little squeak that wouldn't warn anybody. The horn in a car blows when a relay switch closes to allow current to flow to the horn, which is a spring-loaded electrical device operated by a pair of electrical contact points that are part of another electromagnet. Confused? Don't worry about it.

The contact points are normally closed and when current flows through them an electromagnet is formed that pulls them apart, breaking the circuit. The diaphragm spring then pulls them back together and the electromagnet is again formed. This happens many times per second, and each time the diaphragm flexes it makes a sound. A cone-shaped metal section then amplifies the sounds, which occur so fast that the result is one continuous blast of noise.

None of this current can flow until the original relay is electrically grounded, and that is what the horn button does.

First, find the horn. It is under the hood and easily spotted. The horn relay is a little more difficult to find, but it is a little metal can either plugged into the fuse box or taped to the wiring harness somewhere near the fuse box. If you find it now, whenever you have a problem you will know where to look. You can be sure by pulling one of the bayonet clips off the horn then having someone press the horn button. The relay will click and you will know which unit it is.

The worst problem comes when the horn won't stop blowing. This generally happens in the middle of the night, or in a quiet zone. First, pull off one of the bayonet clips on the wires leading to the horn. That will stop the noise while you collect yourself. You can also remove the ground wire from the battery if that seems easier at the time. Then pull off one of the horn wires and reconnect the battery.

Press the horn button. If the relay doesn't click, the problem is in either the horn button or the relay. You can tell which it is by having a friend disconnect the battery ground cable, then touch it to the post again and again as you listen to the relay. If you hear it click, the problem is in the button. If it doesn't click under this condition, the problem is that the relay is stuck.

If the problem is in the horn button, it could be the type that is built into the steering wheel and you might want to consider a remote horn button rather than a new (and expensive) steering wheel. Just clip off the wire from the relay, solder on a new, longer wire, and run it to a new horn button you can attach to the steering column. Then run another wire from the horn button to ground.

If the problem is in the relay, replace it. They are inexpensive.

If the horn won't blow, the problem is usually in the horn relay, a defective horn button, or a defective horn. To check the horn, just run a wire from it directly to the battery. If it blows, it is working fine.

With the horn still disconnected, press the button and listen for the click in the relay. If it doesn't click, replace the relay. If the horn and relay check out, your problem is with the horn button and you might consider installing a remote button.

If the horn sounds weak, the problem is with the horn itself. You could just throw it away and install a new horn, or you might have a horn with an adjustment screw. It'll have a lock nut around it. With everything connected, turn the screw counterclockwise until the horn just stops blowing, then clockwise until the sound is clear. You'll be a nervous wreck if you try to make these adjustments while the horn is blowing, so turn a little then blow the horn, then turn a little more until you get it the way you want it.

If the horn works part of the time and doesn't work part of the time, the problem is in the wiring and you'll have to check it out to see where the short is. It is a simple circuit and the short should be obvious.

Adjusting a Manual Clutch

A manual clutch is a device to permit the car to stop while the engine is running by disconnecting the engine from the drive shaft. It also permits gear changing.

The main part of a clutch is the friction plate, a disc with friction material on both sides. This disc always turns with the transmission shaft, but it can be moved fore and aft on the transmission shaft. A large plate called the pressure plate fits over the friction disc and is bolted to the engine flywheel. When the clutch is engaged, spring fingers on the pressure plate press on the friction disc and hold it firmly to the flywheel. Power from the engine can flow to the transmission.

When you step on the clutch, you can separate the engine from the transmission through a series of linkages. A throwout bearing moves the pressure-plate fingers, disengaging them from the friction disc, and the connection between the transmission and the flywheel is broken.

Problems can develop when the pressure-plate spring fingers lose some of their grip, or when the friction disc surface wears down or becomes contaminated with grease.

You step on the gas and the engine speeds up, but the car seems to lag behind where it should be. The clutch is "slipping" and the only real cure is to replace the clutch, generally a job for a professional mechanic.

But if the clutch is slipping for another reason, you can do something about it. Test it this way. If you slowly depress the clutch, you'll feel a point at which something is happening, something is pushing against something. Up to that point is said to be "free play" in the clutch. Free play should be no more than about 3/4 to 1 3/8 inches on most cars. If there is no free play, the clutch might not be fully engaging. If there is too much free play, the spring fingers may not be fully depressing. Then the friction disc is never really disengaged and the friction disc will quickly wear out. When you try to shift gears, the transmission shaft will not be fully stopped, as it is when the clutch is fully disengaged, and parts in the transmission shaft will clash. Also, since the throwout bearing is in constant contact with the spring fingers, it will wear out prematurely.

You can help to prevent these problems with a clutch-linkage adjustment. The procedure will depend on the type of car you have, but generally you will have to jack up the front of the car and support it on safety stands. Ask a helper to work the clutch pedal in and out so that you can find the clutch linkage. You'll then see the adjustment screws to fiddle with. As with most linkage adjustments, you might not hit it the first time, but it will either be better or worse. That'll tell you which way to go on a second, or even third try, until you get the free play just right.

Once you do this job, the next time will be routine, and you'll be adding years to the life of your clutch.

Automatic Transmission Maintenance

When an automatic transmission goes away, it is an expensive proposition. Generally, they will want to rebuild it, and that might be just what is needed. There are a couple of routine procedures you can do that will add years to the life of your automatic.

They aren't difficult. They involve changing the oil and the filter inside the transmission. This is an interesting job for a weekend mechanic who doesn't mind getting under the car. As you know, oil in a transmission can wear out from overheating and other hard use, and the filter in a transmission continues to collect debris in this unit with complex inner workings.

At the bottom of the transmission is an oil pan. It will be

obvious on your transmission if you have the car on a lift or up on safety stands. It is the flat, bolted-on bottom pan. Place a large pan just under the transmission, bringing it as close as possible to the oil pan.

As you remove the screws from around the pan, oil will begin to seep out, so as you remove it be careful that the oil goes into the drain pan. It might appear that gallons of oil are coming out, but the fact is only a fraction of the oil in the transmission comes out when the pan is removed (about 2 1/2 to 3 1/2 quarts as a general rule). But when this much oil is replaced, it is enough to rejuvenate the remaining oil inside.

You'll see the screen or filter, which can be removed when you unscrew the screws that are holding it. You'll also see, if you inspect the old filter, bits of debris that it has removed from the system.

Install the new screen or filter, then check the mating surfaces on the pan and body of the transmission to be sure they are clean. Place the new gasket on the pan, then lift the pan to the transmission and install the screws. Tighten them in a crisscross fashion just as you do a wheel, or you can start in the center and work out to the end on both sides of the pan.

Put as much new oil into the transmission as you have drained out the bottom. If you aren't sure, add oil, then start the engine, put the transmission in park or neutral, and check the dipstick. You want the oil level to be at the full mark.

Finally, start the engine and have a helper shift back and forth through all the positions on the transmission as you watch underneath for any evidence of oil leaks.

Some transmissions utilize a "vacuum modulator" to help regulate shifting. It is connected by a hose to the base of the carburetor or the intake manifold and screwed into the side of the transmission. If your car is rough shifting, disconnect the vacuum hose and ream it out with a pipe cleaner. If it comes out dirty, replace the modulator, which is leaking. It is an inexpensive part that can be replaced with a wrench or even with pliers.

Repairing Paint Chips

Touch-up paint is a great invention, but you must work slowly and carefully, and if you expect the job to be almost professional, use the *right* paint. The trick is to fill the chip, not to

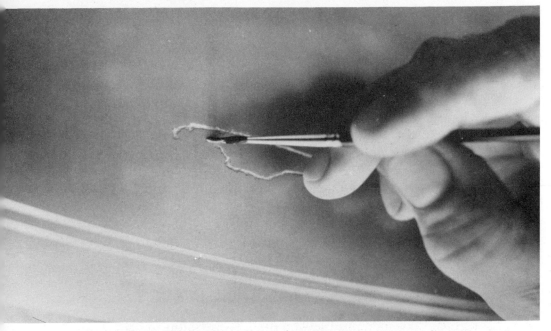

Touch-up paint is a great invention. It'll take care of many small scratches.

paint over the whole area. This can mean repeated applications, allowing plenty of time for drying between, before the job is complete. So go slow and easy.

Any auto parts store worth its salt can match your paint with touch-up paint if you give them the year, make, and model of your car and the original paint color. The original color is important, since they have charts at the store.

Chances are the paint will come in a small vial with a little brush. First, clean the surface you intend to fix. You don't want wax or any dirt in the small ding. Shake the bottle thoroughly, then shake it again. The paint should be well mixed or the job won't look good.

Remember, the idea is to *fill* the ding, not cover the original paint, so barely touch the end of the brush in the paint. Then, working very carefully, touch the brush to the damaged area. Allow the paint to flow into the ding, not around it. This is not a quickie job if you want it to be as neat as possible. When the paint has filled and covered the damage, stop.

Look at the bottle. It will tell how long it takes to dry. Give it that much time and more, until the paint you have applied is completely dry. Don't panic if it isn't a perfect match. The color on your car has probably faded a little, so the repair will get better with age.

Try the same technique again, working just as carefully, to add more paint to the ding. If you get out of the damaged area, wipe it off and start again. Do this as many times as it takes to completely fill the chipped area, a job that might take all week. But your patience will be rewarded. As the area completely dries, it will fade into the car's surface, and where it might not be as good as completely repainting the car, it will do.

You can even repair long scratches in this manner. Suppose your car has been "keyed" by some restless vandal who envies your station in life as reflected by the beautiful vehicle you drive. So a long, ugly scratch results.

Work the same way. One of the tricks, directly from Harrah's vintage-car experts, is to use a brush that is smaller than the scratch. For example, use a sixteenth-inch brush for an eighth-inch scratch.

Try a squeegee technique, filling the scratch then going over the surface with a sharp-edged cardboard and a clean rag to scrape and clean up any excess outside the scratch. Such a repair, with a little time to "cure," can be almost invisible. And you will have saved several hundred dollars.

Repairing Minor Dents

OK, it happens. You've taken great care of your car's finish. Then a rock flies up from the wheels of a semitruck and dents the body. Or you carelessly run into a fence post, or open your door at the wrong time and hit something hard. This is more than a ding, it has become a *dent*.

The trouble is, the paint is damaged to the point that the bare metal will begin to rust if something isn't done. Besides, it looks so tacky. You can fix it yourself and do a near-professional job if you take your time.

The first job is to carefully pound out the dent. This sounds much more involved than it is. You might even try pulling it out with a bathroom plunger. Or if the dent is small, you might want to just leave it there and proceed directly to the section on filling with plastic body filler on pages 268–69.

If you are going to pound out the dent from behind, get a hand-dolly anvil for a few dollars. Hit the dent from the rear

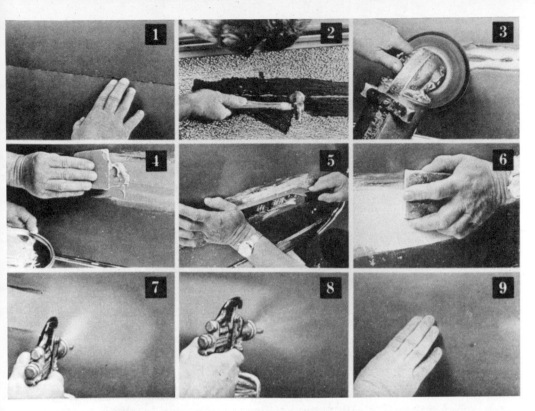

Can you fix a dent yourself and save money? Yes, if it's a relatively minor dent. Remember that a little dent can mean a lot of work. You just have to decide whether it's worth doing yourself. Here are the steps I use (pictured above): 1) Carefully determine the extent of the damage. 2) To take the dent out, try to get behind it and pop it out with your hand, or tap it out with a mallet or hammer. If you can't, you will probably have to drill holes and use a "dent puller." 3) Sand the damaged area to bare metal. (Safety eyeglasses should be used here too.) 4) Fill with premixed filler. 5) While the filler is still "cheesy," use a "cheese grater" file to form the general contour. If imperfections remain, reapply filler and file again. 6) Block sand with #80 dry paper. "Feather edge" the filler and old paint into the metal. If necessary, apply more filler and resand. Then block-sand with #220. 7) Wipe surface clean. Apply primer and let dry. Blocksand with #320 paper. Repeat until all coarser scratches have disappeared and all bare metal has been primed. 8) Hand sand lightly with wet #400 paper. Clean large area with solvent to remove wax, then paint. After paint is thoroughly dry, rub lightly with fine rubbing compound to smooth and polish. 9) If you've used the right tools, with enough time and patience, you should see a job well done. A dent like the one in the photo could cost around $150 if repaired by a body shop. Reference books are available with more details on body repair.

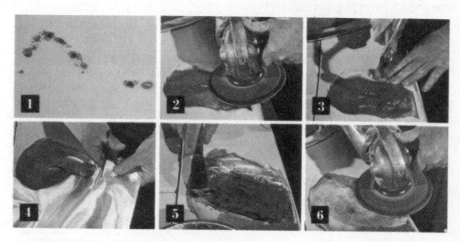

1. Rust holes on fender 2. Sand the rusted area to bare metal with #24 grit coarse sandpaper. 3. Depress the area to allow for the thickness of the patch. 4. After the fiberglass patch has been cut to size, saturate it with resin and hardener mix. 5. Put it in place, work out all the air bubbles with a spreader and allow to harden. (For extra safety wear rubber gloves and safety eyeglasses.) 6. Then sand again and follow steps 4 to 9 in the illustration on dent repair.

with the dolly. This will cause a bulge on the outside of the dent. To get a relatively smooth surface that you can work with, hold the dolly at the back of the dent and hammer down the front bulge. The metal has stretched from the original dent, and you'll have to work with it. Hit it again from the rear, then from the front, until you get a relatively smooth surface.

It is also possible with some dents to drill holes and use a "dent puller" from outside to pull the metal back up to where it should be.

None of this is helping the painted surface, of course, but we'll worry about that later.

Use a straight edge such as a yardstick to keep a check on the uniformity of your work. Continue to work on the damaged surface until you get it as smooth as possible, then sand away all the ruined paint and primer in and around the pounded-out area. Unless you are the world's greatest pounder, you're going to have some irregularities in the surface to fill. Most auto body fillers have to be mixed before they are used, so follow the mixing directions very carefully. They will be on the container of the filler.

Using a putty knife, spread the filler on the area. Take a rubber squeegee and mold the filler into the dents. Use your artistic skills here to move the filler about until it is as smooth as possible, filling the low points in the damaged area but not bulging up over the high points. Most fillers will harden in a half hour or so.

Using a rasp, remove the excess filler then start sanding the area. Begin with a #36 grit production sandpaper and finish with a #100 grit paper until the area is smooth as glass.

Mask off the surrounding areas and spray on a primer coat. Be careful. Many spray cans of paint and primer will spatter at first, so test the spray on a piece of paper before you aim at the surface you are repairing. It is usually best to hold the can about a foot from the surface and, holding the button down, spray once across the surface. Then shut off the spray. Begin again, going across the surface. You don't want the primer to build up each time you change directions. Apply the primer very thinly, two or three times, allowing the coat to dry between applications. Drying will take about a half hour.

The next step is very important. You must wet sand the primer coat. As you sand, keep a trickle of water from a garden hose running down across the area under repair so that the sandpaper doesn't dig into the primer but floats across the surface. Sand smoothly in one direction only, and apply only a minimal pressure. Start with #360 grit sandpaper then switch to #400 grit for final finishing.

Allow the primer to dry for at least twenty-four hours before the next step.

You have obtained the correct color in spray cans from your dealer or auto parts store by giving the year, make, model, and color of your car. If your car is "Sunburst Red" or "Evening Gray" or some other exotic color, state that color and not simply bright red or metallic gray. They have books they can look in to find the exact match. Once again mask off the surrounding areas, then hold the can (which you have pre-sprayed to get rid of spatter) about a foot from the area and move across as you spray. This will be the first of five coats you plan to put on the damage.

Once you have started, keep going. Don't stop or you'll have a runny spot in the paint and they are difficult to hide. Spray thinly. You should still be able to see the color of the primer coat after the *third* coat of paint. That's how thin these coats of paint should be. Wait ten minutes after the first coat, then increase the waiting time between coats. Plan to wait at least twenty-four hours before the next step to allow the paint to dry thoroughly.

If you find flecks or bubbles in the paint when you return the next day, don't panic. Just get some #600 grit sandpaper and wet sand the area very gently.

You want the same high gloss on the repaired area that you have on the rest of the car. The way to get it is with rubbing. Use a rubbing compound on a soft cloth pad and start rubbing at the edges of the repair in a circular motion. As the area begins to match up, move inward into the center of the repaired area. Don't bear down and don't rub any more than is necessary. When the rubbing is done, wax the entire area and the job is done.

An Easier Way

There are repair kits on the market today and they will do a reasonable job of getting rid of a damaged area on a car's body. These patching kits usually contain plastic body filler paste, a bridging material such as fiberglass sheets, powder and hardener, sand papers, and applicators. All but the painting can be handled in a different, easier way.

Meanwhile, the repair can be sanded, primed, and painted exactly like the original metal. In fact, some of the manufacturers claim that the repair is stronger than the original metal.

The area to be patched must be clean of all paint, dirt, grease, or anything else. It must be sanded to bright metal extending beyond the damage. If you can depress all of the metal where the damage is, so much the better since you will be filling.

The fiberglass sheet included with the kit should be cut to a piece large enough to cover the damage with perhaps an inch or so of overlap.

Mix the epoxy according to the directions with the kit. If you go the wrong way with one ingredient, the mixture won't harden. If you go the other way, it will harden too soon. Wet the fiberglass with the mixture and lay it on the damaged surface. Work out any bubbles with a spatula, bearing in mind that if the damage is severe you might want to use a second or third fiberglass sheet to cover. Work out the air bubbles each time, striving for a smooth surface. The fiberglass will bond best to bare metal. Remember, this surface you are smoothing is the final, hard surface you will finish. The fiberglass should cure and harden so that a fingernail scratch won't show.

When that happens, you can finish the repair the same way you did before. The surface can be treated just like metal. It is best to do all of these repairs at room temperature, certainly not on a cold, damp day.

Handling Rusted-out Spots

A repair kit works better than anything for a spot on your car that has rusted through. The fiberglass cloth, after curing, can be treated just like metal. So cut away the ragged, rusty edges, sand away the paint where the fiberglass will be bonding, and do the job just as though you were filling a dent, though you won't need the filler.

Instead, the fiberglass will become the new metal. Soak it in the mixture of epoxy and resin (and this must be mixed exactly according to directions), then drape it over the cutout. Stretch it tight while it is still wet, making sure that the edges are on the bare metal you have sanded. If you want to add another layer, do so. The more layers, the thicker the repaired area will be.

Finish it as before, with sanding, priming, painting, rubbing, and polishing.

You can help to prevent rust in your car by keeping it as clean and dry as possible. Some manufacturers claim that modern automobile paints don't need it, but a good wax job still helps a lot. Wax often and use chrome polish on the bumpers to keep moisture off the metal. The worst rust, by the way, starts from the inside, so when you wash your car be sure to clean the dirt from underneath, too. A dirty undercarriage holds moisture and accelerates rusting, especially if road salt is used in your area.

Undercoating will fight rust that starts under the body, but it can't help other high-moisture areas like the chrome strips around the rear windows. If you have your car undercoated, don't coat the driveshaft. This could unbalance the shaft and cause excessive vibration. Of course, don't cover the exhaust system either. Objectionable odors could result.

Repairing a Vinyl Top

Not only does a rip in a vinyl top look bad, but moisture can get underneath and begin to rust the metal of the roof. The best solution is probably to get a new top put on, but you can help if you don't mind a little loss of appearance. Immediately put some type of waterproof tape on the tear. Tape matching the color of the top won't look too bad.

Vinyl tops can be repaired, and they should always be kept clean with a top cleaner or mild soap.

Then get a vinyl repair kit from the auto parts store. Generally, you will apply the vinyl glue to the tear and tape the edges together until the glue sets. Kits come with a variety of colors if you want to try to match, or in a clear solution for any color. Follow the directions with the kit for a job that is more than passable, and which will certainly protect your top from moisture.

There are special vinyl top waxes to clean and help protect your repair and the whole top.

The same kit can be used for repairs to vinyl upholstery. Tape is usually included in vinyl repair kits to strengthen the repair when used with upholstery.

Repairing a Burn in an Auto Rug

A cigarette burn is unsightly, yet they do happen. There is a solution to this problem. First, cut out the burned section with a single-edged razor blade. Then make a pattern of the piece you have removed.

Slide the seat back as far as it will go, reach back, and cut a piece of carpet from underneath. Make it the same size as your pattern. Put the patch in place and carefully squirt some carpet glue around the edges, then place a piece of wax paper over the repair. Weight it with a heavy object until the glue is dry. The wax paper will keep everything from sticking together, except where you want it to stick.

When the glue has dried, remove the weight and the wax paper, then rake across the patch with a dull nail to help blend the nap of the old carpet with the nap of the patch. The repair will be almost invisible.

Removing Stains from Upholstery

First of all, never use gasoline or naphtha as a cleaner. They are dangerous to breathe and can be harmful to your skin. Not only that, but a careless spark could blow up the car—and you.

Use a cleaner specified for either vinyl or fabric, or an all-purpose cleaner that can be used for both. Do not use laundry soap or bleaches, and if you use a cleaning agent, clean a whole

1. Cut out the burned section with a single-edged razor blade. 2. Match the hole you cut with a piece of carpet cut from beneath the seat. 3. Make the patch about the same size as the hole. 4. Put the patch in place and carefully squirt carpet glue around the edges.

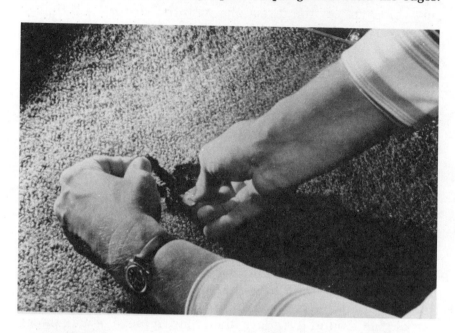

Weight with a heavy object (and a piece of wax paper to keep it from sticking) and allow to dry. Then you can rake across the nap with a dull nail to help hide the repair.

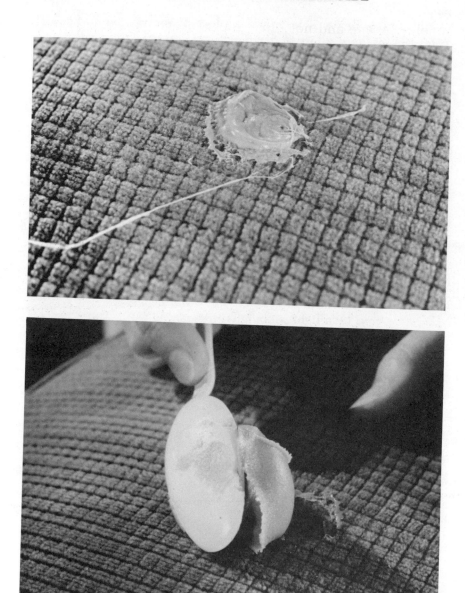

panel at a time and not just the spot. That way, the cleaned area will blend in with the rest.

There are some stubborn stains that need special treatment.

- Chewing gum. Ice will harden the gum so it can be scraped away. And believe it or not, on most upholstery *peanut butter* works too. Spread a teaspoonful on, leave it about fifteen minutes, then clean with soap and water. The oil in the peanut butter helps to unstick the gum and make it come off easier.
- Car sickness. Scrape away the excess, then sponge the spot with a cloth saturated in cold water, followed by washing with mild soapsuds and warm water.
- Grease. Use warm water and soapsuds.
- Blood. Use a rag and cold water. Change frequently to clean sections of the rag, then apply household ammonia cleaner directly to the spot.
- Chocolate. Warm water and mild soapsuds will work, followed by a light rubbing with cleaning fluid.
- Nonchocolate candy. Use very hot water followed by a light rubbing with a mild soap solution.

Peanut butter will remove gum from upholstery.

Index